D1118765

Dickinson and the
Strategies of Reticence

DICKINSON AND THE STRATEGIES OF RETICENCE

The Woman Writer in
Nineteenth-Century America

JOANNE DOBSON

INDIANA UNIVERSITY PRESS

Bloomington and Indianapolis

Library of Congress Cataloging-in-Publication Data

Dobson, Joanne
  Dickinson and the strategies of reticence.

  Bibliography: p.
  Includes index.
  1. Dickinson, Emily, 1830–1886—Contemporaries.
2. Dickinson, Emily, 1830–1886—Criticism and interpretation.   3. Women and literature—United States—
History—19th century.   4. American literature—Women
authors—History and criticism.   5. American literature—
19th century—History and criticism.   6. Self-denial in
literature.   I. Title.
PS1541.Z57D57   1989   811'.4   88-46030
ISBN 0-253-31809-2
1 2 3 4 5   93 92 91 90 89

for Dave

CONTENTS

ACKNOWLEDGMENTS

I wish to express my appreciation to the following people, who read and commented on the manuscript, or portions of it, at various stages: Nina Baym, Joyce Berkman, Frank Couvares, Margo Culley, Judith Fetterley, Susan Harris, Timothy Morris, David Porter, Cheryl Walker, and Sandra Zagarell. Their knowledge, incisive editorial advice, and enthusiastic support have added much to the final version of this study. And to my husband, David Dobson, I owe my greatest debt: an unfailing encouragement and practical assistance that greatly enabled the completion of this project.

INTRODUCTION

Emily Dickinson is a writer who seems peculiarly ahistorical. Stylistically she is ahead of her time; in the compression and indirection of her poetics Dickinson foreshadows aesthetic modes of the early twentieth-century American modernists. In her exploration of the meaning of individual existence in a universe whose existential terms are often uncertain she anticipates twentieth-century thematic preoccupations. Further, in the disregard of her poetry for the great public issues of America in her era—abolition, the oppression of the Indian, women's rights, the plight of the working poor—she dissociates the subject matter of her work from its social and political context.

These features of her work have led teachers and scholars to define Dickinson almost exclusively as a proto-modernist poet whose work foreshadows the disjunctive, innovative, culturally dissenting idiom of twentieth-century poetry. Yet, in spite of its seeming anachronism, Dickinson's writing is firmly rooted in its era and culture in ways that are only now being examined. The current interest in reconstructive literary history and contextual criticism is beginning to show us a Dickinson whose consciousness was as permeated with the lively, sentimental, eccentric, even grotesque images of popular nineteenth-century American culture as it was with the more exalted concerns and language of Shakespeare, Herbert, and Emerson, with whom she has often been compared. In this study I am concerned in particular with Dickinson's surprising and largely unexamined connections to a conventional ideology of womanhood and of "feminine" expression pervasive in the culture into which she was born. Art mediates in complex, nuanced, and often highly conflicted ways between individual experience and cultural imperatives. And Emily Dickinson *was* a nineteenth-century American woman writer. To make the assumption that she was affected by that fact in ways that defined her and influenced her expression—even as she rebelled against the constraints of that definition—seems only logical. A critique based on that assumption offers new insights into the origins, nature, and significance of her poetry.[1]

The cultural ideology of respectable womanhood in mid-nineteenth-century America was structured on the assumption of women's innate and unique morality. It defined ideal feminine morality in large part as altruism, selflessness, and reticence. Certain features of Dickinson's work—her at-

traction to the conventional feminine images of the little girl and the wife/
bride, the radical indirection of her style, and her refusal to publish—link
her directly to the common feminine expressive dilemma: nineteenth-
century American women writers, in what they said and in the manner in
which they handled language, were expected to reveal nothing that would
clash with prevailing conventions of morality and personal reticence. For
women, the expression, especially in any public mode, of personal experience—that is to say, the unique experience of the individual woman as
opposed to cultural stereotypes of femininity—was fraught with taboos.

The response of women writers to this code of reticence was significantly
varied. No cultural imperative is ever completely hegemonic, and women's
expression ranged from strict or anguished conformity by the majority to
outright flouting of expectations on the part of a few conscious rebels and
in the more lurid productions of the popular and reformist press. Although
a few mainstream writers did produce work that was fueled by personal
experience, they did not do so without emotional conflict that is reflected
in both their lives and their narratives. Dickinson's reaction can be seen to
be full of that conflict too. Implicit in her life and in both the convention-
alities and the innovations of her poetry is a relationship compounded of
assent and dissent, a relationship that is recognizably cognizant of and
responsive to strictures on self-disclosure. Her "slant" expressive strategy,
non-publication, and frequent use of conventional feminine images allow
Dickinson a poetics in which personal disclosure is screened through a
series of fail-safe devices designed to allay anxiety about nonconforming
articulation.

Dickinson's birth and education exposed her relentlessly to the nineteenth-century American ideology of feminine reticence. Although the full
range of American publication included much that was sensational and
subversive, in the culture of the white, literate middle class from which
Dickinson came, women's writing was severely delimited in ways designed
to screen out personal expression. The intention was to present Woman
as a moral ideal rather than represent any particular woman as a multi-
dimensional individual. Through her socialization and reading Dickinson
would have known, as would any literate woman, expressive restrictions
so stringent and so ingrained that they amounted to a culturally endorsed
and culturally monitored feminine community of expression. The impetus
was always to be moral, and moral in a distinctly culture-specific manner.
"So if a woman enter the field of authorship," advised an editorial in the
Springfield Republican in 1864, "let her do it always in the spirit which seeks
for other rewards than the world can give; let her feel that the mission of

her poem is to elevate and bless humanity, that she always speaks for the right, the true, the good" (Capps 146).

A decision to write in violation of the web of proscriptions that resulted from the core perception of woman's altruistic morality invited psychic conflict and anxiety for most female poets or novelists. In 1833, in a discussion of Mme. de Staël's *Corinne*, Harriet Beecher Stowe suggested that because of the "constant habits of self-government which the rigid forms of our society demand," American women automatically repressed "vehement and absorbing" feelings like those expressed by the French writer (*Life and Letters* 82). Dickinson is occasionally compared to her great male contemporaries, most often to Emerson, but she was caught in a particularly female conflict between the urges of the unique articulative self and the strictures of her social identity; to express herself fully and directly would have been to deny her "womanhood." Male writers experience similar conflicts, but in a manner more likely to jeopardize social reputation and respectablility than gender identity. Dickinson felt it necessary to tell Thomas Wentworth Higginson that her poems were not personal. "When I state myself, as the Representative of the Verse," she wrote to him in 1862, seemingly in response to a statement in a letter of his, "—it does not mean—me—but a supposed person" (L 268).[2] In light of the contemporary constraints on personal expression by women we can understand her need so to inform him; to place gender identity in peril is a psychologically dangerous endeavor. Yet the fact is that Dickinson's poetry provides the most comprehensive and immediate experience of individual passion created by any American woman writing in the nineteenth century.

Dickinson's longing for cultural approbation is manifestly evident in her work. Her fascinated use of feminine stereotypes like the little girl and the wife/bride shows her attraction to (although ultimate rejection of) the possibilities for self-expression these conventional figures offered her. Further, the heightened rhetoric and extreme "slantness" of Dickinson's writing most likely issue from anxiety generated by an awareness, perhaps to a large degree unconscious, of her failure to conform, her own expressive "deviance." Not only are her exploration of popular stereotypes and her stylistic indirection congruent with contemporary strictures and practice, so also is her refusal to publish in an era when women's publication was socially sanctioned only in cases of financial need or of moral imperatives. Dickinson's life and writing were informed and shaped by her responses to a feminine community of expression which mandated personal reticence.

Dickinson's adaptation of contemporary practiçes evidences deviation as well as conformity; she recreates popular images so that they exhibit characteristics unique to her work, and she takes both the obliquity of her style and the privacy of her writing to an extreme. Further, her lack of a primary focus on presenting a moral message opposes Dickinson's literary concerns to the didactic orientation of most contemporary women writers. In particular her disregard of public issues places her poetry outside the expressive boundaries of the literature of social advocacy, a literary mode that allowed mainstream women writers particular freedom in subject matter and stylistic forcefulness. And in her intense and extended exploration of the significance of a woman's personal experience Dickinson is in direct violation of the most pervasive and stringently observed proscription on women's expression—thé interdiction on the presentation of a woman's passional life.

In coming to understand the ways in which a significant number of Dickinson's more problematic decisions about her life and work stem from a conflicted relationship of both assent to and dissent from the cultural logic of women's discourse, we can begin to reassess certain biographical and critical assumptions about Dickinson and her work. For instance, contextual investigation suggests that her non-publication is not evidence of the suppression of her poetry by family, friends, and editors but that, in conformity with the attitudes of her female contemporaries toward the private nature of personal lyrics, she herself chose not to publish. Dickinson's writing dealt to a significant degree with personal feelings, indeed often with anguished passions, of love, anger, fear, and loneliness; she would have felt compelled to keep it, at least during her lifetime, from the public eye. When she told Higginson in 1862 that publication was as "foreign to [her] thought, as Firmament to Fin—" (L 265), Dickinson was most likely telling the truth. Rather than responding to constraints on personal expression by eliminating the personal from her writing, as many of her contemporaries did, Dickinson withdrew her writing itself from the public eye; she declined to publish. The method was different, but the result was the same: private experience remained private.

Contemporary ideals of femininity also suggest to us that the "little girl" pose Dickinson often adopted in her daily life—Higginson describes her behavior as "childlike" three times in his account of his initial meeting with her (L 342a)—her little girl and wife/bride poetic personae, and her frequently extreme stylistic indirection do not have their origins in unique personal maladjustment but, rather, are consistent with a cultural identity and a set of expressive strategies contemporary women's writing offered her.

Dickinson's work, like that of many of her contemporaries, reveals evidence of the common dilemma of trying to express the self while still screening uniquely personal experience from expression. The "supposed person" of her poetry often violates proscriptions on passionate feelings, creating for Dickinson an expressive situation that renders her, like her contemporaries, subject to expressive reactions designed to make articulation "safe." Like other women writers she was attracted to the more culturally approved, "respectable," literary images of woman's identity. Further, she adopted, and carried to an extreme, stylistic and tonal strategies of indirection if not identical to, at least related to, those used by other women writers. Dickinson, like some of her contemporaries, turned to irony, ambivalence, and the disruption of expected patterns of sequence in order obliquely to express proscribed experiences and feelings. These reactions suggest that non-publication was not sufficient protection from expressive anxiety—that Dickinson had internalized cultural expressive proscriptions at such a deep psychic level that their effects on her articulation were ineradicable.

It would be inspiring, but not, I think, realistic, to believe that Dickinson sprang into poetic utterance as a full-fledged and sophisticated feminist/ modernist; there is little in her life or letters to encourage that belief. Instead we see in her work the complex interplay between her individual genius and her role as a woman in that particular society. At times what we need to know to fully understand a writer's work has less to do with greatness than it does with the writer's individual treatment of literary materials and responses made available by his or her society.[3] High art and popular art spring from the same cultural matrix, although they stand in differing, at times even oppositional, relationships to it. Myra Jehlen reminds us that although "greatness involves a critical penetration of conventions," it does "not necessarily or even frequently [involve] a radical rejection of them" (579). Historically, women's culture has found productive ways of dealing with the restrictions of patriarchy, and these accommodations have allowed women to function in an otherwise disabling environment. Dickinson was a woman writing in nineteenth-century America and the conventions that resulted from reaction to expressive constraints satisfied for her the same socially inculcated needs they met for her contemporaries.

Examining Dickinson's life and work in light of what we know about other writers of her gender, place, and era proves invaluable in revealing societal sources for certain of her actions and preoccupations and in highlighting the extreme uniqueness of others. For, certainly, no artist stands in splendid isolation from the shaping factors of the social world in which she came to individual and social consciousness. As David Reynolds has recently commented, "her tortured, elliptical poetry was far more than the anguished record of one trapped woman's private struggle. It can be profitably viewed as the highest product of a rich [woman's] literary movement" (413). Between Dickinson and her contemporaries exists a cultural commonality that includes shared influence and shared reaction.

Her contemporaries, in writing about the special problems of the woman artist, have left evidence as to just how difficult the exercise of artistic freedom was for them, and must, by implication, have been for her. In the *Atlantic Monthly* for July 1864 Dickinson would probably have read Rebecca Harding Davis's featured tale, "The Wife's Story." "It seems but just," begins the narrator of this story about a talented woman's desire for a career as an opera singer in spite of the conflicts of marriage and motherhood, "that one should be so left, untrammelled, to chose between heaven and hell: but who can shake off trammels,—make themselves naked of their birth and education?" (1).

Davis's protagonist is unable to do so, and a close look at Dickinson's life and work in its cultural context shows that she too was affected, in ways that have been insufficiently examined, by her birth and education. Given her genius, Dickinson re-shaped and gave new dimensions to the conventions that the culture offered her. Her intensely idiosyncratic reconstruction of received feminine images constitutes at once an attraction to and a critique of those modes of being, suggesting a deeply rooted conflict in her own sense of identity. Her radical intensification of contemporary stylistic modes of indirection shows an acute and poignant need to screen her expression. But in Dickinson's stylistic exploration of the expressive potential of literary and linguistic indirection, we see, along with conformity, the workings of the individual creative spirit freeing itself for expression within a set of rigid limitations. Using devices of elliptical expression occasional, but significant, in the work of her contemporaries, she intensifies and exploits to the fullest the potential of disorder and of tonal nuance for creating an oblique aesthetic, fashioning a poetry that is in the indirection of its statement far ahead of its time. In an era when reticence was considered a primary requirement for the respectable female, Dickinson's stylistic strategies allowed her to address proscribed areas of women's personal experience, particularly anger and forbidden passion, safely—but also with honesty, precision, and strength of feeling.

Thus while Dickinson's poetic achievement constitutes in part an acquiescence to expressive constraints, it also reflects a brilliant usurpation of the limited terms of expression they offered her. In the gentle satire and ambiguity of a comment in a letter to her brother when she was twenty, she anticipates a lifelong struggle: "I dont [sic] have much to fear—," she wrote to Austin, "I've got all but *three* feelings down, if I can only keep them!" (L 42). To keep them, or to keep them down: in a century of feminine constraint on strong emotions and on their expression, this was a defining dilemma.

Dickinson and the
Strategies of Reticence

I

"A CERTAIN PREJUDICE"
THE COMMUNITY OF EXPRESSION

LITERATURE IS . . . SAID TO BE PERMITTED
[TO WOMEN]: BUT UNDER WHAT PENALTIES
AND RESTRICTIONS?

—HARRIET MARTINEAU, 1837

Emily Dickinson came of age in an America burgeoning with literary activity. From the novels, poems, essays, and philosophical treatises of those writers we have come to define as classic American spokesmen, through the mainstream novels and poems of popular writers such as Susan Warner and Henry Wadsworth Longfellow, the poignant narratives of freed or fugitive slaves, and the more ephemeral, often sensational, productions of the story papers and the pamphlet press, American literature was diverse, energetic, colorful, pervasive, influential, and alive. The writing of her era as Dickinson would have experienced it was not an American literature that we of the twentieth century, whose reading in nineteenth-century literature is largely confined to the classic writers, would immediately recognize as such. Dickinson would not have known a body of writing characterized primarily by mythic portraits of the American isolato battling the wilderness within and without. As American literature presented itself to her, it was a literature of variety, characterized by low as well as high ideals, by cultural consensus as well as dissent, by sentiment as well as stoicism, by realism as well as romanticism, by humor as well as high seriousness, by attachment as well as isolation, by polemical intention as well as by the urges of artistic ambition. The multifaceted body of texts with which Dickinson would have been bombarded—and not unwillingly as the range of her reading shows—constituted not the American Renaissance as F. O. Matthiessen has presented it to us but rather a far more culturally embedded American literary rebirth with roots in the popular imagination of both men and women, whites and blacks, the well-educated and the nominally educated.

Most of all, and once again contrary to modern perceptions, American literature in this era was a body of writing that welcomed the work of women. The publication scene in nineteenth-century America was distinctly favorable to feminine literary production. The era between 1830 and 1850, for instance, saw sixty-four new "ladies magazines" begin publication (Papashvily 40), and women's novels were the first best sellers—*Uncle Tom's Cabin* (1852) by Harriet Beecher Stowe sold over 20,000 copies within the first three weeks of its publication (James D. Hart 110), and *The Wide, Wide World* (1850) by Susan Warner is generally considered to have been the first novel to sell over a million copies. And newspapers and story papers abounded in the work of women poets, novelists, short story writers, and columnists. This affirmation of women's writing was flattering and lucrative and constituted a social sanction—at least under certain conditions—for female writers. It was in this climate of acceptance that Dickinson was socialized; she read her American contemporaries in the popular periodicals to which her family subscribed and in the novels and poems she shared with, and discussed with, her relatives and friends.

The cultural affirmation of women's writing, however, did not offer *carte blanche* for woman's utterance. And this Dickinson would have known as well. By and large, affirmation was based on compliance with stringently delimited terms designed to reinforce conservative cultural assumptions about woman's identity. In other words, the accepted women's discourse operated, as codified genres tend to, as a discourse designed to direct social mores and inhibit social change. In Fredric Jameson's terms, the accepted modes of women's expression ultimately served as "strategies of containment," rather than as explorations or experiments in personal or cultural change. Dickinson would have known that the chief assumption of the dominant mode of writing by and about women was a belief in and reverence for what was perceived as woman's uniquely innate moral nature. This perception placed strong and particularized constraints on women's expression, screening out in various ways passionate personal expression—which might well be perceived as conflicting with an altruistic feminine morality. Specifically absent from, or apologized for, or negated in the writing of most women of the white middle class in that period are what were seen as "deviant" qualities for women—sexual passion, personal (as opposed to altruistic) anger, and aspiration for achievement or recognition outside the private sphere of the family. Although some women wrote in open violation of these expressive tenets, mainstream women writers, many of whom were excellent stylists and perceptive commentators on the cultural scene and women's place in it, had to find avenues of expression either within the boundaries of the acceptable, or at least not in obvious violation of expressive norms.

Much of Dickinson's work, of course, is generated and fueled by personal passions: sexual longing, frustration, and renunciation; a personal anger that doesn't hesitate even at the threshold of the Divine; and an ambition that is at one and the same time overweening and vigorously denied. That she came of age in a period that both encouraged and strictly delimited women's literary expression had a profound impact, nonetheless, on Dickinson's stance vis-à-vis expression. The common belief that the classic antebellum writers were marginal to their society, David Reynolds suggests, may well be mistaken. Certainly with Dickinson we can see that, as he says about these writers in general, "far from being estranged from [her social context she] was in large part created by it" (3). Dickinson's flirtation with widely circulated stereotypes of women's identity indicates a certain poignant longing for a stable cultural identity. And the radical indirection of her poetry, her letters, and her recorded personal conversation is congruent (in kind if not in degree) with the elliptical style of a significant number of her contemporaries. Most likely it constitutes a reaction to precepts of proper feminine discourse that would have been an integral part of the socialization they shared as well-educated, well-read, well-bred, middle-class women.[1]

Further, a not inconsequential percentage of Dickinson's poetry is in conformity with contemporary expectations, not only for women's expression but for poetic expression in general. An examination of the bulk of her poetry shows more of an interest in the themes and conventions of her era than a strict concentration on those poems currently defined as major would suggest. Poems like "The Beggar Lad—dies early—" (717) or "The grave my little cottage is" (1743), for instance, if they had appeared in contemporary newspapers or magazines, would have caused no adverse comment. These are poems that, like many others, have received little if any modern critical attention because they do not provide what most modern critics desire from Dickinson—a modernist, existentialist, feminist poetic vision.

If we are truly to know this brilliant poet, in her roots as well as her branches, it is imperative that we look at the gendered ideology of expression in which she was acculturated. That ideology had as a central tenet the injunction against personal expression. The Rev. John Dudley, who was a friend of Dickinson's,[2] serves as a cultural spokesperson in a sermon on the Virgin Mary he gave in 1871: "Oh! how womanly, because how reserved; not ambitious of talk, of self-display, of self-manifestation, but divinely reticent. . . . How still I have been, many a time reading those great words, *pondered in her heart!* Chaste, reserved, hiding, exalted" (Leyda II 171–72). The essence of feminine gender identification is here stated as a personal reserve not cultural in origin, and thus open to dissent, but linked to *spiritual* imperatives: a reticence that is divine, and thus incontrovertible. This mandate of reticence may well have been the "angel" with which Dickinson struggled, in an ambivalent, fluctuating, self-contradictory manner, throughout her poetic career. Cristanne Miller notes that Dickinson's need for approval was a gendered determinant in the creation of her particular poetics (184). That approval would not have been limited to approbation from others. Dickinson, a conventionally socialized nineteenth-century woman writer, may well have struggled in her life and poetry with a talent, insight, and vision she herself did not always completely understand or approve.

When I say that women writers needed to eliminate "personal" experience from their work, I mean the literal details of their own lives, but, more particularly, experiences reflecting passionate and intimate human energies, whether they are presented as the author's own or whether her exploration of character simply reveals knowledge of them. Eros, anger, and ambition were particularly suspect for women in nineteenth-century America, and were subject to rigorous censorship, both external and internal. Obviously, not all literature needs to be the expression of personal feeling. But writing whose style and subject matter is severely constrained by rigid societal or political strictures from reflecting the personal concerns, preoccupations, and experiences of the artist—whether they are presented as his or her own or explored through the life of a protagonist—will of necessity manifest limitations of scope and style. And a body of writing under divine mandate as the expression of women to be "the world's redeeming influence," (153) in the words of the Rev. John Abbott, author of the popular advice manual, *The Mother at Home* (1833)—a book owned by the Dickinsons—is a body of writing multiply constrained by social, institutional, and personal biases favoring a conventionally moral expression.

Although Dickinson's writing is characterized by what many would consider a higher morality, the imprint of the conventional is not eradicated from either her subject matter or her style, both of which sometimes show reactive strategies designed to make expression safe and sometimes exhibit outright conformity. What follows is a delineation of the conventional ideology of literary expression for women in which Emily Dickinson would have come to consciousness of herself as a literary woman and with which she, either by rejection, modification, or accommodation, would have had to come to terms. It is my contention that all three of the above responses—rejection, modification, and accommodation—characterize the striking and idiosyncratic body of articulation, both personal and poetic, that Emily Dickinson has bequeathed us.

Women and Morality

Rufus Griswold opens his preface to *The Female Poets of America* (1848) with a presumption that "the moral nature of women" (3) is a determining factor in the quality of women's writing. He then focuses on the particularly intense appreciation in America of women and their moral function in society:

> The most striking quality of that civilization which is evolving itself in America, is the deference felt for women. As a point in social manners, it is so pervading and so peculiar, as to amount to a national characteristic; and it ought to be valued and vaunted as the pride of our freedom and the brightest hope of our history. It indicates a more exalted appreciation of an influence that can never be felt too deeply, for it is never exerted but for good. (4)

For Griswold, as for his contemporaries, feminine moral influence was essential to the development of a free and progressive nation. The hyperbole of his language—"the pride of our freedom," "the brightest hope of our history"—is in itself a testimony to the depth of feeling surrounding this issue. And the cultural reverence for that quality is *central* to the identity of the "evolving" nation: "the most striking quality of that civilization." A more cool-headed evaluation by French historian Alexis de Tocqueville confirms the contemporary perception of the unique function of gender in American society. In *Democracy in America* (1835), de Tocqueville proposes that "the singular prosperity and growing strength of [Americans] ought mainly to be attributed . . . to the superiority of their women" (214). And he too defines this essential and beneficial superiority specifically as woman's morality. "No free communities ever existed without morals, and . . . morals are the work of woman" (198). In the common cultural perception the future of the nation depended directly on how well women adhered to and fulfilled their moral function.

In an even more extreme extension of this ideology the future of civilized society in the world at large was seen to depend on woman's influence. Ralph Waldo Emerson, in an address to a women's rights convention in Boston in 1855, defined women as the "civilizers of mankind." "What is civilization?" he went on to ask. "I answer, the power of good women" (*Miscellanies* 409). And Catharine Beecher, in "An Address to the Christian Women of America," specifies the exact nature of woman's "power": she is to be the great moral teacher. "Woman's great mission is to train ignorant weak immature creatures to obey the laws of God—first in the family, then in the school, then in the neighborhood, then in the nation, then in the world" (Parker 149). National freedom, prosperity, and strength; the "civilizing" of mankind; the training of the world in "the laws of God": in the conservative ideology of femininity that pervaded middle-class American culture during the nineteenth century these exalted imperatives were the responsibility of women. "Schooled in virtue," Mary Kelley notes, "the Christian helpmeet was to meet her responsibility to the republic by being the exemplar and teacher of virtue to husband and sons" (*Private Woman* 60–61). On men shaped and influenced by virtuous women the nation's development and prosperity depended. Woman's redeeming role was an indirect one, but without it the nation would lack the moral ballast necessary for political, economic, and social stability.

The Community of Expression

With such an exalted value placed on woman's social function, it was seen as essential, not only for the individual and the family, but for the nation and the world as well, that women remain true to their uniquely moral nature. Femininity was a cultural construct of momentous import, powerful in its influence, but fragile in its nature and subject to contamination both from without and within. Women writers were under a heavy obligation to introduce nothing into their writing that would disturb preconceptions about woman's moral nature, or that would sully the souls of impressionable readers. Accordingly, the concept of woman's innate morality and the perceived importance of that morality to the culture became the generative core in the dominant white middle class of a complex network of personal biases, cultural directives, economic initiatives, and publishers' preferences. These imperatives, both spoken and unarticulated, structured and defined for women in nineteenth-century America a "community of expression" having a marked effect on the subjects and style of women's writing.[3] The "community of expression" I present in this dis-

cussion is a conceptual model reflecting—in lives and in literature—out-
lines, dynamics, and results of the cultural expectations that structured
women's literary expression.

This community of expression, which amounts to a tacit expressive al-
liance, was characterized by omissions and evasions designed to screen
out or veil, in any one of a number of fashions, the reality of an individual
female, as opposed to stereotyped "feminine" experience—as if something
in the nature of uncensored female experience might be innately disruptive
to social order. Expression of the full range of women's personal experience
was strictly proscribed, and the woman writer was severely trammeled in
her expression. On an institutional level her writing was screened by editors
and subject to the close gender-specific evaluation of reviewers. On a personal level she was subject to public scrutiny; to be a popular writer in
nineteenth-century America was to invite public attention of a sort that is
now reserved for politicians and show-business celebrities.[4] Further, she
had to deal with her own anxiety about violating proscriptions which in
the process of her socialization she would have internalized.

Merely being present in the public forum, as Mary Kelley tells us, was
problematic enough for individual women writers: "although these women
achieved fame, as private women they were uncomfortable in the world
beyond the home. At best they felt ambivalent, at worst that they simply
did not belong there" (*Private Woman* 29). This sense of displacement, of
illegitimacy, reveals itself in various psychological manifestations: "they
had difficulty coping. . . . a continuing crisis of identity. . . . conflicted
and contradictory responses" (111). Women were afflicted by a sense of
guilty anxiety about having, in the first place, penetrated the public world:
an alien, unnatural, and unsexing sphere. "[W]omen of the home," Kelley
describes them, "[they] simultaneously came to assume the male roles of
public figure, economic provider, and creator of culture" (111).

Perhaps the anxiety many women felt about the possible abuse they
might experience in a public realm can be most vividly seen in a fictional
mode. In Augusta Evans Wilson's *St. Elmo* (1866), Edna Earl, the protagonist, is an aspiring young writer. As she begins her career, her kindly
minister, with all good intentions, tells her:

> "The history of literary females is not calculated to allay the apprehension
> that oppresses me, as I watch you just setting out on a career so fraught
> with trials of which you have never dreamed. As a class they are martyrs,
> uncrowned and uncanonized; jeered at by the masses, sincerely pitied by a
> few earnest souls, and wept over by the relatives who really love them.
> Thousands of women have toiled over books that proved millstones and
> drowned them in the sea of letters. How many of the hundreds of female

writers scattered through the world in this century will be remembered six
months after the coffin closes over their weary, haggard faces? You may
answer, 'They made their bread.' Ah, child! it would have been sweeter if
earned at the washtub, or in the dairy, or by their needles. It is the rough
handling, the jars, the tension of the heartstrings that sap the foundations
of a woman's life and consign her to an early grave" (252).

The grotesque nature of this jumbled compilation of exaggerated imagery—
lost souls, martyrs, millstones, and corpses—indicates the workings of a
kind of anxiety that rises from irrational, unconscious, internalized fear,
rather than from objective reality. Whether the author intends this to reflect
her sense of the actual situation or as a parody of public hysteria is difficult
to ascertain; Edna Earl is very successful, but she does suffer inordinately
because of her career, and eventually gives it up at her husband's request.
In either case, the dynamic of hysterical anxiety regarding women's articulative presence in the public sphere is clearly delineated.

The anxiety created initially by intrusion into a defeminizing sphere was
then compounded by the imperative to screen nonconforming sentiments
or experiences from public expression. In order to allay her own anxiety,
as well as to assure acceptance by, and lack of personal censure from, the
popular audience—and this was almost without exception the audience
for which women wrote—the woman writer filtered her utterance through
a grid of social proscriptions that, in effect, denied the existence of women
as individuals, as persons with unique sexual, emotional, and professional
experiences. Among elements of human socialization so intrinsic as to become intuitive is a sense of when to hold our tongues. The sociolinguist
K. H. Basso tells us that "a knowledge of when not to speak may be as
basic to the production of culturally acceptable behavior as a knowledge
of what to say" (Giglioli 69). And in nineteenth-century America women
writers learned only too well the lesson of "when not to speak." With
personal female experience as the central taboo of women's literary expression, articulation of any aspect of a woman's experience not in conformity
with the prevailing ideal of altruistic feminine selflessness was screened
out of women's writing. Nina Baym, in her study of book reviewing in
America at mid-century, suggests that this taboo amounts to cultural secret
policing. "The highest examples of female characterization, according to
reviewers, approximate the woman to a type. The 'best' women characters
are not individuals . . . and certainly have no secrets to be laid bare. They
are 'Woman.' In the discourse on characterization of women the substitution of norms for observation or discovery is so pervasive that one feels
oneself close to a major cultural deception" (98).

This cultural bias toward idealized feminine characterization was by no means universal or unanimously observed. Women writers were far from being expressive automatons, and this study will discuss nonconforming writers—those women who, like Fanny Fern (Sara Parton), in all consciousness of the norms for women's speech, chose to violate them—as well as conforming ones. By and large, however, the work of women fiction writers and poets shows unmistakable signs of having been severely constrained by a set of strongly felt expressive expectations dominant in what was considered "respectable" society throughout most of the nineteenth century in America.

When I speak of a "community of expression" I am paraphrasing Roger Fowler's description of a speech community as an arena within which exists a set of rules for expression. "We are dealing," he says, "in bodies of people who subscribe to, and employ, distinctive networks of [speech] varieties; these networks are necessitated by, express, and to a large extent create, modify and define cultural patterns of a multiplicity of non-linguistic kinds" (*Understanding Language* 216). The concept of a "community of expression" enlarges upon this description to include varieties of *discourse* that are "necessitated by, express, and to a large extent create, modify and define cultural patterns." I propose that the writing of nineteenth-century American women at mid-century, particularly in the manifestly "literary" genres of poetry and fiction, shows characteristics of just such an expressive community—constituting a discourse distinctively and discernibly patterned by cultural assumptions regarding the nature of womanhood and her "divine reticence." Constraints imposed by these assumptions, particularly those stemming from the core proscription on the expression of women's personal experience, are evident early in the century, pervasive at mid-century, and begin to dissipate by the 1870s.

Women writers conformed to these expectations in more or less varying degrees according to how conservative they were, and also according to the genres they chose. But education and socialization included strict training in feminine proprieties, and that training combined with their reading of contemporary literature would have made all women writers aware of expressive expectations. As Raymond Chapman says: "No one who uses an artistic medium can remain . . . unaware of the way in which that medium operates in the community as a whole" (29). And contemporary social commentator Gail Hamilton notes in 1862 her cognizance of both internal and external constraints: "There are obstacles [to women's writing] without as well as within. A certain prejudice against female writers 'still lives.' It is fine, subtle, impalpable, but real" (*Country Living and Country Thinking* 188).[5]

Harriet Martineau also notes delimitation of women's writing. In *Society in America* (1837) she says: "Literature is . . . said to be permitted [to women]: but under what penalties and restrictions"? (293). These "restrictions" are nowhere stated, but they are apparent in women's texts, where they are manifested in absences, apologies, and displacements. Literary texts speak in their evasions as clearly as they speak in their insistences. "It is in the significant *silences* of a text," Terry Eagleton says, "in its gaps and absences, that the presence of ideology can be most positively felt" (*Marxism* 35). In nineteenth-century American women's writing, with rare exceptions, sexuality is "silent," almost entirely eliminated. The silence of ambition, both in the author and in her female protagonists, takes another form; ambition is screened through elaborate apologies, rationalizations, and renunciations. Anger is present, by and large, only if it is altruistic (and then, significantly enough, it often amounts to rage); *personal* anger is silent in its own way, often initially present, but almost always "corrected" in the course of the narrative.

Although minor characters might deviate from the ideal, protagonists were severely stunted by the eradication of these personal aspects of women's lives from contemporary women's texts.[6] In poems and novels, the writer's personal awareness of the complex reality of the self was almost inevitably subsumed by a stereotyped ideal, severely restricting creativity and breadth of inquiry.

Genre was a determining factor. Particularly free from constraints (although reticent enough by modern standards) were essayists like Margaret Fuller, Gail Hamilton (Mary Abigail Dodge), and Fanny Fern. Writers of regional sketches like Caroline Kirkland and Alice Cary, for instance, also were remarkably unconstrained, especially in the directness and energy of their styles.[7] As Judith Fetterley says, "nineteenth-century American women found it easier to write well in forms that appeared less literary, artistic, and serious because such efforts more accurately coincided with their sense of who they were and what they could do" (*Provisions* 15).[8] It must be noted that these genres—the essay and the local-color sketch—are not the ones traditionally most closely associated with expression of *personal* feeling and experience.[9] The genres of poetry and the novel, more traditionally "literary," and more amenable to the in-depth presentation of women's lives and feelings, are where the constraints on feminine expression most clearly reveal themselves in marked omissions and evasions. These genres, particularly poetry, were problematic for women writers. They, more than other modes of expression, checked women's liberty in the creation of persona or protagonist and limited the inventiveness of their style.

I do not intend to imply that the writing of men in mid-century America was, in contrast to women's writing, completely unconstrained. Obviously that is not the case. Evidence of a peculiarly nineteenth-century decorum and restraint can be seen in the writing of men as well as of women. It is not within the scope of this discussion, however, to address the issue of men's writing. The gendered community of expression for male writers in nineteenth-century America has not yet been investigated and the cultural history of masculinity is only beginning to be written. But the wider scope of experience provided in men's writing of the period and the increased stylistic freedom their work exhibits indicates that constraints upon discourse were not as restrictive for men as they were for women. Male writers were not bound by an ethos identifying them as innately, uniquely, and restrictively moral and threatening their gender identity for any deviation. Cultural monitoring was far more gender-specific for women than it was for men. In book reviews, for instance, "the womanliness of a piece of writing was a matter for discrimination and praise in a way that manliness was not" (Baym, *Novels* 254). A look at men's writing of the period—particularly of those writers who have come to be perceived as classic American artists—shows that male writers felt somewhat freer than women did to address their own experience, and that, without question, they provided protagonists—both male and female—with a wider range of personal passions than women writers did.[10]

When Louisa May Alcott wished to publish her sensational tales of passion, she chose a male pseudonym, a very unusual occurrence in America, where women's pen names tended to be even more feminine than their actual names. The following passage in a letter from her editor, James R. Elliott, stresses the "masculinity" of her authorial persona: "You may send me anything in either the sketch or Novelette line that you do not wish to 'father,' or that you wish A. M. Barnard, or 'any other man' to be responsible for" (Stern, *Publishers for Mass Entertainment* 125). The characters in these tales were sexually passionate, ambitious, angry, even violent, hardly products of the imagination a proper woman would wish to acknowledge. Alcott's choice of a masculine "author" for these works reflects the greater freedom allowed men in literary expression.

The Era

The community of constraints that characterized women's poetry and fiction was evident early in the century, continued as a pervasive and determinant presence through mid-century (perhaps not coincidentally the time period that saw the inception of serious women's rights agitation in

America), and began to abate during the 1870s. Certainly the moral ideal for woman's expression was well in place by 1815 when Lydia Huntley Sigourney, eventually the author of over sixty-five books of poetry and prose, published her first volume, *Moral Pieces in Prose and Verse*. Catharine Maria Sedgwick's first novel, *A New England Tale* (1822), was also moral in intention, initially conceived as a Unitarian religious tract. Both women thus began literary careers with a moral impetus at a time when careers in the public realm were distinctly uncommon for women.

While Sigourney and Sedgwick were empowered by this impetus, the constraints of the contemporary definition of feminine morality had the obvious disadvantage of hindering the range of their literary inquiry. Sigourney in particular, as a contemporary, Ann Stephens, notes in an undated pamphlet biography, refused to allow "one sentiment which angels might not acknowledge" (Haight 100). And Sedgwick, writing in 1851 after having read *The House of the Seven Gables*, deplores the "raw head and bloody bones" of Nathaniel Hawthorne's imagination (*Life and Letters* 328), saying that she desires the "kindliest resources of the art of fiction." By this she means that she wants fiction to be uplifting and inspirational. In this perception of literature, its purpose is not to *record* the "tragedy of life," but rather to provide "elixirs" and "cordials" for it (329).

With the notable exception of Hope Leslie, most of Sedgwick's female protagonists, beginning with Jane Elton of *A New England Tale*, conform to contemporary expectations of ideal femininity.[11] She states that ideal in her description of Hawthorne's "Little Phoebe." Phoebe, she says, "is the redemption of the book [*The House of the Seven Gables*]—a sweet and perfect flower amidst corruption, barrenness, and decay" (*Life and Letters* 328). In his 1848 anthology, *The Female Poets of America*, Rufus Griswold at once defines and prescribes for women's poetry a similar ideal. In his description of Emiline Smith's work he approves it as being characterized by "a religious delight in nature, and a contentment with home affections and pleasures, which in one form or another are the matériel of the finest poetry of women" (250). Women in writing that conforms to conventional expectations are to be depicted as sweet, perfect, pious, domestic, and content.

In the 1850s the two most popular women's texts were noticeably affected by the restraints on the expression of female experience. Both Stowe's *Uncle Tom's Cabin* and Warner's *The Wide, Wide World* are charged with moral purpose. *The Wide, Wide World* is a tale of a young girl's training in obedience and selflessness and was considered to be a moral exemplum for young women; a contemporary reviewer in the *Newark Advertiser* declared it to be "capable of doing more good than any other work, other than the Bible" (Papashvily 3). Stowe's *Uncle Tom's Cabin* was also engendered from a moral base, conceived with the intention of showing the nation precisely what an evil thing slavery was. Warner and Stowe chose differing methods for dealing with the problem of the author's strong feelings. Warner, like many of her peers, chose a little girl for a protagonist, and "corrected" Ellen's childish rebellion in the course of the narrative.[12] Stowe, rather than focusing on a woman's experience (or even a girl's) vented her intelligence and passion on a great public issue, that of slavery. Neither novel has an adult female protagonist. The presentation of a fully adult woman with a story interesting enough to carry an entire novel would have run the risk of violating the proscriptions.[13]

By the 1870s constraints had begun to slacken, and women's writing shows the liberating results in both poetry and fiction. In his 1874 revision of Griswold's 1848 anthology, R. H. Stoddard notes the change, saying that "a new race of female poets . . . with a wider range of thought in their verse, and infinitely more art" had come into existence since the collection was first issued (7). He says that earlier readers would not have liked the "force" and "originality" of the poets he had added to the volume, suggesting that he was aware of a change in the evaluative priorities of the readership. A preface statement in *Our Famous Women* (1886) confirms the contemporary understanding that values were shifting: "Causes both economical and moral," said the editor, "have tended to break up old habits of life and thought" (Kelley, *Private Woman* 133). Elizabeth Stuart Phelps, in her novel *The Story of Avis* (1877) reflects that change as she presents her powerful portrait of a complex and passionate woman, Avis Dobell, a talented and ambitious artist. This novel heralds the breakup of the communal proscriptions and anticipates such groundbreaking women's novels of the later century as *The Yellow Wallpaper* by Charlotte Perkins Gilman, published initially as a short story in 1892, and *The Awakening* by Kate Chopin, published in 1899.[14] These later works examine at length and with great honesty the previously proscribed areas of sexual attraction and personal ambition, and they do so with a sense of personal anger that is seen to be legitimate, and thus remains uncorrected.

Regulation

Conforming writers adhered to the precepts of the community of expression, encouraged by a network of those pressures that result from cultural ideology and come to bear on any writer: pressures of genre, conventions, scope of permitted experience, reviews, the marketplace. Women's expression was screened by the literary establishment, and with what seemed to be an incontestable rationale. The editors of *Godey's Lady's Book* in an extended policy statement in January 1837 promised to make certain "that nothing be introduced to undermine those sacred relations of domestic life, in which the Creator has placed the sceptre of woman's empire" (5). Reviewers, as Baym tells us, also served as monitors, taking "it on themselves to write as preceptors, making novel reviewing the occasion for instructing women on their sexual duties and sexual natures" (*Novels* 183). And, of course, the factor of sales was important; with financial need a prominent rationale for women's writing, few women had any interest in writing "deviant" books they might well not be able to sell.

Institutional factors, however, were not the only monitors. Women were aware, at both a conscious and unconscious level, of the potentially disastrous personal consequences of cultural deviance. De Tocqueville describes the problem: "in the United States the inexorable opinion of the public carefully circumscribes woman within the narrow circle of domestic interests and duties and forbids her to step beyond it . . . she is not slow to perceive that she cannot depart for an instant from the established usages of her contemporaries without putting in jeopardy her peace of mind, her honor, nay, even her social existence" (201). The emphatic diction of this description—"inexorable opinion," "carefully circumscribed," "forbids," "jeopardy"—focuses our attention upon the strength of the constraints that bound most women in a limiting identity and explains why women experienced profound anxieties about deviating in any way. "Any deviation," Baym notes, "on the part of speaking women, from an ideal of the female voice became the occasion for a generalized gender terror" exhibited in just one way in the frantic condemnations, both personal and literary, of book reviewers (*Novels* 266).

The truth of de Tocqueville's observation about women's "jeopardy" can be seen in the experience of the poet Elizabeth Oakes Smith. Her departures from custom caused caustic comment both from her acquaintances and in the press. The first woman ever to lecture before the lyceums of the country, Smith recalls that Sarah Josepha Hale, editor of *Godey's Lady's Book*, who had been her good friend, wrote her "a severe letter of condemnation" and refused to see her or to call on her after Smith began, in the 1850s, speaking in public on woman's issues (*Autobiography* 97). Censure of women's outspokenness was severe, and Smith, for one, was "cruelly abused by the press" (153) after she abandoned the conservative stance that had characterized her earlier years. So virulent were the attacks that she felt them as a "martyrdom" (37).

Emma D. E. N. Southworth, initially one of the liveliest writers of the era, also felt the brunt of social excoriation. Hale accused *her* of a "freedom of expression that almost borders on impiety" (John Hart 215). Southworth, in spite of criticism, stayed with fiction, but as her career progressed her work gradually came into conformity with the limitations on woman's expression. In her seventies she wrote to her daughter about a visit from a Professor Powers: "He told me the first book he ever read was my 'Deserted Wife' which his father a Babtist [sic] minister brought him from Washington. I told him it was a wild story, the work of my younger days" (*Hidden Hand* xiii). As she created increasingly more constrained characters and plots, her uniqueness as a writer, which had been largely dependent on her ability to create unconventional, lively women characters like the "wild" Hagar in *The Deserted Wife* (1849), diminished.

More effective than external censure in constraining woman's expression was the carefully nurtured self-regulation, both conscious and unconscious, by which women were characterized—the result of a rigorous training of young women in self-government. "Believing," de Tocqueville said, "that they had little chance of repressing in woman the most vehement passions of the human heart, they [Americans] held that the surer way was to teach her the art of combating those passions for herself" (199). In a letter to Austin Dickinson in 1850, Emily Dickinson's girlhood friend Jane Hitchcock attests to the pervasiveness of this education in repression. Writing from Ipswich Female Seminary, Hitchcock says: "The Teachers here every day preach to us about *restraining* our *feelings* (Leyda I 163, her emphasis). Caroline Gilman in her 1838 *Recollections of a Southern Matron* reveals results of her feminine training when she comments that a woman's "first study must be self-control, almost to hypocrisy" (297). And Susan Warner's refusal, in 1839 at the age of twenty, to reveal her "most private sentiments and most secret thoughts" even to her own private journal shows us the anxious conflict this ethic caused for women writers. "Perhaps I should be willing to write in that fashion if I was very sure nobody would ever see it," Warner said. "And it is even possible I may do it, *at all risks*, but not just now," she concluded enigmatically (Anna Warner 190, my emphasis).

Warner's comment reveals the kind of anxiety that was in itself a monitoring factor. Certainly the lives of even the most conformist of women writers would have included a more or less occasional flare of anger, spurt of ambition, or spasm of sexual longing. But anything resembling these "most private sentiments and most secret thoughts" is screened from both protagonists and poetic personae. In the expression of these aspects of life, mainstream women writers felt themselves to be at "risk," testifying to the imperative necessity to maintain the cultural construct of femininity in spite of the pressing awareness of aspects of the self in contradiction to that construct.

In her discussion of Mme. de Staël's *Corinne*, Harriet Beecher Stowe testifies to anxiety about and rigid self-monitoring of feminine passions in America at this time, and in so doing she implicitly addresses the issue for the woman writer. Stowe says that she feels an immense sympathy with Corinne: "But in America feelings vehement and absorbing like hers become still more deep, morbid, and impassioned by the constant habits of self-government which the rigid forms of our society demand. They are repressed, and they burn inward 'til they burn the very soul" (*Life and Letters* 82). That no Corinne, passionate and self-defining, appears in popular American women's literature in this era should not surprise us once we have understood the dominant ideology of femininity. As Stowe's description suggests, such a creature of the imagination would have caused "burning" anxiety for her creator, and she would have been screened from articulation before she ever reached the page.

Stowe's description of "repression" and "soul burning" is suggestive of the activity of the unconscious. That the dynamic of screening was not wholly unconscious—that conforming women writers were often consciously aware of the presence of the ideology of reticence as a factor in their writing—we know from comments in their work. In *The Hidden Path* (1855), a novel in which one of the two protagonists is a writer, Marion Harland (Mary Virginia Terhune) addresses the question directly. In a discussion about the need of woman writers for expressive reserve, Bella, the non-writer protagonist, argues thoughtfully that, although women may be "better adapted for the task" of writing novels because they are "purer in heart and purpose," they are indeed hampered in their literary freedom: "if [women] have fewer frailties, they are such as meet with stinted charity. A girl learns concealment from her cradle" (48). Harland affirms here what she sees as the necessity for feminine concealment.

Ann Stephens, ironically enough the author of the first of the sensational "dime novels," is yet another writer who reveals the kind of willing self-censure that was prevalent among women writers. Discussing her antipathy to registering a character's profanity, she says: "I will risk a feebler description in my own language rather than for one instant break through the rule of a life" (*Fashion and Famine* 287).[15] For these writers the claim of propriety, the "rule of a life," was superior to the urge for precision in artistic expression. Taught from childhood to repress all aspects of experience that conflicted with conventional morality, most women writers internalized the cultural precepts at such a deep psychic level that, both consciously and unconsciously, a "feebler description" was preferable to a violation of expressive proscriptions.

The Protagonist

The proscriptions on women's expression had several effects on women's fiction and poetry, but none was more pronounced than the stunting of the female protagonist. The emphasis on domestic morality precluded investigation of individualism—that is to say, personal experience—in women characters. Mid-century book reviewers welcomed individuality in *male* characters, Nina Baym tells us; in *female* characters it was anathema. And the venom directed at nonconforming characters spilled over onto the authors themselves. The attack on Charlotte Brontë by a reviewer in *Graham's Magazine* is a case in point: " 'the authoress, in fact, is a strong-minded woman, a hardy, self-relying egoist from the very strength of her individuality; and she has stores of vitriolic contempt and scorn for her weak sisters' " (*Novels* 99). "Strong-minded," "hardy," "self-relying"—these adjectives would seem at first glance to be complimentary. These characteristics, however, in the reviewer's perception, render the author devoid of empathy, compassion, affection—the essential "feminine" personality traits. The fear was that individuality would "unsex" a woman.

The restrictions on the woman at the center of a text were severe, but they can be more concretely seen by their flouting in a nonconforming text than by listing absences in any number of conforming texts; presence is always easier to chronicle than absence. Elizabeth Stoddard in *The Morgesons* (1862), a novel much influenced by Brontë, creates a superbly nonconforming protagonist, passionate and self-defining Cassandra Morgeson, and the unsettling effects of her personality upon others show us that core perceptions of woman's identity were being challenged. Ben Somers, Cassandra's former suitor, defines the nature of her deviance, and his description is central to our understanding of what was being screened from other texts.

> Then, to my amazement, I saw that, unlike most women, you *understood your instincts*; that you *dared to define them*, and *were impious enough to follow them*. You debased my ideal, you confused me, also, for I could never affirm that you were wrong; forcing me to consult abstractions, they gave a verdict in your favor, which almost unsexed you in my estimation. I must own that the man who is willing to marry you has more courage than I have. (226, emphasis mine)

Stoddard in this extraordinarily insightful passage states the presence of the constraining ideal, interprets her heroine's uniqueness, and affirms it;

Cassandra understands her instincts, defines them, and follows them. She rejects piety, the essential component of feminine morality. She is a woman who focuses at length and in depth on her own needs and development. In particular she is a sexual woman, falling deeply in love, first with a married cousin and later with a handsome, dissolute alcoholic. Cassandra is "personal"—shattering the boundaries of the ideal.

Stoddard delineates, too, the kind of censure that stands in the way of the presentation of non-ideal women characters. Charges of "impiety" and "debasement" were common for women who deviated from the ideal, as was the claim that they had "unsexed" themselves. Women's writing, limited as it was by anxiety about the potential, both personal and national, for moral disruption that might be created by a full disclosure of woman's nature, produced few female protagonists like Cassandra. Readers in general did not respond well to a nonconforming heroine; she confused them, just as Cassandra confused Ben. Cassandra, with her sober self-involvement, unrelieved by comedy, romance,[16] or renunciation, was an unsettling protagonist, and, most likely as a consequence, *The Morgesons* did not have a wide popular reception.

Reactions: Conventions and Strategies

Aside from stunting literary protagonists, proscriptions on women's expression caused other reactions, leading to conventions and strategies that follow discernible patterns. Publishing conventions were pronounced. The conforming writer would only publish if her work was to be "an instrument of good," as the popular poet Lydia Sigourney said about the impetus for her life's work (*Letters of Life* 324), or if she needed the money, as many women writers, including Sigourney, did, to support her family. In both cases her ambition would be altruistic, not personal, and she would not be open to censure, either by the public or by her own sense of what was "womanly."[17] Further, in their work women writers developed certain strategies of expression affecting character presentation, subject matter, and style.

Rather than presenting individualistic women protagonists, women writers usually relied on stereotypes of feminine identity, among the most popular of which was the image of the "little girl." It was one way to avoid the presentation of an adult woman character, and from Jane Elton, orphaned at the age of twelve in Catharine Maria Sedgwick's pioneering *New England Tale* (1822), through saintly little Eva of Elizabeth Oakes Smith's long poem, *The Sinless Child* (1843), the multitudinous little girls of Susan Warner's novels, naughty little Gerty of Maria Cummins's 1854 *The Lamplighter*, boyish Capitola of E.D.E.N. Southworth's 1859 newspaper opus, *The Hidden Hand*, and the March sisters of Louisa May Alcott's *Little Women* (1868), the little girl protagonist was markedly present in the literature of conventional women. She served at least two very important functions; she bypassed the freighted issue of adult female sexuality, and she offered a legitimate outlet for female anger.

Warner's *Queechy*, which consists largely of a love story between the protagonist, Fleda Ringgan, and Mr. Carleton, an English aristocrat, is an example of a text using the little girl protagonist in a manner that both suggests and evades issues of sexual passion. The story begins when Fleda, still a little girl, attracts Mr. Carlton's eye as the apotheosis of womanly perfection. The story of the growth of their mutual love continues throughout the entire novel, sexualized occasionally, as in the following passage about a tandem horseback ride that at first terrifies little Fleda:

> But Mr. Carlton's arm was gently passed round her, and she knew it held her safely and would not let her fall; and he bent down his face to her and asked her so kindly and tenderly, and with such a look too, that seemed to laugh at her fears, whether she felt afraid?—and with such a kind little pressure of his arm that promised to take care of her,—that Fleda's courage mounted twenty degrees at once. And it rose higher every minute; the horse went very easily, and Mr. Carlton held her so that she could not be tired, and made her lean against him; and before they had done a mile Fleda began to be delighted. Such a charming way of travelling! Such a free view of the country! . . . and she sat silently and gravely looking at it, her head lying upon Mr. Carlton's breast, her little mind very full of thoughts and musings, curious, deep. . . . (I 141)

Sexuality is very indirect in this novel, coded in terms of affection and care offered to a child, revealed in the peculiar emphasis of the language and imagery in such scenes. In most women's novels, however, the little girl protagonist allows an almost complete eradication of sexuality.

Anger, however, *was* permitted to children; ostensibly they didn't know any better. Many novels use the "childish" anger of little girls as an important expressive device. Maria Cummins's Gerty, for instance, hurls a rock through her former guardian's window in *The Lamplighter* (1854), and Warner's Ellen in *The Wide, Wide World* has been so mistreated by her guardian that she has come to hate "the very look of her bonnet hanging up on the wall" (165). This anger is "safe," however, because once expressed it can then be denied by being "corrected" in the course of the narrative; both Gerty and Ellen mature into ideal selflessness. Nonetheless, the proscriptions have been circumvented; anger and rebellion *have* been expressed.

Another strategy for handling anger was to direct it outward at important public, humanitarian, issues. Thus both anger and literary ambition would be altruistic rather than personal. Stowe in *Uncle Tom's Cabin*, Rebecca Harding Davis in "Life in the Iron Mills" (1861), and Helen Hunt Jackson in *Ramona* (1884) are three of the notable writers in this category. Stowe's novel is directed against the enslavement of black Americans. Davis's short story exposes the exploitation and abuse of the working class. And Jackson chronicles the cruel displacement of American Indians from their ancestral land. Women's perceived moral superiority sanctioned altruistic anger in their writing, and public issues engendered many fine nineteenth-century American women's texts. In this case social biases worked to the advantage of women, for, as a result of the cultural conditioning that encouraged them to express concern for others if not for themselves, women's fiction and poetry of social reform was politically influential in its era, foreshadowing the powerful social realist fiction of the twentieth century.

Feminine style, too, was restricted by expectations as to the nature of woman. Style as well as subject being an expression of self, most women writers did not wish to appear "bold" in their mode of expression, for fear of being perceived as unfeminine. Standard forms—the sentimental novel and conventionally rhymed and metered verse—dominate women's writing. And the kind of language essayist Gail Hamilton calls "drawing-room grammar"—a genteel parlance eliminating concrete, vigorous diction— was expected (95), although certainly not universally adhered to.

A tendency in some women's writing of the period to resort to tactics of indirection displays the authors' ingenuity in finding means of expression in spite of proscriptions. Ambivalence, irony of tone, and sequential disordering of narrative provide women writers ways of obliquely expressing sentiments that they might hesitate to state directly. These devices offer safe—because more or less covert—outlets for proscribed feelings and are used in varying degrees by both conventional and nonconforming writers. The conventional Warner in *The Wide, Wide World*, for example, has so completely overlaid personal anger with conventional piety that she guards herself from all but the most subtle reading of proscribed subjects. It is the extraordinary ambivalence of her characterizations that reveals Warner's true feelings. The sinister undertones of the autocratic "hero" figure make Ellen's automatic obedience worrisome. Even though the Rev. John Humphries is presented as a masculine ideal, the problematic elements in his character reveal, on one hand, Warner's sublimated fury at what she, on the other hand, sincerely sees as the necessity for feminine submission to masculine authority. When the writer cannot speak in her own voice, her ambivalence speaks for her.

Fanny Fern, an often dissenting writer, is more open in her use of indirection as an expressive device. In her satiric short essays this author often uses heavy irony to make statements that sound conventional when taken literally, but that, because of tonal implications, reveal themselves to be not only unconventional, but anti-conventional. For instance, in "The Tear of a Wife," a short journalistic essay, Fanny Fern urges her married women readers to smile instead of cry, calling marriage the *"summum bonum,*—the height of feminine ambition." But the hyperbole of her language in a context where she has previously described marriage as an ongoing nightmare of "back-aches, and side-aches, and head-aches, and dropsical complaints, and smoky chimneys, and old coats, and young babies" (*Ruth Hall and Other Writings* 236–37) reveals a strongly ironic stance, making it clear that she is mocking the cultural ideal of marriage as "the height of feminine ambition."

In *Hitherto* (1869), novelist A.D.T. Whitney uses indirection differently, not in terms of tone, but of genre expectations, disrupting the sequence of conventional narrative to make her point. The conventional narrative of the women's novels with which Whitney's readers were familiar moves from the sorrows of childhood to the "happy ending" of the wedding day. Whitney begins as expected—with the miserable childhood experience of Anstiss Dolbeare, her very sympathetic protagonist—and takes us through her wedding day. But Whitney doesn't stop there; the bulk of the narrative concerns itself with a close investigation of the first seven years of her marriage, focusing on the "disappointment and endurance" (4) Anstiss must undergo as she finds out that her marriage does not fulfill the needs of her intelligence and sexuality. At the end, following a religious conversion, Anstiss dwindles into wifehood, becomes, in truth, as her husband wants, "married to [him], through and through, every thought and fibre of her" (459). The resolution may be, finally, conventional, but the seven-year insertion that disrupts narrative expectations presents a subtle but effective condemnation of the personal diminution required by conventional marriage.[18]

Although many women writers did acquiesce, at least overtly, to conventions of woman's identity and social role, constraints on their expression occasionally required them to resort to tactics of stylistic indirection, such as the use of ambivalence and irony in tone, or the disruption of sequential expectations in narrative, to allow them to present nuances of complexity unavailable to direct expression.[19]

Nonconforming Writers

For the largest part of the century style and subject matter in the genres of the novel and poetry were heavily constrained. Louisa May Alcott was one writer who felt the cultural admonitory finger directly. "I think my natural ambition is for the lurid style . . . ," she said toward the end of her life, "[but] I shall always be a wretched victim to the respectable . . . " (Stern, *Books* 168).[20] Hawthorne understood the problem and noted in 1853 that women's books were sure to possess "character and value" only when they jettisoned the expressive constraints, or what he called "the restraints of decency" (*Letters* 78).

Some did. And in the experience and comments of these "deviants" we can begin to see how problematic the issue of women's expression was.[21] Hawthorne admired Fanny Fern, author of *Ruth Hall* (1855); he felt she wrote "in little more than her bare bones, her heart pulsating visibly and indecently in its cage of ribs. Still there are ribs, and there is a heart" (*Letters* 78). What Hawthorne meant was that the character of Ruth Hall, Fanny Fern's protagonist, comes to life (is *embodied*, according to his metaphor) as a passionate woman in a way that was unusual for contemporary women's fiction. *Ruth Hall* was considered by many to be a very scandalous book. The reviewer for *Putnam's Monthly* said the book was full of "unfemininely bitter wrath and spite." And *Godey's Lady's Book* refused to review it (Wood, "Scribbling Women" 3–4). This was partly because it was a *roman à clef* in which Fanny Fern revealed mistreatment received at the hands of her socially prominent family. Partly, however, the scandal stemmed from the author's presentation of a female character who deviates strongly from the ideal.

Ruth Hall is an angry and ambitious woman. Like her creator, Ruth is a writer who violates expressive proscriptions and is charged with "unsexing" herself: "All sorts of rumors became rife about 'Floy' [Ruth's pseudonym], some maintaining her to be a man, because she had the courage to call things by their right names, and the independence to express herself boldly on subjects which to the timid and clique-serving, were tabooed" (133). Because of the scandal attached to the novel and because of flamboyant publicizing by its publisher, *Ruth Hall* was popular, selling more than 50,000 copies in eight months (Kelley, *Private Woman* 5). Stoddard's

The Morgesons, a more serious-minded study of a woman's individuality, was not well received by the public; although it was favorably reviewed, it did not sell (Stoddard xix). However, both authors center on a similar trait in their characters, that of emotional honesty in self-expression. Ruth had "the courage to call things by their right names." So did Cassandra. "But one thing," she says, "I know of myself then—that I concealed nothing; the desires and emotions which are usually kept as a private fund I displayed and exhausted. My audacity shocked those who possessed this fund. My candor was called anything but truthfulness . . . " (58–59). Both Ruth and Cassandra violate the unwritten laws of feminine reticence and are condemned for that violation. Their creators, in singling out this particular issue for explicit mention, stress their awareness of the constraints on women's expression.

Adah Isaacs Menken, an actress and poet whose flagrant self-exposure both in life and in print during the 1850s and 60s made her a pariah to conservative Americans, was another nonconforming writer. Menken wrote with passion about all aspects of her experience, saying "audacity is divine" ("Genius," *Infelicia* 63). The Albany, New York *Sunday Argus*, as late as 1877, nine years after her death, remembered her with "holy horror" ("A Strange Woman," July 15, 1877). In an era when women's literature was expected to present a feminine ideal, Fern, Stoddard, and Menken transgressed the codes of feminine articulation. Menken was able to do so because she was an outlaw to begin with—a "free lover" and an actress who, billed as "the Naked Lady," appeared on stage clad only in flesh-colored tights. Menken had nothing to lose. She had no interest in being accepted by the genteel and although she was often verbally abused, designated as "merely [a] sensuous animal" (*Sunday Argus*), any calumny she received from the public most likely would have meant little to her; she called popularity "the mess of pottage that alienates the birthright" ("Genius," *Infelicia* 65). Menken's penalty for her expressive deviance was to be vilified by the respectable public and press. Stoddard's penalty was to be ignored. She received little reward for *The Morgesons*, a well-written and honest piece of fiction. It took a particularly strong and canny writer like Fanny Fern to defy the proscriptions on women's expression and still be successful with both the writing establishment and the respectable public.

But the consequences of deviance weren't usually as happy for women writers as they were for Fanny Fern. In her short story, "Marcia," Rebecca Harding Davis tells the fascinating story of Marcia Barr, a nonconforming writer, unschooled but brilliant and original. Marcia has been brought up in social isolation on a remote plantation and her training has not included the proprieties. In this she serves almost the function of an experimental

control case. She has been kept apart from the contamination of the expressive strictures, and the results show in the vivid, unconstrained realism
of her writing. She wrote about "the hot still sunshine . . . the slimy living
things in the stagnant ponds . . . the house and negro quarters with all
their dirt and dreary monotony . . . " (273). And she did not censor her
language: "There was . . . in all that she said or wrote an occasional gross
indecency, such as a child might show: her life on the plantation explained
it. Like Juliet she spoke the language of her nurse. But even Shakespeare's
nurse and Juliet would not be allowed nowadays to chatter at will in the
pages of a family magazine" (273). And neither was Marcia. Her insistence
on "strong and vivid" (273) writing in her own manner leads her not to
success, but to poverty, illness, and starvation. After a failed suicide attempt she succumbs to what she perceives as a fate almost literally worse
than death—marriage, manifestly desperate on her part, to an "honest and
kindly" man who takes her away from "rubbishy book-makers" because
he wants her to "live like a lady" (277, 279).

Davis suggests here that to "live like a lady" and to write literature
uncensored by the expectations of a restrictive culture are contradictory
and irreconcilable goals. "Marcia" is a curious story, partly a thoughtful
study of the clash between individual genius and the literary/cultural establishment and partly a cautionary tale. But its message is clear: little room
for expressive deviation is allowed, and the punishment can be severe.

Women writers thus faced a difficult situation in nineteenth-century
America; they had a clear mandate to write, and a clear sanction against
complete and honest expression. A feminine literature, to be acceptable to
conventional writer and reader, had to screen out, sublimate, or otherwise
disguise insistent but culturally threatening personal energies. The result
is that in nineteenth-century American literature the personal was a problematic subject for women in a way that it was often not for men.[22] We
know that Emily Dickinson, the leading poet of woman's personal experience in nineteenth-century America, persistently refused to publish. But
Emerson, although his own work is reticent enough about his personal
life, extolled personal candor, saying of the ideal poet in 1844: "The poet
has . . . a whole new experience to unfold; he will tell us how it was with
him" ("The Poet," *Selected Writings* 310). And Walt Whitman focused a
large portion of his poetry on aspects of human experience usually considered personal—most notably on sexuality. The very title of Whitman's
major long poem, "Song of Myself" (1855), emphasizes the deliberateness
of his dissociation from the personal reticence that characterized much
contemporary writing.

For the most part, however, women writers either avoided the personal altogether, as Stowe did in *Uncle Tom's Cabin*, and focused their literary energies on public issues, or they attenuated personal experience by adopting stereotypes and appropriating the traits of the conventional domestic heroine for their protagonists. Rather than creating their protagonists each time afresh out of their own experience of a woman's life, women writers generally compromised their writing by presenting only the "acceptable" aspects of a woman's life. Sigourney's attempt in 1841 to write an American epic poem focusing on the life of Pocahontas, for example, was doomed by the author's inability to imagine her protagonist as anything other than a domestic heroine, and the Indian maid's resultant sweet compliance is hardly the stuff of which epic poetry is made.

Thus, in nineteenth-century America, women's writing was a literature that was significantly restricted in its possibilities. When Margaret Fuller attempted in 1846 to describe her hopes for American literature, she could only perceive it in a gender-based image, as being written by "simple *masculine* minds seizing upon life with unbroken power" ("American Literature" 230, my emphasis). Women were in a position where they were permitted to write, but only with "broken" power, and that so many of them, including Dickinson, wrote as well as they did is testimony to their determination and to the strategies of discourse the more interesting writers among them developed. In studying any of these writers we must always keep in mind the rigid cultural monitoring that afflicted them. What the younger Elizabeth Stuart Phelps said in 1896 of her mother, a writer also named Elizabeth Stuart Phelps (1815–1852), we can say of many of these women, and certainly of Emily Dickinson: "Her nature was drawn against the grain of her times and of her circumstances; and where our feet find easy walking, hers were hedged" (*Chapters* 13).

II

"MY AUTHOR EXISTENCE"
LIVES OF WOMEN WRITERS

> Nothing but deadly determination enables
> me ever to write; it is rowing against wind
> and tide.
>
> —Harriet Beecher Stowe, 1850

In the domestic seclusion and self-willed non-publication of her adulthood Emily Dickinson chose to live very differently from the largely progressive and outgoing women writers who were her contemporaries. Her background was similar to theirs. Like Dickinson many of these women had come from well-to-do homes and well-respected families. Like Dickinson they, for the most part, had received good educations. Some rejected—not without conflict—their religious upbringings. Others suffered debilitating emotional problems or had been disappointed, in one way or another, in love. These factors—gentility, religious conflict, emotional instability, and heartbreak, alone or in combination—have been mentioned as factors in Dickinson's withdrawal from society and from publication. Yet, in spite of the co-existence of these writers in similar cultural conditions to Dickinson, not one reacted to her circumstances by choosing to withdraw her person and her writing from an active engagement with that culture. The surprising fact is that, while many other women writers did battle with the restrictions that would have kept them silent and at home, Dickinson's life in many ways appears congruent with conservative norms for modest, domestic femininity.

Although women writers by and large in their writing extolled domestic commitment for women, setting domesticity up, as Nina Baym says, "as a value scheme for ordering all of life" (*Woman's Fiction* 27), they themselves lived lives that went far beyond the home. Lydia Sigourney and Frances Osgood, for example, broke the codes for acceptable, modest, domestic feminine living with assertive professional or personal behavior that, restrained as it may seem to twentieth-century readers, appeared immodest and free-wheeling to their contemporaries; Sigourney was an expert at professional self-promotion and Osgood, though married, carried on a well-publicized flirtation—perhaps even a love affair—with Edgar Allan Poe. Alice Cary, like Dickinson unmarried, lived an independent and satisfying life in New York City's literary social circles, supporting herself by the proceeds from her writing. Catharine Maria Sedgwick, Elizabeth Oakes Smith, and Harriet Beecher Stowe flouted the ideal of feminine reticence by speaking out boldly on important public issues, such as religious and racial despotism and women's rights. In spite of pressing domestic claims on their time and energy, both Stowe and Elizabeth Stuart Phelps (mother of the later Phelps) wrote prolifically. And Susan Warner saved herself and her family from financial destitution by writing novels.

Warner, by far the most conservative personally of this group of well-known and prolific women, was a reluctant author. Only severe economic hardship caused her to enter the public sphere, and she did it with initial anonymity. If circumstances had allowed, she certainly would have chosen modest seclusion over the public visibility she eventually attained. Other women writers experienced varying degrees of ambivalence about their public exposure. As Mary Kelley notes: "Unlike a male, a female's person was to be shielded from public scrutiny. . . . After all, her proper sphere was the home. . . . Even her exercise of moral, social, or personal influence was to be indirect, subtle, and symbolic. . . . In essence, hers was to remain an invisible presence" (*Private Woman* 111). But even a constant immersion in such a doctrine of female seclusion did not prevent many women from exercising their talents, whether out of financial necessity or for the purposes of moral influence. Some like Warner experienced something close to agony about their intrusion into the public sphere. Others like Osgood and Sigourney seemed to revel in public acclaim. Most found themselves somewhere in between, able to tolerate visibility for the sake of realizing their literary purposes.

The lives of these eight women—writers, for the most part, whose ambitious careers and wide-ranging social and political activities strikingly contradict the domestic ideals they espouse in their writing—suggest that a wide diversity of lifestyles and professional opportunities existed for women writers, even within the bonds of "respectability." Since these were writers whose careers were at a peak before Dickinson began in her late twenties her own commitment to poetry, she would have known something at least of their lives and work; the press was very freehanded in reporting on the lives of women authors. Thus she did have role models for far different life-possibilities for herself as a writer than the domestic seclusion she eventually chose.

Both Dickinson's domestic seclusion and her refusal to publish show signs of conformity, not to the examples that these women set in their lives, but to the conservative tenets of the ethos of femininity that pervaded middle-class American culture and most women's writing during the nineteenth century. Dickinson's seclusion was to some degree affirmed by the feminine ideal of domesticity; it was seen as a woman's obligation to dedicate herself to the needs of home and family. However, in light of the active involvement of other women writers in society in spite of their domestic concerns, we can see that her seclusion, in its exclusive extremity, did not stem from cultural *imperatives* but seems rather to have been a manifestation of pressing personal needs which usurped the ideal of domesticity for their own purposes. Further, given the well-defined rationales of moral teaching and financial need that attached themselves almost inevitably to women's publication, Dickinson's refusal to publish shows cultural logic. In contemporary terms her writing satisfied neither of these criteria: she showed little desire to bring a moral message to readers and she was not economically needy. The facts of Dickinson's life, when set up against the lives of her peers, suggest that strong conservative traits, particularly the ideal of the private nature of feminine existence, to a greater or lesser degree, regulated her self-image and her interaction with the public world. In the extreme exclusivity of her attachment to home and family, Dickinson's life, among the lives of nineteenth-century American women writers, was unique.

I

The family background of Catharine Maria Sedgwick (1789–1867) displays striking parallels to Dickinson's. Sedgwick too was born into a prominent Massachusetts family. Her father was, like Dickinson's, a lawyer and a member of Congress, and he was often away from their Stockbridge home for months at a time on government business. Although Sedgwick did not have the excellent formal education that was available to Dickinson, she praised the "uncommon mental vigor" of her home life for compensating the deficiencies in her training (*Life* 46). Sedgwick and other members of her family struggled with and eventually rejected the rigid Calvinism they were born to. Like Dickinson's mother, Mrs. Sedgwick seems to have suffered long periods of mental depression, as did Sedgwick herself. At the time of her brother Robert's marriage, Sedgwick suffered an emotional crisis such as has often been conjectured to have happened to Dickinson at the time of *her* brother's marriage (Kelley, "Woman Alone" 216–17).

But Sedgwick's reaction to all this was radically different from Dickinson's. Her spinsterhood combined with her financial security offered her an autonomy that she, unlike Dickinson, took full advantage of. She traveled widely and had many friends. She maintained residences in New York City and in Stockbridge, where she was centrally involved in the literary camaraderie of what has come to be known as "The American Lake District." It was at a gathering in her home in 1850 that Hawthorne is reputed to have met Melville for the first time. Sigourney and Harriet Martineau are among literary women known to have visited her there, as well as the renowned actress Fanny Kemble, who became a close friend.

It is particularly relevant to note here that Sedgwick's social and financial circumstances, so like Dickinson's, did not deter her from involving herself in a literary career that brought her much public attention. Nor did they prevent her from speaking out with a bold literary voice on major social issues. A novelist, Sedgwick was a fine stylist and an excellent regional writer. She was in some ways an early social reformer, tackling the hypocrisy of the prevailing Calvinist Christianity in her first novel, *A New England Tale* (1822), and racial and religious despotism in *Hope Leslie* (1827). *A New England Tale* was initially conceived as a Unitarian tract deploring the sad effects on individuals of narrow-minded adherence to outdated religious principles. *Hope Leslie*, a novel that merits increased attention, speaks out passionately for the rights and dignity of Native Americans at a time when there was very little sympathy in American society with that cause.[1]

Sedgwick, like many women writers of her day, did not think of herself as an artist. "My *author* existence," she told her journal in 1835, "has always seemed something accidental, extraneous, and independent of my inner self" (*Life and Letters* 249). However, long before she died at the age of seventy-eight, Sedgwick was indeed recognized as an artist, renowned among her contemporaries along with Irving and Cooper as one of the founders of the new American literature that dealt with native, as opposed to European, characters and concerns, in local and realistic, as opposed to exotic and romantic, settings. In fact, Sedgwick's lively and insightful contributions to American fiction, although forgotten or undervalued in much twentieth-century discourse, were central to the development of a uniquely American literary voice.

The poet Lydia Huntley Sigourney (1791–1865) was raised in circumstances very different from Dickinson's and Sedgwick's; her career demonstrates the increasing democratization of literature in America and the social and economic opportunities a literary career offered. She was born the daughter of a gardener in Norwich, Connecticut, and was educated by her father's employer, who took a great interest in the bright young girl. Her consequent acquaintance with the influential Wadsworth family of Hartford was an initial factor in her rise to poetic fame. From her early life in social obscurity, Sigourney found literature to be an avenue to social prominence, independence, and security.

She began her career in Hartford as a schoolteacher. In 1815, with the sponsorship of Daniel Wadsworth, she published her first book, *Moral Pieces in Prose and Verse*, as Lydia Huntley, but ceased publishing upon her marriage to Charles Sigourney, a hardware merchant. Disappointed both emotionally and financially in her marriage—her husband proved to be cold and critical, and shortly after their marriage he fell into financial difficulties—she was soon in the position of supporting her family by her writing. At times, because of her husband's disapproval, she had to smuggle manuscripts in and out of the house. Her books, sixty-seven in all, include poetry, novels, biographies, religious meditations, gift books, and travel sketches. Her articles and single poems in periodicals number in the thousands. At one point she was the largest single contributor to literary annuals in the United States.

In a wry account of what she considered "The Album Persecution" (*Letters* 368ff) Sigourney gives us an enlightening insight into the special public social role of the publishing poet in nineteenth-century New England—a role that Dickinson, obsessively private, would have found extremely uncomfortable. Called upon by friends, acquaintances, and often even by strangers, Sigourney was expected to turn out a steady stream of original verse for all comers. Elegies, epitaphs, and epithalamions were her specialties, but she was available also to the wandering admirer who showed up at her door to have his prosaic album rarefied by a few lines from the pen of this revered poet. In nineteenth-century America, unlike today, poetry was comfortably interwoven into everyday life. It was published in the newspapers, sent to friends in letters, read aloud around the kitchen stove; it provided enhancement to daily routine and to the rituals of life and death, as well. Viewed in this context, Dickinson's practice of sending poems or scraps of verse to her friends, or even to strangers, to mark special, or even mundane, occasions is not at all unusual. However, she kept her verse private; unlike Sigourney she did not enter the public arena.

To a modern reader much of Sigourney's work seems bland, but occasionally her writing manifests an eerie intensity that maintains its interest, as in the strange tale, "The Father" (Fetterley, *Provisions* 105–16), where a bereaved parent is found trying to tear his way, night after night, into his daughter's grave. "The Suttee" (*Poems* [1827] 126–27), a poem which portrays a beautiful young Indian woman bound to the rotting corpse of her dead husband and screaming for the loss of her child as she burns, is another notable piece.[2] Sigourney also took up unpopular social causes, such as that of the slave and the Indian. But, most often, she was a canny popular poet who maintained her lucrative popularity by presenting comfortable, noncontroversial generalizations about life in familiar verse forms. She made no pretense about the quality of her work. "If there is any kitchen in Parnassus," she concluded in her autobiography, "my Muse has surely officiated there as a woman of all work, and an aproned waiter" (376).

Perhaps the aspect of Sigourney's literary career most significant for a study of women writers is the fact of her professionalism in an age that extolled feminine literary amateurism. In spite of her stance as a woman whose primary concerns were domestic—a major aim of her career, she said, was "not to interfere with the discharge of womanly duty" (*Letters* 324)—Sigourney was a thoroughgoing professional. She was a pioneer for women writers in several ways. In public relations Sigourney was expert, regularly sending letters and gift copies of her books to leading literary and public figures. She also revealed a sharp professionalism in negotiating favorable contracts with publishers and setting up a book distribution system that operated from her own home, and she was one of the first women writers in America to publish under her own name. Although she was often condemned for her "unfeminine" behavior (and curiously enough that censure continues in modern criticism),[3] it marks a significant step in the progressive professionalization of women's writing as well as in the commercialization of literature that characterized the century.

Elizabeth Oakes Prince Smith (1806–1893), poet, novelist and public lecturer, like Dickinson and Sedgwick, was a member of an old New England family. Born in Maine, she was married reluctantly (at her mother's urging) at sixteen to the humorist Seba Smith, then twice her age. During her youth Smith had been an avid student. She had learned to read at the age of two and throughout her girlhood nourished dreams of a college-level education and a school of her own. With marriage, however, and the births of five sons, she was forced to devote herself to domestic concerns. She recalls with poignancy in her autobiography the alteration in her expectations: "I . . . transformed myself to an utterly different creature from what had been native to me" (45).

Upon her husband's financial failure in the 1830s Smith was liberated from her domestic role by the need to earn money to help support her family, and she began an attempt to make a living by her pen. She found a warm reception from the public and from other writers as well, soon becoming a popular figure in New York's literary circles. She was friendly with many of the leading writers of the time, published poems and essays in major journals, and wrote several novels. Smith's best-known work, "The Sinless Child" (1843), a seven-canto narrative poem published originally in Poe's *Southern Literary Messenger*, was a best seller in book form in the 1840s. The character of Eva, the visionary child/woman of the title, epitomizes the stereotype of the ethereal little girl then so popular in women's writing, and Smith's early promulgation of this exemplary figure stands in ironic contrast to her later career as a woman's rights activist.

In the 1850s Smith gave up literature, except for an occasional potboiler, to travel and lecture on the rights of women. She felt that the moral claims of feminism superseded the aesthetic claims of literature. "My literary career had not been devoid of recognition," she relates in her autobiography, "but in this new field, designed to reveal woman to herself, I realized an inconceivable satisfaction. True, many long endeared friends were vexed at me, and did not fail to remonstrate, and I was cruelly abused by the press; but I did not falter . . . " (153).

Smith was a courageous woman. In spite of much condemnation, she took to the lecture circuit, and later extended her scope to religion—becoming in 1877 an ordained minister serving an independent congregation in upstate New York. Indeed, Smith had been a rebel from childhood, commencing to doubt her family's Puritan theology at the age of six. Like Dickinson, who never joined the church and who expressed doubts about conventional Christian beliefs in a number of poems, Smith broke with her religious background. Her later reform activities she saw as a result of this bold and exciting break: "I was reaping the benefits of stepping outside of my Puritanic bondage. Brought up as I had been, I had so much to renounce and so much to do that I almost danced over my freedom" (*Autobiography* 153). That Smith saw her "freedom" from "Puritanic bondage" as an opportunity to go out into the world and attempt to effect important social changes contrasts sharply with Dickinson's dedication to home, family, and the writing of a poetry that was private to an extreme.

The life of Frances Sargent Locke Osgood (1811–1850) also exhibits a degree of freedom uncharacteristic for a nineteenth-century American woman. Born in Boston into a mercantile family, Osgood was encouraged to write at an early age and was publishing in Boston's *Juvenile Miscellany* at the age of fourteen. Osgood seems to have been a passionate and impulsive individual. In her early twenties, while sitting for her portrait, she

was charmed by the romantic personality of the young artist, Samuel Still-
man Osgood, and married him, following him to England in 1835. After
two children and an estrangement from her husband, Osgood was involved
in a very public literary courtship (in the pages of the *Broadway Journal* for
the most part) in the mid-40s with Edgar Allan Poe. This courtship has
often been conjectured to have developed into a love affair but does not
seem to have seriously damaged Osgood's reputation with her contemporaries. She was a widely beloved poet, publishing several collections of
prose and verse, and her work appeared in most of the prominent American
periodicals. Her death at the age of thirty-eight from tuberculosis brought
forth expressions of regret from major literary figures. A memorial volume
edited by Mary Hewitt in 1851 contained contributions from Nathaniel
Hawthorne, Sigourney, Smith, Rufus Griswold, Sarah Helen Whitman
(Poe's fiancée), and others.

Osgood's poetic interests are in love, domestic affections, time, poetry,
and nature. It is in the area of love and passion, however, that Osgood's
poetry is most unusual for her time. In an era that discouraged feminine
candor, she is relatively bold in her approach to this most personal subject,
writing, for instance, about illicit sexual attraction in "Oh! Hasten to my
Side":

> I try to calm, in cold repose,
>   Beneath his earnest eye,
> The heart that thrills, the cheek that glows—
>   Alas! in *vain* I try!
>
> (Watts 113)

and expressing blunt and bitter disappointment in marriage in "Song":

> I loved an ideal—I sought it in thee;
> I found it unreal as stars in the sea . . . .

she says, and expresses hope that her thwarted capacity for love

> . . . may wake in some better and holier sphere,
> Unbound by the fetter Fate hung on it here.
>
> (Griswold 287).

This is strong language. As Emily Stipes Watts notes, Osgood said things
in verse that would not be said again in America by a woman until the
1890s (106). She means, of course, in published and socially sanctioned

verse; Adah Isaacs Menken's scandalous posthumous volume, *Infelicia*, was published in 1868, and Dickinson was dealing, in her own very private and oblique way, with what seem to be the most rigidly proscribed subjects for women—sexual passion, ambition, and anger. But what is notable about Osgood is that she seems to have managed to evade in her own psychology the more stringent proscriptions, especially against the expression of sexual attraction, and that she published her passionate lyrics, seemingly without serious personal consequences.[4]

Probably as a result of her pressing need to please the public—she, like Sigourney and Smith, supported her family by writing—Osgood's verse sometimes suffers from the repeated use of conventional images and diction. At her best, however, she is a poet whose honesty of feeling is exceptional in an age characterized by suppressed feminine passions.

Elizabeth Stuart Phelps (1815–1852) led a more conventional life than Osgood. Wed at twenty-seven to a minister who later became a professor of religion at Andover Newton Theological Seminary, she came late to the conflict between her two careers—as writer and as mother—that elicited some of her best work. As a popular writer and as the mother of two young children, Phelps suffered profound conflict in her daily life; she was "torn by the civil war of the dual nature which can be given to women only," as her daughter later remembered it (*Chapters* 12). Phelps had been born in Andover, and was brought up in an academic atmosphere. By her late teens she was a publishing writer of religious articles. Her personality was characterized by a marked intensity, both psychological and religious, as she struggled throughout her life, in a manner reminiscent of Dickinson, with depression, religious doubts, and an obsession with death. As her husband noted in a memorial after her death: "Life was to her eye, a passage through a great *emergency*" (*Last Leaf* 36).

Phelps first came to be noted as a writer in 1851 with her publication of *The Sunnyside: or The Country Minister's Wife*, which sold 100,000 copies in this country alone within the first year and was subsequently translated into French and German for European sale. Dickinson had in her library a copy of Phelps's posthumous book, *The Last Leaf from Sunnyside* (1853), so we have confirmation that she was familiar with this author. That she had also read *The Sunnyside* is indicated by a comment in a letter to Susan Gilbert in June 1852, where Dickinson says, "I think of each 'sunnyside' where we have sat together . . . " (L 93). The emphasis by quotation marks indicates a literary allusion, and this novel was in the height of its popularity at that time. That this "sunnyside" allusion should be followed by the much-commented-upon "man of noon" paragraphs is not surprising, considering that the novel focuses upon marriage and its obligations. Marriage here transforms a lively young girl named Emily—whose only image of being the proper minister's wife she wants to be is to picture herself "in a straw bonnet trimmed with green ribbon" (*Sunnyside* 18)—into a shabby, albeit willing, domestic drudge.

Phelps's best book, however, and one that is beginning to receive attention currently from feminist critics, is *The Angel Over the Right Shoulder* (1852), a slender autobiographical volume which, as Nina Baym nicely puts it, is a tale of "domestic schizophrenia" (248). Better than any other contemporary work it illustrates the dilemma of the talented woman whose pressing domestic responsibilities make a life of artistic or intellectual endeavor difficult, indeed impossible. Mrs. James, the protagonist of *Angel*, is, like Phelps herself, a wife and the mother of two children. The narrative follows her doomed attempt to structure for herself a daily schedule that will allow time for the serious intellectual life she craves. The opening sets the tone of frustration that pervades the tale:

> "There! a woman's work is never done," said Mrs. James. "I thought, for once, I was through; but just look at that lamp, now! it will not burn, and I must go and spend half an hour over it."
> "Don't you wish you had never been married?" said Mr. James, with a good-natured laugh.
> "Yes"—rose to her lips, but was checked by a glance at the group upon the floor, . . . (Fetterley, *Provisions* 209)

That group, of course, consists of her husband and children tumbling together in a drudgery-free romp.

After seeing in a dream two angels recording her "selfish" and her selfless deeds in an eternal book, Mrs. James renounces her intellectual ambitions. The message of the tale, as of the largest part of the contemporary literature of women, is that the needs of a woman's family far outweigh her own ambitions in importance. Phelps herself, however, did not succumb to silence, but wrote until her death in childbirth at the age of thirty-seven.

Harriet Beecher Stowe (1811–1896) was another woman who combined the careers of mother and writer. She was born in 1811 in Litchfield, Connecticut, into the family of Lyman Beecher, a prominent Congregational minister, and was educated at home as well as at the well-known Miss Pierce's School in Litchfield. Although she had published several stories over the years, Stowe was forty years old and, in her own words, "a mere drudge" (Charles Stowe 92) married to a conspicuously eccentric professor of religion and the mother of five children before she turned to writing in earnest.

Stowe's experiences with the oppression of blacks in the border city of Cincinnati where she lived with her family for eighteen years combined with her Christian convictions regarding the moral responsibility of the individual to make Stowe a committed abolitionist. Her convictions were galvanized into fury by the Fugitive Slave Law, which penalized citizens who were found guilty of helping slaves escape from bondage. When her sister-in-law wrote suggesting that Stowe use her writing talents to strike a blow against slavery, she agreed, saying, "As long as the baby sleeps with me nights I can't do much at anything, but I will do it at last. I will write that thing if I live" (*Life and Letters* 130). *Uncle Tom's Cabin*, a brilliant epic indictment of slavery, was the result.

Exhortation ran in the Beecher blood; all seven of Stowe's brothers became ministers. But in mid-nineteenth-century America the only pulpit open to women was the printed page. Stowe's fiction thus had a strong moral component. A novel, she said in the New York weekly newspaper, the *Independent*, in 1856, was "understood to be a parable—a story told in illustration of a truth or fact" (Kelley, *Private Woman* 250). She used that medium with open and sweeping didactic intent: to reach a large audience, to motivate individual and political action, to help change the course of history. The impetus for Stowe's expression and the impetus for Dickinson's were in this way diametrically opposed. Where Stowe's writing was directed outward to effect change in the world of social and political reality, Dickinson's work dealt largely with the personal and internal realities of individual consciousness.[5] Stowe did not escape unscathed from her flouting of the ideal of feminine reticence; her notoriety after the publication of *Uncle Tom's Cabin* was probably greater than any woman in America had hitherto experienced. Her great public visibility, however, and the attendant unpleasantness, did not prevent Stowe from continuing an often controversial writing career.[6]

Susan Warner (1819–1885) is the most conservative writer in this study, the most extreme adherent to the ideal of "true womanhood." She was born in New York City, the daughter of a wealthy lawyer who saw to it that she had an excellent education at home—she studied music, Italian, history, literature, and the classics—and associated with the genteel families of New York society. When, in 1837, he suddenly lost his fortune, Susan and her younger sister, Anna, were forced to retreat from society to an old house that had been purchased as a summer home on Constitution

Island. There it soon became evident that their survival depended upon their own efforts in gardening, housekeeping, and whatever money-making projects they could devise on their own. This change in her way of life was a painful blow to Warner, and her bitter resentment of inept, irresponsible males who cause hardship for the women in their care is evident throughout her books. However, Warner was a devout evangelical Christian and strictly interpreted biblical and cultural commands of subordination to men; the bulk of her substantial literary earnings, for instance, went to further her father's futile lawsuits though she and Anna were at times reduced to raising and selling vegetables for a living.

Warner had always been an adept storyteller, sharing her impromptu narratives with her family. At a time of extreme financial desperation for her family, help came from that quarter. As her sister told it years later, Warner was drying dishes with her Aunt Fanny who suddenly exclaimed, " 'Sue, I believe if you would try, you could write a story.' Whether she added 'that would sell,' I am not sure," Anna continued, "but of course that was what she meant." According to her sister, Warner wrote the opening words of *The Wide, Wide World* that very night (Anna Warner 263). That phenomenal best seller was published in 1850, followed shortly by *Queechy* (1852), and then by a myriad of other novels far less noteworthy. Both *The Wide, Wide World* and *Queechy* were the work of a writer of great ability and passion, whose imaginative horizons were strongly culturally determined. Nonetheless, noted writers enjoyed her books as much as did the rest of the reading public. Elizabeth Barrett Browning wrote to her friend Miss Mitford, "Tell me if you have read Queechy? I think it very clever and characteristic. Mrs. Beecher Stowe scarcely exceeds it after all her trumpets" (Browning III 393), and Henry James found Warner's work to be a more successful transcription of local color than the novels of Flaubert (Foster 48).

As a conservative woman, Warner was sanctioned in her literary ambition only by her severe financial need. Her desire to do good also helped to allay the anxiety caused by her sudden notoriety. Anna Warner tells us that when *The Wide, Wide World* proved to be a success, Susan was deeply concerned that her talent should be "thoroughly sanctified" (Anna Warner 342–43). Initially Warner published under the pseudonym of Elizabeth Wetherell, but her anonymity did not last long. Her response to the fame immediately attendant upon the publication of *The Wide, Wide World* in 1850 is typical of most contemporary women's socially inculcated preference for privacy, and it enlightens us as to the roots of Dickinson's fierce protection of her own obscurity. Warner tried desperately to maintain her anonymity, but within months of publication her true identity was known and widely disseminated. In their issue of May 8, 1852, shortly after the publication of *Queechy*, the *Springfield Republican*, following a process of involved and circuitous reasoning, triumphantly, and incorrectly, announced her identity as "Elizabeth Warner." "Now," they continued with unabated avidity, "where does she live?" Like other conservative women writers Warner was extraordinarily anxious about her sudden visibility in the public eye, confiding cryptically and ambivalently to her journal in 1851: "Nay, fame never was a woman's Paradise, yet" (Kelley, *Private Woman* 28).

Alice Cary (1820–1871), popular poet and writer of regional sketches, was born in the frontier state of Ohio, and brought up in an atmosphere of rural poverty and marginal literacy. Her education consisted of brief periods in a country school and long evenings poring over religious magazines, Pope's *Essays*, *Charlotte Temple*, and whatever other reading came her way. In spite of a disapproving stepmother, Alice and her sister Phoebe wrote early, and Alice's first poem was published in Boston and Cincinnati during her teens. As her writing filtered into Eastern publications, Cary was encouraged by literary luminaries such as John Greenleaf Whittier, Horace Greeley, and Rufus Griswold. Upon the failure of a love relationship, Alice, with her sister Phoebe, took the bold move of relocating to New York with the express intention of making a living by writing.

By 1856 Alice had earned enough to buy a small house on 20th Street, for the next fifteen years the center of an influential literary clique. The lively Sunday evening receptions at their home drew, according to their biographer, Mary Clemmer Ames, "not only the most earnest, but many of the most brilliant Americans" of that era (60). The wide range of disparate minds and interests represented there is indicated by the names of several of those who visited often: the journalist Horace Greeley was a regular; another journalist, Dickinson's friend, Samuel Bowles, attended when he was in New York City; as did Bayard Taylor, yet another journalist and a world traveler. The woman's rights' activist Elizabeth Cady Stanton came often, as did social reformer Robert Dale Owen, the lecturer Anra Dickinson, New York *Ledger* editor Robert Bonner, writers Elizabeth and Richard Stoddard, journalist and lecturer Kate Field, the poet John Greenleaf Whittier, and the master showman Phineas T. Barnum. At about the same time that Emily Dickinson was withdrawing increasingly from society, the Cary sisters, in spite of their humble social origins, opened up for themselves a stimulating life among some of the most forward-thinking people of their era. For them, literature was socially as well as economically liberating, offering a wide world of congenial companionship from which to pick and choose.

As a poet Alice Cary was more prolific and more popular than her sister Phoebe, who, ironically, was often the better poet. A parodic stance in Phoebe's poetry sanctioned discussion of unromantic and nonsentimental realities, while Alice's poetry is often conventional in subject, dealing with love, religious renunciation, and death. Certain poems, however, stand out for their understanding of the complex and difficult lives of women. In "The Bridal Veil" Alice Cary presents a loving bride whose outspoken refusal to submit her spirit, in spite of conventional expectations, is striking: "I have wings flattened down and hid under my veil . . . And spite of all clasping, and spite of all bands, / I can slip like a shadow, a dream, from your hands" (*Ballads* 144). At its best, as here, her verse is lyrical, with clear syntax and an unforced line. On the whole, however, her poetry is conventional in its employment of stock images and standard verse forms and in its avoidance of controversial subject matter.

It is in her regional sketches that Cary's writing excels. *Clovernook*, in both the first and second series, contains superb realistic sketches of the harsh, limited lives lived by frontier people, especially women. Perhaps because Cary was not writing in a codified genre—her tales are presented not as fiction but rather as "recollections"—she found herself freed of the constraints of the writing community and able to express with stark clarity the pain of individuals forced to live at a level of minimal economic and emotional sustenance. Dickinson, too, deals with emotional deprivation. But, whereas she concentrates on the experience of *personal* emotional impoverishment in poems such as 612, beginning, "It would have starved a Gnat— / To live so small as I—," Cary takes her critique into the larger world, particularly concentrating on the emotional toll taken by the harsh life of the American frontier. The popularity of the *Clovernook* tales led not only to a second series but to a children's version in 1854 and *Pictures of Country Life* in 1859. During the course of her career Cary published eleven volumes of poetry and prose on her own and three with her sister.

Refusing several offers of marriage, Alice Cary and her sister lived together in New York until, in 1871, they died within six months of each other.

The writers whose lives I have presented here span a period of over fifty years of women's writing and publishing—from Sigourney's earliest book in 1815 to Stowe's and Warner's publications in the 1860s and 70s. By far the largest part of their work was done, however, before Dickinson began

her own writing career in her late twenties. These are writers she would
have read about and heard about as she was growing up and entering
young adulthood. As a group they present her with role models for a wide
variety of experience; they traveled widely, led varied social lives among
interesting people, spoke out on important social and political issues, were
financially independent, published widely to much acclaim, and at least
one conducted a passionate public romance. In sum, these were women
who took risks, who lived much freer lives than was usual for American
women in that era. On the whole, although they for the most part did
preach a gospel of domesticity, the momentum of their lives was *away* from
the home, out toward an active involvement with society. The momentum
of Dickinson's life, on the other hand, led her in the opposite direction—
from a socially active childhood and youth to a virtual self-imprisonment
within her home. For the last twenty-five years of her life, as far as we
know, she left her home only for visits to Boston for medical treatments.
Except for a few select visitors she refused to see anyone. And, except for
ten poems that may well have been submitted without her knowledge, she
did not publish. In Dickinson's life, the ethos of feminine domesticity and
privacy pervading women's writing was lived in actuality and to an extreme
unimagined in the novels or poems of her contemporaries.

II

   That Emily Dickinson was a domestic woman, we know. Her domestic
obligations began early in her life. In a letter to Jane Humphrey in January
of 1850, when she had just turned nineteen, she complained about the
claims on her time that had kept her from writing to her friend: " . . . and
my two hands but *two*—not four, or five as they ought to be—and so *many*
wants—and me so *very* handy—and my time of so *little* account—and my
writing so *very* needless . . . " (L 30). In May of the same year she wrote
at length to Abiah Root about the arduous job of keeping the house while
her mother was ill. During this ten-day to two-week period, she did the
cooking, washed the dishes, dusted and cleaned, sat with the invalid,
provided for her needs, and cared for her father and brother as well. "God
keep me from what they call *households*" (L 36), she exclaimed to Abiah in
summing up the experience. But this period of intense domestic labor was
only the beginning of lifelong responsibilities for Dickinson in the home.
   In nineteenth-century America, domesticity was the arena in which a
woman's active life was expected to be played out. It was a private arena
as opposed to the great public arenas of commerce and government, but

it was not the less important for its privateness. In *The American Woman's Home*, Harriet Beecher Stowe and Catharine Beecher elevate the domestic role to the highest social function:

> Surely, it is a pernicious and mistaken idea that the duties which tax a woman's mind are petty, trivial, or unworthy of the highest grade of intellect and moral worth. Instead of allowing this feeling, every woman should imbibe from early youth, the impression that she is in training for the discharge of the most important, the most difficult, and the most sacred and interesting duties that can possibly employ the highest intellect. (193)

It was through the moral influence of home and mother that the nation was to develop and maintain a viable set of moral values. "Genius," as literary talent was almost inevitably called, transgressed the codes and caused personal conflict for the woman writer, placing contradictory claims on her time and energy and jeopardizing her sense of identity. Domesticity encompassed an ideology of the public and the private that structured women's understanding not only of their responsibilities but of their desires as well. Far more than simply consisting of the daily obligations of household maintenance and child rearing, domesticity offered for women a secure identity, a definition of who they were. Dickinson's sense of herself as a private, domestic woman, sanctioned by the cultural ideal, most likely played a significant role in her increasing seclusion within the home and her decision not to publish the poems that by her early thirties she was writing almost daily.

An understanding of the cultural ideal of feminine privacy and domesticity helps us to see that Dickinson's withdrawal into the home and her refusal to publish were not aberrations rooted in psychological alienation from her society. Rather—however deeply rooted in pressing personal needs they may have been—they were the logical, if exaggerated, extremes of compliance to contemporary codes of feminine behavior. In relation to contemporary women writers Dickinson seems to have followed the old adage: "Do as I say, not as I do." Although the ethos of ideal domesticity was at the heart of the message imparted by women's writing in that era, the lives of most women writers themselves were in conflict with, if not in direct contradiction to, this ethos. Dickinson, however, because of the urgent demands of an idiosyncratic psychology, seems to have lived, with an almost reactionary integrity, a life congruent with the conservative message of feminine domesticity preached by the women writers whose progressive lifestyles she did not emulate.

Dickinson's domestic life was not that of a lady of leisure. The Dickinson family usually had a servant to do the heavier housework; Margaret O'Brien was with the family for ten years during the late 1850s and early 1860s, and Maggie Maher came in the late 1860s and stayed until Vinnie's death in 1899 (Sewall, *Life* 609–10). It still fell to the women of the family, nonetheless, to do much of the cooking and housecleaning. Dickinson made bread and desserts, and was known for her excellence in both. "People must have puddings," she told Thomas Wentworth Higginson on his first visit. "*Very* dreamily," he added, "as if they were comets" (L 342a).[7] In her letters over the years she makes reference to, among other chores, cooking, washing dishes, dusting, cleaning lamps, knitting, and caring for her invalid mother. Doubtless she had many other daily tasks; social class did not necessarily excuse a woman from domestic drudgery. Harriet Martineau in 1837 noted the obligations at the highest social levels: "All American ladies should know how to clear-starch and iron: how to keep plate and glass: how to cook dainties: and, if they understand the making of bread and soup likewise, so much the better" (302). Since it was upon the quotidian chores of women that the comfort and order, and indeed the health and harmony, of a household depended, the responsibility was a heavy one. That Dickinson took her domestic work seriously we can assume from a comment by Joseph Lyman, a friend of the Dickinson sisters in their youth, that, whereas Vinnie was sometimes "afraid of soiling her little fat hands," "Em is an excellent housekeeper" (Sewall, *Life* 87).

It is difficult for modern readers accustomed to labor-saving devices to have an adequate sense of just how all-consuming an obligation housework was in the nineteenth century. Being "an excellent housekeeper," a far more arduous occupation than it is today, must have seriously fragmented the time Dickinson had available for writing poetry. Susan Strasser in *Never Done*, a fascinating study of American housework, investigates the many facets of daily domestic functions: baking, cooking, keeping the fires, heating the home, lighting the home, drawing water, disposing of water, washing and ironing clothes, making and mending clothes, shopping, cleaning, nursing the sick, caring for and educating children—the list is endless. And each one of these functions breaks down into multiple tasks, most of them daily. Strasser notes the complications that attended just one aspect of one of these jobs—the initial preparation of food. Merely to get food to the stage where one could *begin* to cook it was a job in itself!

> Few manufactured products relieved the housewives' tasks once they had brought the food home. All year round, food arrived in the kitchen unprepared. Shoppers returned from the market with live chickens that had to be killed, or dead ones that had to be plucked; their work at home matched

that of the farmer or the poor urban chicken keeper. Even purchased fish had scales; even purchased hams had to be soaked or blanched. Roasting and grinding green coffee, grinding and sifting whole spices, cutting and pounding lump or loaf sugar, sifting heavy flour that might be full of impurities, soaking oatmeal overnight, shelling nuts, grinding cocoa shells, seeding raisins, making and nurturing yeast, drying herbs: tasks like these accompanied nearly every ingredient of every recipe, whether it came from the garden or the market. (29)

Along with her other housekeeping chores, Dickinson is known to have done much baking. Strasser's delineation of the multitudinous steps of food preparation helps us to understand just how much daily drudgery was involved in producing the family bread and baked goods and enlightens us as to how much time Dickinson must have spent at this task. The conflict between literary talent and domestic claims may well have been a draining one for Dickinson; Apollo and Hestia are both demanding task-masters.[8] But we must remember that to some degree Dickinson chose that conflict. Like Catharine Maria Sedgwick, Dickinson as an unmarried woman from a well-to-do home might well have chosen to relinquish the domestic role in favor of literary endeavors. For most women writers that was not an option; the writing/housework conflict was the central struggle of their daily lives. Dickinson's contemporaries leave record that the struggle was often debilitating. "I did my best by my house, my school, my sick child, and my publisher," the novelist Emma D.E.N. Southworth (1819–1899) writes in an autobiographical note, "yet neither child, nor school, nor publisher received justice" (John Hart 214). Southworth, deserted by her husband, was attempting to support herself and her two children by working as a schoolteacher when she began her writing career, and she became seriously ill as a result of the struggle to balance responsibilities.

And Harriet Beecher Stowe, mother of six, in a letter to her sister-in-law at the time she was writing *Uncle Tom's Cabin* describes an arduous round of petty but essential domestic activities:

During this time [the weeks after her last baby's birth] I have employed my leisure hours in making up my engagements with newspaper editors. I have written more than anybody, or I myself, would have thought. I have taught an hour a day in our school, and I have read two hours every evening to the children. The children study English history in school, and I am reading Scott's historic novels in their order. To-night I finish the "Abbot;" shall begin "Kenilworth" next week; yet I am constantly pursued and haunted by the idea that I don't do anything. Since I began this note I have been called off at least a dozen times; once for the fish-man, to buy a codfish; once to see a man who had brought me some barrels of apples; once to see a book-

man; then to Mrs. Upham, to see about a drawing I promised to make for
her; then to nurse the baby; then into the kitchen to make a chowder for
dinner; and now I am at it again, for nothing but deadly determination
enables me ever to write; it is rowing against wind and tide. (*Life and Letters*
128)

These are hardly the conditions under which we can conceive of great
literature coming into being, but Stowe persevered and *Uncle Tom's Cabin*,
written amid this domestic chaos, is a literary masterpiece and, in its day,
was a political bombshell as well.

Two women writers of this era have left detailed literary records of the
clash between inclination and domestic obligation. These texts are, significantly, the work of mother and daughter—the two Elizabeth Stuart
Phelps. The elder Phelps's novella *The Angel Over the Right Shoulder* and
the younger Phelps's novel *The Story of Avis* (1877) approach the problem
in different ways and with differing degrees of insight. But both clearly
reveal the pain and human waste of talents undeveloped and dreams un-
fulfilled because a woman's time and energy were essential to domestic
well-being, indeed, to survival.

Although the older Phelps feels intense sympathy for her protagonist's
plight, she can only advise renunciation of Mrs. James's desire to transcend
her daily round and pursue an intellectual life. She does so through the
device of a dream in which an angel watching over her left shoulder records
Mrs. James's "selfish" deeds and an angel over her right shoulder records
those actions taken to benefit her family. Her subsequent renunciation of
intellectual ambition is sincere on the part of the protagonist, but the tale
itself is fueled by ambivalence. The younger Elizabeth Stuart Phelps, in
The Story of Avis, a novel that is in many ways a fictionalized biography of
her mother, takes a cautionary approach. In her study of Avis Dobell, a
brilliant artist who, deeply in love, marries in spite of her awareness that
genius and family will not mix, she eloquently delineates the effects of
conflicting duty and desire. The younger Phelps does not *advise* renunciation; rather, in a careful step-by-step account of the daily clashes between
the artistic and the domestic spheres, she reveals its tragic *inevitability*. From
a young girl who early decides that she will have no part of domesticity—
in her teens informing her scandalized aunt, in the words of Elizabeth
Barrett Browning, that "carpet-dusting, though a pretty trade, was not the
imperative labor after all" (54)—Avis becomes a slave to the needs of her
family to the point where her artistic capacity is destroyed:

Women understand—only women altogether—what a dreary will-o-the-
wisp is this old, common, I had almost said commonplace, experience,

"When the fall sewing is done," "When the baby can walk," "When house-cleaning is over," "When the company has gone," "When we have got through with the whooping cough," "When I am a little stronger," then I will write the poem, or learn the language, or study the great charity, or master the symphony; then I will act, dare, dream, become. Merciful is the fate that hides from any soul the prophecy of its still-born aspirations. (272–73)

For its time *The Story of Avis* is unique in the extent of its exploration of the domestic dilemma of the woman artist. Avis loses her art as a result of the relentless claims of domesticity, and the younger Phelps does not condone that loss, but deplores it. For her the angel over the right shoulder is not constituted of divine imperatives, but rather of inequitable social arrangements and expectations; in no way can that spirit be considered a *good* angel.

Dickinson's involvement with the "prickly art" (L 907) of housekeeping was probably not as overwhelming as it was for Southworth, Stowe, or the elder Phelps. Dickinson had no children to make claims on her time and energies, but she did have a mother who for long periods was an invalid, requiring much careful attention. Dickinson, indeed, considered her mother's illness a "holy" claim.[9] Further, her father's prominent position as a lawyer, community leader, and treasurer of Amherst College entailed a considerable amount of entertaining; every year, for instance, the Dickinsons hosted at their home an Amherst College Commencement tea that drew up to two hundred people. These entertainments would have required a great deal of work on the part of the women in the family. And the ordinary day-to-day maintenance of the Dickinson's large home would, in itself, have been a demanding responsibility. Dickinson did have serious domestic claims on her time. Unlike the women in the stories, but like the other writers in real life, she wrote and wrote prolifically nonetheless. Whatever effect domestic conflict had upon the themes, images, and structure of her work, it did not keep her from writing.[10] In fact, it is quite possible that the culturally sanctioned identity of domestic woman empowered her writing, serving to allay anxieties that the identity of professional writer would have elicited. Dickinson's obvious commitment to home and family may well have enabled her to write with the dedication and seriousness of purpose of a professional without experiencing the gender conflict that such a self-definition caused other women writers.

Domesticity seems to have played a different role in Dickinson's life than it played in the lives of most other women writers. Rather than taking advantage of her social and marital status to free herself from quotidian obligations as Sedgwick, to a large degree, did, Dickinson took her domesticity seriously. And she took it farther than other writers did: what women like Stowe and Southworth struggled to overcome, Dickinson seems to have acquiesced to, and perhaps exploited. She told Higginson she experienced "a Cowardice of Strangers" she could not control (L 735), and her life of severely limited social contact affirms that weakness. Her domesticity not only offered her a culturally acceptable identity definition, it also allowed her the extreme seclusion she evidently needed in order to protect herself from irrational anxieties induced by normal social contact.

The extent of Dickinson's break with society may well have been abnormal, but she would have found much in the ethos of feminine domestic privacy that women's writing generally extolled to sanction her self-restriction to the home; her sister-in-law, Susan Dickinson, in a *Springfield Republican* obituary (May 18, 1886) said that Dickinson's "instinct that a woman's hearthstone is her shrine" was "simple and strong." In the domestic obligations that went with the secluded domestic role, Dickinson found work at which she could well consider herself, not fearful and eccentric, but necessary and useful. In this way she would have been able to alleviate her extreme anxieties about social contact, to write with seriousness of purpose, and still allow herself a way of life that had the sanction of the cultural ideal.

It has been common wisdom among some Dickinson scholars that Dickinson's reclusiveness was necessary for her artistic survival as a woman in a repressive society. Millicent Bingham says Dickinson's withdrawal was the "only sane response" to a world in which there was too much "matter-of-fact" (*Home* xv). And Suzanne Juhasz sees Dickinson's "movement into her house and then her room as paralleling the movement into her mind that her poems document, because both actions were undertaken for the purpose of maintaining her self against pressures from the world to lose it" (11). This may well have been true for Dickinson's own particular psychic economy, but it is time we came to recognize that her isolation was not an *inevitable* reaction to her situation as a nineteenth-century American woman writer. Rather, it was a particularly unique response. Assumptions about the nature of women affected women's lives in obvious ways, and Dickinson's domesticity is congruent with those assumptions. But the extreme oddity of Dickinson's cloistered seclusion in the context of the often very public lives of the women writers who were her contemporaries testifies to the enormous amount of psychological need that must have combined with deeply embedded social prescriptions for feminine reticence and withdrawal to cause such an excessive reaction on Dickinson's part as her refusal to meet strangers or leave the family grounds.

Perhaps the most striking contrast between Dickinson and her contemporaries who published successfully is the remarkable boldness most of the latter displayed, in spite of the prevailing ethos of domesticity and privacy for women, in their forays into the public world. Sigourney, of course, was a consumate businesswoman, managing her own public relations and distribution at a time when these were pioneering activities. Sedgwick's first novel, *A New England Tale* (1822), was written as an open attack on Calvinism, the dominant religious orientation of her day. In spite of the fact that she had few friends in the East and no financial resources, Alice Cary in 1850 moved to New York City with the express intention of becoming a professional writer. Elizabeth Oakes Smith risked social anathema by speaking in public on women's rights issues. And Stowe, after the international furor caused by *Uncle Tom's Cabin*, was probably the most public woman in nineteenth-century America. What is important to note, however, is not that these women should have provided point-by-point models for Dickinson but, rather, that their lives show the wide range of possibilities for women writers in her day and highlight Dickinson's seclusion as the uniquely personal response that it was. She was not forced inevitably into seclusion, but, rather, chose it.

Mabel Loomis Todd's initial mention of Dickinson in her journal in 1882 focuses on what she sees as the deliberateness of the poet's seclusion: "[She] is called in Amherst 'the myth.' She has not been out of her house for fifteen years. . . . She is very brilliant and strong, but became disgusted with society & declared she would leave it when she was quite young" (Leyda II 377). But reports of those who knew her better, and indeed her own words, indicate that her behavior was probably not a deliberately chosen strategic withdrawal but the result of overwhelming irrational anxieties. "In all the circumference of Expression," Dickinson wrote to Todd's parents, the Loomises, in 1884, "those guileless words of Adam and Eve never were surpassed, 'I was afraid and hid Myself' " (L 946).

In a letter to Mary J. Reid in 1895, Dickinson's sister Lavinia contrasts Dickinson with her friend and fellow poet, Helen Hunt Jackson, linking the "timidity" of the former to her feminine refinement: "Helen Hunt Jackson was a brilliant, dashing woman of the world, fearless and brave, while Emily was timid and refined, always shrinking from publicity" (Bingham, *Ancestors'* 320). Thomas Wentworth Higginson, a perceptive contemporary observer of the human scene, experienced Dickinson as having been characterized by "an excess of tension, and . . . an abnormal life" ("Emily Dickinson's Letters" 453). In a comment to his sister in 1873 he indicates that he found her seclusion to be akin to psychosis: "I saw my eccentric poetess Miss Emily Dickinson who *never* goes outside her father's grounds & sees

only me & a few others. . . . I'm afraid Mary's other remark 'Oh why do
the insane so cling to you?' still holds'' (Leyda II 213). And Susan Dickinson
tells us that Dickinson herself found her way of life to be less than grati-
fying. In a letter to Higginson in 1890 Sue says: "She hated her peculiarities
and shrank from any notice of them as a nerve from the knife" (Bingham,
Ancestors' 86).

   In order to develop as accurate a picture of her life as possible, it is
important to place Dickinson's self-limiting behavior in a proper perspective. Although Dickinson's withdrawal most likely had cultural roots (Sue
told Higginson in the same letter that "she [Dickinson] as deeply realized
that for her, as for all of us women not fame but 'Love and home and
certainty are best'''), it was *not* the inevitable response of a woman writer
(even a brilliant one) to her talent and social position. Nor was it a personal
triumph. When Sandra Gilbert and Susan Gubar speak in *Madwoman in the
Attic* about Dickinson's long sequestration as one component of an "aesthetic" that "helped her to free herself from social and psychological constraints which might otherwise have stifled or crippled her art" (586), they
suggest a personal transcendence of constraints on Dickinson's part that I
find overly hopeful.

   Let us not romanticize Dickinson's withdrawal. While isolation may well
have been her particular necessary condition for creation, we must not
forget that her fear and seclusion cost her dearly in personal pain and
limited the range of her experience. Whereas other women writers forged
satisfactory social and professional lives for themselves, often courageously
flouting convention to do so, Dickinson retreated into the home and es-
chewed—as a refined woman was taught to do—the jostling and strife of
the world. In marked contrast with the groundbreaking activities of her
contemporaries, this behavior appears conservative, indeed, strongly acquiescent to cultural demands.

   Dickinson's lack of publication has been the occasion of much comment
over the years. The consensus has been that she greatly desired to be a
publishing poet but that her contemporaries were unappreciative of her
poetry. Ruth Miller is perhaps the most insistent proponent of this theory,
saying that Dickinson "besieged" Bowles and Higginson with her poetry
in hopes of encouraging them to publish it and that her disavowal of desire
to publish was a mask (4). Richard Sewall, too, says, "Emily's disavowal
about publishing can hardly be taken literally" (554). But recent publication
discoveries reveal that Bowles and others of Dickinson's contemporaries
were receptive to her poetry. Karen Dandurand documents twenty Dickinson publications, including reprints, in her lifetime, and speculates that

there may well have been more. "Within two months [in 1864]," she notes, "five poems made a total of ten separate appearances in four cities" ("Civil War Publications" 17). Poems appeared over the years not only in the *Springfield Republican* but also in the *Drum Beat*, a New York newspaper devoted to Civil War fund raising, the *Boston Post*, the *Round Table* (New York), the *Brooklyn Daily Union*, and *A Masque of Poets*, an anthology of poems published by Roberts Brothers. In addition, the anthologized poem was quoted in full in a review of the book in Boston's *Literary World* (Dandurand, "Publication" 7). The fact that editors were not only willing to publish her poems but that other editors liked them enough to "clip" them for their own publications makes it evident that Dickinson's decision to keep her work for the most part unpublished was not due to a lack of receptiveness from others. Nor was it most likely due to editorial tampering with her poetry. Dandurand documents an alteration in a poem published initially in the *Daily Republican* that was corrected in the reprint in the *Weekly Republican* ("Publication" 7); Dickinson, had she chosen, could have had as much control over her publications as any writer. The truth seems to be that Dickinson was serious when she told Higginson that publishing was "foreign to [her] thought, as Firmament to Fin—" (L 265).[11] (See Appendix 1.) Her reluctance to expose her personal thoughts and feelings to public scrutiny was quite consistent with the feelings of her contemporaries.

In that era women's anxiety about the presentation of self in the public eye in print (as well as in any other way) was profound. Caroline May in her 1848 collection of women's poetry, *The American Female Poets*, indicates an almost pathological reluctance on the part of the poets to have any part of their lives made public in the brief biographies she appended to the poems. When she wrote to poets asking for personal data the response was sparse: "several of our correspondents declared their fancies to be their only facts; others that they had done nothing all their lives; and some— with a modesty most extreme—that they had not lived at all" (viii). In her autobiography, *A New England Girlhood* (1889), Lucy Larcom, a popular writer of poems and stories at mid-century, declares: "I could never imagine a girl feeling any pleasure in placing herself 'before the public.' The privilege of seclusion must be the last one a woman can willingly sacrifice" (222). And Catharine Sedgwick at the time of the publication of *A New England Tale* wrote to her brother, Theodore: "I have a *perfect horror* at appearing in print and feel as you have seen me when I have been trying to make up my mind to have a tooth out." "To be the subject of public inquest," she later wrote to another brother, "is not agreeable to a woman of any womanly feeling" (Kelley, *Private Woman* 130). As Mary Kelley says, "commercial publication was steeped in significance. To enter the public realm was for the woman to enter a new realm of being" (*Private Woman* 125).

Dickinson's determination to keep her writing private, for herself and a few friends, is conservatively consistent with this context. "How can you . . . print a piece of your soul!" she is credited with having said in consternation to Helen Hunt Jackson (Bingham, *Ancestors'* 166). And she resisted the entreaties of Jackson and other friends and well-wishers to make her poetry public. "If you will give me permission," wrote Jackson to Dickinson in 1878, "I will copy them—sending them in my own hand-writing—and promise never to tell anyone, not even the publishers, whose the poems are. Could you not bear this much of publicity? only you and I would recognize the poems" (L 573a). Dickinson evidently said "no," for the poems never did appear.

In the most conventional view, only two motives for publication were seen as viable for women: the desire to be "an instrument of good" (chapter 4 investigates ways in which this rationale pervaded women's written expression) and a pressing need for money. As Baym puts it: "the claim of need for any woman or the rationale of a public service motive for the comfortable would sanction female authorship" (*Woman's Fiction* 175).[12] A comment in a letter from Calvin Stowe to Harriet Beecher Stowe cites moral motivations: "God has written it in his book that you must be a literary woman, and who are we that we should contend against God?" (*Life and Letters* 105). What becomes evident, however, is that doing good was only *one* motive for Stowe; the financial pressures on her were probably as great as the moral pressures. "There is no doubt in my mind that our expenses this year will come two hundred dollars, if not three, beyond our sala-ry. . . . I can earn four hundred dollars a year by writing, but I don't want to feel that I must, and when weary with teaching the children, and tending the baby, and buying provisions, and mending dresses, and darning stock-ings, sit down and write a piece for some paper" (*Life and Letters* 132), she wrote to her husband in 1850.[13] But sit down and write she did. Still, while under very real financial pressures, Stowe was in a better position than many women writers. Some of them were destitute; the biography of nine-teenth-century American women writers is replete with absconding hus-bands and bankrupt husbands, fathers, and brothers.[14]

Elizabeth Oakes Smith was one writer who entered the publishing arena under these circumstances; her husband's bankruptcy in the 1830s enabled her to publish with public approbation the poetry she had been writing for years. In *Female Poets of America* Griswold praises her for her "shrinking and sensitive modesty" that did not publish until financial stress made it necessary (177), and John Neal introduces Smith's *The Sinless Child* in the same manner, saying that she writes with "steadfast determination to do all that might become a woman, for the help of her husband" (xxv-xxvi). Louisa May Alcott, like many other women writers, completely discounts artistic or expressive motives for her writing when she tells her publisher, James Redpath, in 1864 not to talk about "genius": "the inspiration of necessity is all I've had" (Saxton 261). By "necessity" she meant severe financial need. Susan Warner's career originated specifically in her need to support her family—herself, her sister, her aunt, and her father—and continued from the same motivation. Many women writers were in similar positions. But, as writers, their misfortune was, in a way, their fortune: it permitted them to write without censure, either from without or from within.

As I have said, Dickinson had neither conventional rationale for publishing; she did not write with didactic intent nor was she economically needy. In Dickinson's refusal to publish, as in other aspects of her life, it is impossible to state definitively her motivations. But a *practical* result of this decision was to allow Dickinson, as a writer, the identity of the literary amateur—not an uncommon stance for economically secure women—rather than the identity of the literary professional. Dickinson did not write, as a professional poet would, for public distribution. She wrote for herself and a small circle of friends and acquaintances, and in the role of feminine literary amateur she would find herself recognized and appreciated. In this she was like Mrs. E. C. Kinney, a contemporary poet who Griswold says wrote without any of "the usual incentives, except the desire of utterance, and the gratification of friends" (195), and like Emma Embury, a poet about whom Elizabeth Oakes Smith said, "I fully respected the genius that was buried in too much prosperity" (*Autobiography* 89).

Indeed, one of Dickinson's contemporaries astutely cited "too much prosperity" as a factor in the development of Dickinson's idiosyncratic style. Upon reading the manuscript of the first edition of her poems, the poet Arlo Bates told the editors of Roberts Brothers publishing house: "Had she published, and been forced by ambition and perhaps by need into learning the technical part of her art, she would have stood at the head of American singers" (Bingham, *Ancestors'* 52). He attributes the stylistic deviances of Dickinson's poetics to what he saw as an ineptitude perpetuated by a privileged social and economic status that did not make publishing a financial necessity. That her financial security fostered, not ineptitude, but experimentation is beside the point. Her lack of "need" allowed her to write without the commercial considerations that might well have—but not inevitably—resulted in artistic compromise.

A more problematic implication of Bates's statement is the question of ambition. "Had she been forced by ambition," he says, implying, without comment, that she was not. To Bates's audience the statement needed no elaboration. It was assumed in nineteenth-century America that a woman *would* be without ambition. The factor that needed comment was, indeed, the opposite; female ambition was a deviation from cultural consensus about the nature of women. The poet Maria James provides a typical example of the apology that pervaded women's published writing: "As I advanced toward womanhood, I shrunk [sic] from the nickname of poet, which had been awarded me: the very idea seemed the height of presumption" (Griswold 66). Many women's books contain a similar disclaimer, to the point where the disclaimer became so much a convention of the preface that Ann Stephens could speak in *Fashion and Famine* about "the usual half-sincere, half-affected apology of haste and inexperience" (v). Literary ambition, that is to say writing for the sole sake of aesthetic creation or of fame, was perceived as an aberration for women. As Grace Greenwood put it, "a true woman shrinks instinctively from greatness" (Wood, "Scribbling Women" 5).

Unlike such modern critics as Ruth Miller and Richard Sewall who, working from modern assumptions, postulate a burning desire for publication on the part of Dickinson, Bates accepts her lack of publication as unremarkable. In truth, Dickinson seems to have conformed quite closely to cultural precepts in this area. Some of her modern commentators cite a desire to avoid artistic compromise as a major factor in her decision to keep her poetry away from publishers. In a discussion of contemporary publishing priorities, George Whicher compares Dickinson to Sidney Lanier:

> Lanier's awareness of differences between what artistic integrity demanded and what it was possible to get into print throws a revealing light on Emily Dickinson's lifelong refusal to submit her poems to publication. She was not one to conform to "these tyrannies" [Lanier's terms for contemporary verse standards], and if the price to be paid for following her innermost convictions was lack of public recognition, she was willing to pay the price. ("Victorians" 237)

Since, unlike most other women writers, however, Dickinson was not economically dependent on her writing, she would not have found artistic compromise necessary for that reason; even if she had published, she would not have needed to alter her poetry in order to please the public and boost sales. If a serious and dedicated ambition to be a professional writer *had* been present, she might even, as Helen Hunt Jackson did in 1870, have paid for the publication of her own book of poems.[15]

Or yet another course was available to Dickinson, had she truly desired to publish. Within the great bulk of Dickinson's poems exists a large body of fairly conventional nineteenth-century poetry—among it a few of her finest poems—that could have been published without censure or artistic tampering at any time during her writing career. If public recognition was a major concern, Dickinson had the potential for publishing however many volumes she wished of these poems, consistent as they are in form and subject matter with contemporary poetic tastes. (See Appendix 2). That she chose, in spite of much coaxing, not to, is yet another indication of her conformity to conventional attitudes in this matter. "Fame of Myself, to justify, / All other Plaudit be / Superfluous—" (713), she wrote in 1863, at a time when her writing was at its productive peak and she would have been most apt to have been thinking about whether or not to publish.[16]

A reading of that much-discussed and little-agreed-upon poem, "Publication—is the Auction," also written about 1863, with the common feminine rationales for publishing in mind suggests Dickinson's conformity:

> Publication—is the Auction
> Of the Mind of Man—
> Poverty—be justifying
> For so foul a thing
>
> Possibly—but We—would rather
> From Our Garret go
> White—Unto the White Creator—
> Than invest—Our Snow
>
> Thought belong to Him who gave it—
> Then—to Him Who bear
> It's Corporeal illustration—Sell
> The Royal Air—
>
> In the Parcel—Be the Merchant
> Of the Heavenly Grace—
> But reduce no Human Spirit
> To Disgrace of Price—
>
> (709)

Publication is associated instantly here with its commercial aspect—the selling of expression for gain—rather than with its communicative aspect. However, both—financial gain and communication for its own sake—are scorned, the former because it's "foul," the latter because, "Thought belong to Him who gave it— / Then—to Him Who bear / It's Corporeal illustration." In other words, ideas bond the muse to the poet in an exclusive, closed relationship. Two exceptions only are allowed: financial need (but only marginally)—"Poverty—be justifying / For so foul a thing / Possibly . . . " says this elite speaker—and moral imperative, the dispensing of God's word—"Sell / The *Royal* Air— / In the Parcel—Be the Merchant / Of the *Heavenly* Grace—" (my emphasis). *Self*-expression, writing that exists for the sake of embodying personal feelings and insights, is explicitly proscribed from appearing in the public eye as the poem concludes: "But reduce no *Human* Spirit / To Disgrace of Price—." The poem suggests that in extreme cases publication is justified by poverty and that religious or moral content also sanctions publication but that the public sharing of the "*Human*" spirit, or, in other words, personal expression, is disgraceful.

This attitude is entirely in accordance with the thinking of the vast majority of Dickinson's social peers. A look at a novel by Josiah Gilbert Holland, a close Dickinson family friend and a very popular writer in several genres, confirms its prevalence. In *Miss Gilbert's Career* (1860) Holland specifically berates women writers who write solely for their own benefit. Fanny Gilbert is a young woman of sixteen who has been turned from what Holland considers to be her proper domestic path in life by the idea of being a writer. Declaring her independence, "I will not live a humdrum, insignificant life of subordination to the wills and lives of others . . . I will have a career" (87), she begins to write a novel. Holland's perception of her motivation for doing so is significant. "Had she been at work for money, or had she been animated by a desire to accomplish some great reform, or had she been engaged in doing some work of duty, as one of God's willing laborers, then she might have been content" (147). But Fanny, having no need for money and no moral motivation, writes only out of a desire for public attention—self-expression and communication aren't even considered by Holland as possibilities—and her career brings her little satisfaction.

Given her close relationship with the Holland family, Dickinson most likely read this novel and may very well have approved its sentiments. It stems from the prevailing climate of expression that sanctioned women's publication only under specific limited terms. Dickinson, not "a' work for money" nor "animated by a desire to accomplish some great reform" nor motivated by religious feeling "as one of God's willing laborers," seems to have acquiesed to the cultural ethos that produced *Miss Gilbert's Career.* "To have a career" is, for women, a twentieth-century ideal. To be a woman in conventional nineteenth-century thinking was to be domestic, secluded, "content." Publication for its own sake was in conflict with those ideals.

Emily Dickinson's life was very different from those of the women writers who were her contemporaries. All lives are constituted by idiosyncratic interminglings of cultural determination and individual need, but she adapted cultural determinants to far different effects than did her cultural peers. She was born into a social milieu that gave her certainly as many advantages and opportunities as these other writers. Undoubtedly, also she suffered similar conflicts between her role as a domestic woman and her career as a writer. However, she made very different choices than her contemporaries. Where they chose to involve themselves in social and political life in ways that were often daring in that cultural context, she withdrew into a domesticity that became absolute. Where they took advantage of every rationale to publish their work, again contrary to the prevalent ideal for feminine behavior, she consistently refused to allow hers into the public sphere. When we look at her behavior in its social context, we see that it is congruent with conservative norms for femininity but not with the progressive behavior of the women writers who were her peers. As surprising as it may seem for this writer whose poetry is revolutionary in its exploration of a personal female experience, it was Dickinson who lived out in her life to an extreme degree the ethos of ideal womanhood—retired and devoted to family and friends—and it was her contemporaries who blazed the trail for the modern professional woman writer.

III

"ARE THERE ANY LIVES OF WOMEN?"
CONVENTIONS OF THE FEMALE SELF IN WOMEN'S WRITING

> Bene vixit quae bene latuir: She has lived well who has kept herself well out of sight.
>
> —Thomas Wentworth Higginson quoting conventional wisdom

In *Women and the Alphabet* (1881), Thomas Wentworth Higginson, Dickinson's chosen "preceptor," a feminist, and an active supporter of women writers, satirizes the pervasive and strongly felt ideology suppressing female individuality. He suggests that the cultural ideal of femininity might well be summed up in the image of "the Invisible Lady," a carnival sideshow attraction whose voice was present, but whose person could nowhere be found.

> The Invisible Lady, as advertised in all our cities a good many years ago, was a mysterious individual who remained unseen, and had apparently no human organs except a brain and a tongue. You asked questions of her, and she made intelligent answers; but where she was, you could no more discover than you could find the man inside the Automaton Chess-Player. Was she intended as a satire on womankind, or as a sincere representation of what womankind should be? ("Temperament" 66)

Although Higginson states that society is in the process of changing its attitudes toward women, he recognizes how entrenched in mainstream thinking the ideal of feminine reticence is, lamenting that "the opinion dies hard that she [woman] is best off when least visible" (67).

For women's writing the significance of the decorum of "invisibility," which amounted to the barring of female subjectivity from the public sphere, was profound; it resulted in a conspiracy of literary discourse that pitted the "feminine"—or the societal definition of womanhood—against the "female"—or the personal experience of womanhood—in such a way that the latter was all but eliminated from women's texts. Anxiety that a full disclosure of woman's nature might contradict culturally prevailing assumptions of feminine morality was intense, producing in middle-class society an ideology of feminine reticence so powerful that Higginson calls it "a gospel of silence" (73). Book reviewers, for instance, as cultural monitors, felt that "the potential of the novel as an agent of female acculturation" was vitally important. According to Baym, "the real function of at least female characterization was to deceive—for some, in order to inspire women to strive toward an ideal; for others, to screen women from the betrayal that the new demands of psychological characterization could not but lead to if they were seriously heeded" (*Novels* 98, 107).

The challenge faced by the conforming woman writer was the debilitating task of expression detached from the self. In Higginson's terms, she was to exert her "brain and tongue" as if they were disembodied, as if the language they produced had no direct connection to a particular adult female with an individual physiological, psychological, and social identity. To Higginson the cultural bias was clear: "To many men, doubtless, she [the Invisible Lady] would have seemed the ideal of her sex, could only her brain and tongue have disappeared like the rest of her faculties" (66).

The expressive bind women writers found themselves in was this: they were writing prolifically and with great popular success, so they did have voices, yet as individuals they were expected to maintain a decorous silence within their texts, in essence, to become "invisible ladies," manifesting nothing that would reveal to the world the presence of any passion or aspiration beyond the ordained. In order to manage such expressive sleight of hand, to be both present as a feminine voice and absent as a uniquely female presence, women turned to specific images—that of the little girl was particularly popular—that would allow them at one and the same time to be somebody in the text and yet remain, as Dickinson asserts in a very familiar poem, "Nobody." By denying aspects of their adult female experience that fell outside the limited, and limiting, norms of respectability, both reader and writer, in their interaction within the text, turned into "Invisible Ladies." The result was that, although peripheral women characters were at times allowed their individuality, the woman at the center of a text, the one most likely to be identified with by her creator, and by the reader as well, became almost universally conventionalized in ways that assured an anxiety-free reader and writer.

The necessity to do so most likely was intensified by the increasingly prurient and scandalous body of subliterature made easily available to readers by the penny newspapers and the pamphlet press. Here aspects of women's life eradicated from mainstream literature—sexuality, ambition, anger—were fulsomely represented, in a manner that objectified, distorted, and perverted them. These texts shattered the constraints on the representation of women, but they in no way provided an outlet or a model for the expression of women's actual life experience; the writers of this sensational fiction seem to have been overwhelmingly male, and prurient objectification could not substitute for honest subjective expression. This widely deplored (but secretly widely read) body of writing only served to heighten cultural fears about what an unmonitored female discourse might reveal.[1]

As she set pen to paper Dickinson must have been aware to a significant degree of the decorum of "invisibility" mandated for women of her class; certainly it was a factor in her non-publication. Yet, in spite of Dickinson's decision not to publish, she continued to write. In so doing she faced the same choices as her contemporaries; her options, if she were to speak about herself at all, were threefold: to speak in conventional cultural terms; to exploit conventions for personal use; to spurn conventions. She adopted, at one time or another, all three options, but it is the first two I wish to address here; the rebellious, proto-feminist aspects of her work have been documented, but the influence of conservative thinking upon her literary self-presentation has not been adequately investigated.

As a nineteenth-century American woman poet Dickinson had the model of Lydia Sigourney, about whom the contemporary novelist Ann Stephens says approvingly: "In her life you find no distorted acts, no wild search after unattainable sympathies and transcendental delusions. She never . . . [allows] . . . one sentiment which angels might not acknowledge" (Haight 99–100). Although this is not precisely true of Sigourney, who, at times, in subtle ways in her stories and poetry manipulates cultural assumptions and stereotypes in a grotesque and intriguingly "distorted" manner, what is significant here is the ideology involved in such an approbation. Stephens describes as the ideal presentation of self the direct opposite of the persona appearing in much of Dickinson's poetry—a self that often does define itself by "distorted," exaggerated, and even grotesque acts.

It is significant, however, that it is often at her most conventional, in her adoption of the little girl figure and its corollary wife/bride image that we see Dickinson's persona at its most distorted, in a vain quest for what might well be considered "unattainable sympathies and transcendental delusions." Although these figures show up in only a small percentage of her poems, her treatment of them is significant, for while Dickinson's little girl and wife personae in their obedient passivity usually conform to the most stringent ideals of feminine subservience, her ambivalent tone in most of these poems stresses ambiguous rather than positive aspects of this pattern of feminine behavior. Therefore, while acquiescent to cultural options, Dickinson's treatment of these stereotypes is also investigative. Jane Tompkins speaks of stereotypes as "cultural shorthand," "instantly recognizable representatives" of cultural categories which "convey enormous amounts of cultural information in an extremely condensed form" (xvi). As such, stereotypes provide for Dickinson potent images of femininity to identify with—and to identify against. While expropriating the advantages of self-definition these figures offer—firm cultural identities and highly charged emotional content—she also reveals an uneasy suspicion of the modes of being they represent.

Poetry and fiction in America in the middle of the nineteenth century were not the genres in which it was appropriate for women to be as honest in their expression as Dickinson, and others as well, obviously wished to be. Elizabeth Oakes Smith, after considerable success as a poet and novelist, renounced these modes of expression to become, in the 1850s, a woman's rights activist. Her rationale for that renunciation is instructive as we attempt to define the precise nature of the strictures on these two genres. "My literary career had not been devoid of recognition, but in this new field, *designed to reveal woman to herself*, I realized an inconceivable satisfaction" (*Autobiography* 153, my emphasis). What can be ascertained from this statement is that although it was possible in certain arenas, for instance in the speeches and essays of the woman's rights activists, for women to be honest about their experience, novels and poetry, in her literary context, were not "designed to reveal woman to herself." Thus they did not provide an arena for either subjective disclosure, or for an honest exploration of the external situations of women's lives, such as the political and legal constraints feminists brought into the public eye.

These self-consciously literary forms of writing as practiced by the majority of middle-class women served, as literary genres often do, as cultural reinforcement, raising problematic questions about women's situation in society but ultimately affirming society's preconceptions. The rigid stereotyping that characterizes women's lives in most women's literary writing throughout this era results in images of a life characterized, not by continuity and progressive growth, but by discrete, discontinuous stages, and by diminishment. "Life's Changes," a poem by Margaret L. Bailey in *Female Poets of America* (1848), expresses nicely the literary fragmentation of women's lives.

A little child on a sunny day,
Sat on a flowery bank at play;
The gentle breath of the summer air
Waved the curls of her golden hair,
And ever her voice rang merrily out
In a careless laugh or a joyous shout.
. . . .

Years rolled by: in her maiden pride
She stood, a gentle and trusting bride—
How beautiful still! though a softening shade
O'er the dazzling hue of that beauty played,
While the tender glance of her soft blue eye
Told of a love that could not die. . . .

Again I saw her: Time had been there,
Tipping with silver her golden hair;
He had breathed on her cheek, and its rosy hue
Was gone, but her heart was pure and true,
As when first I met her a budding flower,
Or a gentle maid in her bridal hour.
As mother and wife she had borne her part,
With the faith and hope of a loving heart;
And now when nature, with years opprest
Looks and longs for her quiet rest,
With holy trust in her Father's love,
Awaiting a summons from above,
She lingers with us, as if to show
To the faint and weary ones below
How oft to the faithful soul 'tis given
To taste on earth of the joys of heaven.

(225)

Purporting to express the continuum of a woman's life, the poem breaks almost equally into three discontinuous stages: the little girl, the bride, and the old woman waiting for death. Childhood, marriage, death: the "changes" in this life are abrupt indeed, completely eliminating the mature woman and allowing no sense of a complex and evolving personality. Dickinson's words "Born—Bridalled—Shrouded— / In a Day—" (1072) attain a new significance when seen in the light of this conventional perception of a woman's existence; a woman's life revolved around the three poles of her childhood, her marriage, and her death.

Interestingly enough, the image of the mother is left out of the three major images of Bailey's survey of a woman's life, mentioned only in retrospect. It is also omitted from Dickinson's highly condensed version,

"Born—Bridalled—Shrouded." Mothers were the focus of much exposition by proponents of the "separate but superior" school of thought on the "woman question"—writers like Catharine Beecher and Harriet Beecher Stowe. But, although mothers show up in women's poetry, often associated with dead children, and are, like Alcott's Marmee and Stowe's Rachel Halliday, presented in supportive roles in fiction, they are, with few exceptions, never during the larger part of the century at the center of a longer text, one that attempts to show the development of a woman's life and identity. This disinclination to focus on mature women in their active years also shows itself in the lack of attention paid to married women in general, and to unmarried adult women. In "Miss Lucinda" (1861), her delightful story of an eccentric New England spinster, Rose Terry Cooke begs her reader's indulgence for choosing such an unlikely protagonist, apologetically calling her tale "only a little story about a woman who could not be a heroine" (151).

Of the three images of women presented in Bailey's poem, readers, especially of novels, seemed most comfortable with the "little girl," and many writers adopted the mode both in their writing and in their public self-presentation. "True feminine genius," said Grace Greenwood (Sara J. Lippincott), "is ever timid, doubtful, and clingingly dependent; a perpetual childhood" (Welter 29). Whether this was a sincere evaluation or a conscious (or even unconscious) strategy devised to allay anxiety on the part of society about female ambition is difficult to ascertain. We do know that the concept of the childlike woman was pervasive, and numerous comments by women's rights activists and other social critics attest to its damaging effect on individual lives and on society as well. "Now there is no woman," said Margaret Fuller scornfully in 1845, "only an overgrown child" (*Woman* 188).

The image of a little-girl woman served more than one function. Not only was female ambition suspect, but female physicality (and thus sexuality) was the subject of an increasing amount of evaluative medical literature—much of it prescriptive and repressive. For instance, Dr. William Acton, author of the widely read *Functions and Disorders of the Reproductive Organs* (1865) states: "The *best* mothers, wives, and managers of households know little or nothing of sexual indulgence. Love of home, children, and domestic duties are the only passions that they feel" (Degler 254, original italics). If the *"best"* women knew nothing about sexuality, the *worst* knew plenty, according to the prolific body of texts disseminated by the sensational press. In them sexual desire becomes unbridled lust and is associated with other "unfeminine" qualities, such as dishonesty and a vengeful nature. And in these texts, a prurient focus on the female body is pronounced

(Reynolds chapter 7). In fiction and poetry by mainstream women, however, most likely as a combined result of this exploitation and the repressive sexual ideology, there is a most significant silence about women's physicality. Elizabeth Oakes Smith's Eva, in her long poem *The Sinless Child* (1843), for instance, scarcely seems to be physically present as she grows toward womanhood. All we see of her is her long golden hair, her soft eye, her white neck and pale cheek—a "pallid cheek . . . tinged with blue" (71–72). The absence of a fully realized physical and sexual woman from almost all popular nineteenth-century American women's writing constitutes an articulate omission, expressing profound anxiety regarding the personal and cultural consequences of female maturity. The use of a little girl protagonist screened out the mature woman with her disconcerting potential sexuality and guaranteed the woman writer a comfortable, and thus approving, audience.[2]

The immaturity of this protagonist resolves anxieties about both ambition and sexuality; the child's ambitions are directed merely toward finding love and care, and her sexuality has not yet begun to make itself intrusive. Speaking of the popular sentimental novels in which these child protagonists most frequently appear, Annis Pratt says: "In this most conservative branch of the woman's bildungsroman, then, we find a genre that pursues the opposite of its generic intent—it provides models for 'growing down' rather than for 'growing up' " (14). And Dickinson knew these models: "I have just read three little books, not great, not thrilling—but sweet and true. . . . pure little lives, loving God, and their parents, and obeying the laws of the land," she wrote to Susan Gilbert in 1852. "Read, if you meet them, Susie, for they will do one good" (L 85).

Certainly, therefore, Dickinson had much precedent for the childlike pose she adopted sometimes as a personal style and upon which her acquaintances commented. When Higginson first met her in Amherst in 1870 he described his introduction to the thirty-nine-year-old poet using the following images: "a step like a pattering child's"; "two day lilies which she put in a sort of childlike way into my hand"; "a soft frightened breathless childlike voice" (L 342a). With literary models for feminine childlikeness everywhere, it is interesting to note that Dickinson seems to have adapted that mode of self-presentation into her living more than into her poetry.[3] "I love so to be a child," she told Abiah Root in 1850 (L 39), and later she said to Austin, "how to grow up I dont know" (L 115). But the percentage of little girl poems in her work is comparatively small. In the entire body of her poetry there exist only about a dozen poems with a distinctly little-girl persona, although in many more the voice has a childlike quality. They are, however, poems that are often anthologized or quoted in Dickinson studies and are thus familiar to many readers.[4] Feminist critics such as Nina Baym, Barbara Mossberg, and Cristanne Miller have read these poems profitably as studies in power and powerlessness. What is not generally considered, however, is that their presence in her canon connects Dickinson firmly to her contemporary writing community.

When Mary Jane Holmes begins her novel *Dora Deane, or The East India Uncle* (1859) with these lines: "Poor little Dora Deane! How utterly wretched and desolate she was," she encapsulates, in the way popular writers do, a widespread, complex, and variously treated cultural motif—that of the little girl. This protagonist, usually orphaned, often neglected by those in charge of her care, and almost always shut out from her rightful place in society and in a warm loving family, was pervasive in women's writing and was obviously enticing to readers.[5]

This child/woman, for such she is although she is seldom allowed to age past the troublesomely pubescent teens, begins her tale in wretchedness and desolation but struggles for, and by the end of the story usually wins, full recognition of her claim to attention. Most often this recognition entails marriage; sometimes it involves death. But in either case the presence of the individual has been acknowleged, and that partially, if inadequately— to a modern reader, at least—justifies her existence. Dickinson puts it this way, no less poignantly than Holmes.

> They wont frown always—some sweet Day
> When I forget to teaze—
> They'll recollect how cold I looked
> And how I just said "Please."
>
> Then They will hasten to the Door
> To call the little Girl
> Who cannot thank Them for the Ice
> That filled the lisping full.

(874)

In the extreme pathos of the image of the little girl silenced by frost, Dickinson almost, but not quite, outdoes Holmes, whose Dora is found half-frozen on a frigid New Year's morning in front of an empty grate, with her arms wrapped lovingly around the body of her dead mother.

Nineteenth-century women writers chose to use the little girl persona or protagonist in one of two distinctly disparate ways: as an expression of feminine obedience and perfection, or as a vehicle of female anger and rebellion—to be chastened, but nevertheless present and attractive.[6] The convention of the saintly little girl and the convention of the naughty little girl exist simultaneously, sometimes in the same book, as attested to by saintly Eva and naughty Topsy in *Uncle Tom's Cabin* (1852) and the spiritual polarities of Beth and Jo in *Little Women* (1868). Taken as a whole these figures ultimately make similar statements: a woman's condition in a society that refuses to acknowledge the implications of her maturity is untenable. Emily Dickinson uses both figures, and her treatment of them exploits brilliantly the pathos that is the essential component of their being.

Although the little girl image served effectively to screen ambition and sexuality, for the most part, from conventional feminine texts, the image of the naughty child allowed anger, another anxiety-ridden quality for women, to escape the superfine mesh of the expressive constraints. From Susan Warner's Ellen Montgomery, who constantly erupts in angry tears (*The Wide, Wide World* [1850]), to Maria Cummins's Gerty, who, in fury, hurls a rock through a window (*The Lamplighter* [1854]), to Harriet Beecher Stowe's Topsy, who is just naturally "wicked," women's anger and rebelliousness express themselves freely in the guise of a child's "innocent" feelings and actions. As Baym has pointed out in *Woman's Fiction*, "the presence of anger is understood as a basic fact of the heroine's emotional makeup" (252). Although the rebellion is infantilized and ultimately "corrected," it is a markedly noticeable presence, especially in the writing of the novelists. The poets were more inclined to treat the little girl, and the woman as well, in the saintly mode.

Although the "naughty" girls I have mentioned above, among scores of others, have differing personalities and situations, they almost all have one thing in common—they have suffered intolerable abuse. "Though we *must* sorrow, we must not rebel," little Ellen Montgomery's mother tells her near the beginning of *The Wide, Wide World* (12), and in the face of massive mistreatment by both God and humanity, Ellen struggles to abide by that maxim. Her beloved mother is dying of consumption and Ellen's cruel father insists on separating mother and daughter. He ships the heartbroken little girl off to his sister's home in the country. Ellen's aunt has no use for the child; she nags her, refuses to send her to school, steals her letters, and in general mistreats her badly. Ellen is shown to be in a constant state of tearful fury, and one would think her anger justifiable. Not Ellen. "I meant—to be a good child," she sobs to a sympathetic friend, "and I have been worse than ever I was in my life. . . . I have been passionate and cross, and bad feelings keep coming, and I know it's wrong, and it makes me miserable" (150–51). By the end of the story Ellen has succeeded in following her mother's maxim. She does so by psychologically dissociating herself from the oppressive emotional realities of her life to such a degree that she does become a model child, chastened and fit for conventional womanhood. Ellen has been redeemed.

Although it would be difficult for anyone other than Warner herself to consider Ellen "naughty" in any real sense, *The Lamplighter*'s Gerty truly is. An orphan, raised in the slums by an abusive harridan, she has developed a survival mode of aproaching the world: "spirited, sudden and violent, she had made herself feared, as well as disliked" (5). A tough, passionate child, she hurls a stick of wood at her guardian's head, smashes her window with a stone, and declares her hatred to anyone who will listen. This behavior, however, is in response to years of neglect, starvation, and beatings. The murder by scalding of Gerty's kitten—the one creature she has come to love—is the culminating factor causing Gerty's rage. Gerty, too, learns "submission," although ultimately in a more gentle manner than Ellen. Although redeemed from her childish anger and rebellion, she maintains, as Ellen does not, a certain amount of personal autonomy in the world.

Topsy, the slave child in *Uncle Tom's Cabin*, is perhaps the apotheosis of this convention. "I's wicked—I is. I's mighty wicked" (360), she describes herself, "I s'pects I's the wickedest critter in the world" (367). Her behavior, too, is in response to intolerable mistreatment. Taken from her mother at birth and raised by a speculator, she has been sold to a "low" restaurant owner, beaten and sworn at, "whipped with a poker, knocked down with the shovel or tongs" (363). As a black child born in slavery, Topsy's position would not seem to be analogous to that of the white, ultimately middle-class girls of the other novels. A modern reader would like to see a sustained, politically enlightened rebellion on Topsy's part. However, she, too, conforms to the nineteenth-century paradigm. More of a moral fantasy than a real child, Topsy undergoes the same spiritual chastening as the other protagonists and emerges culturally redeemed—a model woman, a Christian, and a missionary.

Although these girls ultimately achieve model womanhood, it is only through loss of individuality that they do so. In *The Wide, Wide World*, the paradigm of these texts, it is made clear that the compromise of self is not good for Ellen, but, rather, is a tactic necessary for survival. The narrative interest of each of these three lives lies not with the "lady" the protagonist becomes, but rather with the unredeemed child, passionate little Ellen, furious little Gerty, wicked little Topsy.

One aspect of Dickinson's little girl persona, the child who wades in the water "for the Disobedience' Sake," reminds us of these "naughty" children. She constitutes, however, only a minor aspect of a more complex character. But the important thing to note is that she *does* remain defiant in the text, and that she gives evidence from a more authoritative text, the Bible, which Dickinson radically misreads, to justify her doing so.

> So I pull my Stockings off
> Wading in the Water
> For the Disobedience' Sake
> Boy that lived for "Ought to"
>
> Went to Heaven perhaps at Death
> And perhaps he did'nt
> Moses was'nt fairly used—
> Ananias was'nt—
>
> (1201)

Compromise of one's own will is shown to be a swindle here. Moses was swindled out of the promised land, Ananias out of his life. Moses was a boy who did what he "ought to." Ananias wasn't; he attempted a minor scam on God, and Dickinson suggests he was disproportionately punished. She here equates good behavior and bad behavior; neither is a guarantee of fair treatment by God. One might as well be bad. In a sense, by allowing the personalities of their immature, "bad" characters to outshine the "good" women they become, Dickinson's contemporaries were allowing a similar misreading of their texts. It is certainly the anger of the young Ellen and Gerty, the quixotic "disobedience" of the child Topsy that the modern feminist reader takes away from her reading. The disquieting energies of these experiences were also available to contemporary readers. Although they did not necessarily serve to subvert the "ought to," the moralistic lesson of the protagonists' maturity, they must have served to complicate it.

Elizabeth Oakes Smith may well have established the pattern for the counterfigure, the good little girl, with her 1834 book-length poem, *The Sinless Child.* Influenced by Wordsworth's perception of the innocence and perfection of childhood, she creates Eva as having been from birth a truly saintly human being.

> Her mother said that Eva's lips
> Had never falsehood known;
> No angry words had ever marred
> The music of their tone.

> And truth spoke out in every line
> Of her fair, tranquil face,
> Where love and peace, twin-dwelling pair,
> Had found a resting place.

(50)

It is difficult in our present cultural climate to discuss an ideal like this without mocking it, but this figure did serve an important function. Compensatory for a lack of real scope and power in society, it gave women a sense of power in another and possibly greater sphere—the realm of the spiritual.[7] Eva does not need to be redeemed; she herself is a redemptive figure. One kiss from her chaste lips turns a careless young man away from a life of sin. Mara in Stowe's *The Pearl of Orr's Island* (1862), a brilliant treatment of this convention, and Fleda in Warner's *Queechy* (1852) serve much the same function in more artful and complex ways. Mara, Stowe says, "has no dreams for herself—they are all for Moses" (122). (Moses is her foster brother and, later, fiancé.) Fleda turns a despondent young agnostic (later her fiancé) to a life of faith by a single gesture. "Elfie," he asks her, "how do you know there is a God?" Giving him a searching look she points imperatively to the sinking sun. " 'Who,' " she queries, " 'made that, Mr. Carleton?' . . . Mr. Carleton was an unbeliever no more from that time" (I 163–64).

The ideal was one that defined woman's identity and social role in flattering and seductive ways. *The Sinless Child* went quickly through three editions and Smith remembers Edgar Allan Poe, who praised it highly, saying to her that Eva "is what all women should be, and then we men would be more what we are designed to be, what we are at our best, all of us" (*Autobiography* 124).

However, there was an additional component to this exemplary child, one essential to our full understanding of it. Perhaps the most well known, and the most maligned, instance of this saintly little girl figure is Stowe's Eva in *Uncle Tom's Cabin*. And what most people know about Eva, including many who have never read the book, is that she dies. Beth, too, in *Little Women* is remembered for her extraordinarily good life and her early death. As Judith Fetterley says of the latter, "Beth is the perfect little woman. Yet she dies. . . . to be a little woman is to be dead" (379–80). Smith's Eva dies too—seemingly as a result of her "redemptive" kiss. Mara expires shortly after her fiancé learns from old Captain Kitteridge that "that ar child was the savin' of ye, Moses Pennel" (Stowe, *Pearl* 383). Of the "good little girls" I have mentioned, only Fleda lives to marry, and she falls willingly at that point from a life of independent responsibility into a state of grateful, perpetual childhood.

An inherent contradiction exists, then, in this image; the goodness of this exemplary child is an ideal promulgated for women, but this goodness is seen at the same time as incompatible with adulthood. It is angelic little Mara who asks, when offered a copy of Plutarch's *Lives*, "Are there any lives of women?" (Stowe, *Pearl* 152). The implied answer is "No." The inevitable end of all this goodness and obedience is the eschewal of adulthood by an early death, or by the lifelong "invisibility" of genteel womanhood.

No precise correlation exists between Emily Dickinson's little girl persona in any one poem and the little girl convention of her contemporaries. Rather, we can see in the figure that the little-girl poems as a whole create a presentation of a remarkably complex little-girl-self that contains certain aspects of both the "spiritual" and the "spirited" child.[8] Like her "naughty" fictional contemporaries, this little girl suffers intolerable mistreatment. She is silenced, frowned at, shut out—both from heaven and outside in the cold. She is rejected by "Day," chased by a menacingly erotic ocean, shut up in Prose and in closets, manacled, starved, frozen, and deprived of love. Like the "good" child she is obedient. Her offenses are few and minor; she sings too loud, stops praying, pleads for attention, hankers after strawberries. Only once—and here she significantly adopts a boy persona—does she overtly rebel, pulling off her stockings and wading in the water out of sheer disobedience. She doesn't climb the fence after the strawberries. She doesn't make a break from the jail of Prose. Only her brain is free. All else remains "still," obedient and submissive. Death comes to this child too, her own sobs her only lullaby, her "lisping" filled with the "ice" that freezes expression and denies the treasonous brain its only outlet.

The most striking fact about Dickinson's good/bad little girl is that she lacks one essential feature of each aspect of the conventional child: she is neither redemptive nor is she redeemed. Pathetic, sullen, and lost, she continues in a state of misery. Like Dora Deane she is "utterly miserable and wretched," but without Dora's hope of eventual warmth. Consider the plight of the persona in 874, a poem that is uncanny in its grasp of the essential paradigm. This little girl has been shut out in the cold, her only offense, it would seem, her use of language—the "please" and the "tease"—to ask for recognition and fair treatment.

> They wont frown always—some sweet Day
> When I forget to teaze—

> They'll recollect how cold I looked
> And how I just said "Please."

As with the other fictional children (and Dickinson's fragmented use of the little girl convention does constitute an adapted fiction), she asks only for minimal rights—warmth and acceptance by others. These are denied as long as she continues to be capable of asking for inclusion.

It is her frozen silence, the ultimate "invisibility" of death, ironically, that brings her the solicitous recognition she craves:

> Then They will hasten to the Door
> To call the little Girl
> Who cannot thank Them for the Ice
> That filled the lisping full.

This recognition is cold comfort to the persona, who is left unredeemed and unredeeming, her syllables of ice expressing only radical pathos. The ambiguity of the final two lines indicates conflict. The speaker wishes to be grateful for the attention—belated though it is—but she is hindered by the frozen lips of death. Yet the wording of the line "Who cannot thank Them for the Ice" allows an alternate reading. The speaker finds consolation in that she is ultimately unable to conspire in her own silencing; she "cannot thank Them for the Ice" because of the ice. Silence, which is synonymous with both obedience and rebellion, has been forced on her. Although the child convention is adopted here, Dickinson's refusal to buy the usual compensatory aspects of the stereotype deepens the tragedy of the figure and shows "invisible" life—life in the little girl mode—to be intolerable. The poem goes beyond being "shut up in prose" to embody the essential expressive dilemma of the woman writer: to be silent is to win approval, but to be a silent writer is a deadly contradiction in terms.

Although the little girl convention offered women writers a narrative adequate to contain characters and events of interest to them and to their readers, the image of the conventional woman was less promising. As Baym says of these popular writers, "the constraints of stereotype kept them all from creating fully believable, multifaceted, unpredictable characters" (*Woman's Fiction* 299), and this, as seems logical given the nature of the constraints and the cultural anxieties that had generated them, was much more true of the women characters than of the young girls. Baym excepts Alcott from this judgment but, interestingly enough, Alcott was not—in her most popular work—writing for women; rather she was one of the first women writers to begin to direct her novels to children, and the first volume

of *Little Women* concludes with the four sisters still happily at home together. However, the clamor of her public and her publisher for a "conclusion" to the story forced Alcott to continue. "My little women must
grow up and be married off in a very stupid style," she wrote to her uncle
as she began the second volume (Stern, *Alcott* 190). Her reluctance to "complete" the tale reveals her awareness of the exigencies of plot—the continuation and conclusion of the story in a conventional mode could mean
nothing less than diminishment for her characters.[9] In this knowledge she
is not alone. Sally McNall's psychological study of the popular women's
fiction of the period reveals that one common theme exists in all popular
American women's writing—"ambivalence about growing up to be a
woman" (3).

Why this should be so can easily be summed up in narrative terms;
although marriage was the culturally defined way by which a girl knew
herself to be an adult, in a very real way marriage meant the end of the
story—the ultimate textual invisibility.[10] The married woman, although
often peripheral to the text, almost always vanishes from its center. Of the
innumerable women's novels I am familiar with from this period, only two,
A.D.T. Whitney's *Hitherto* and Elizabeth Stuart Phelps's *The Story of Avis*,
explore at length with any candor the life of a married woman. These novels
were published later in the century, in 1869 and 1877 respectively, when
the expressive constraints were beginning to loosen, and they were both
self-consciously breaking tradition. Whitney begins her tale with a discussion of the reasons for some "old woman" to tell her story: "What can a
girl of twenty know, that she should try to say what disappointment and
endurance are, and what they come to." She advocates waiting until life
has been lived "for years and years; and then let her, if she can and dare,
look back upon those yesterdays and speak. I think the world would hear
a riper and a different story. I think it would truly get a *novel* then" (4).
And *Avis* is an explicitly feminist exploration of the stultifying effects upon
a brilliant woman of conventional marriage. But these were pioneering
texts, reflecting important cultural factors: increasing feminist awareness;
a rise in the respectability of spinsterhood; and a maturing of the audience
for women's fiction. For the largest part of the century in American wom-
en's novels the mature married woman had no story.

The constraints of this conventional perception on literature can be clearly
seen in Lydia Sigourney's long poem *Pocahontas* (1841). Conceived as an
American epic in a time when interest in such a literary production was
high, the poem finds itself in an expressive bind. The demands of epic
form require a movement of expansion and activity—of mastery of the

world. As a female, Pocahontas cannot be conceived of in such a mode; the female narrative demands contraction and "stillness." From childish defiance (which *is* her story), Pocahontas moves to obedience as a "timid, trusting bride" (25), and finally to an early death. In spite of the wildness implied by her "raven locks" and her "olive cheek," she fulfills all requirements for the conventional sentimental heroine. From a savage child she becomes what Higginson would call an "Invisible Lady." And she "make[s] a beautiful corpse," as Miss Roxy in *The Pearl of Orr's Island* says about another dead woman, Mara's mother, Naomi (8).

Woman-as-corpse is the ultimate image of feminine unconsciousness, and much imagery of unconsciousness is associated in women's writing of this period with weddings and marriages. Edna Earl in *St. Elmo*, the most ambitious and accomplished of the young girl protagonists, loses consciousness at her wedding. Even more significant is the fact that Lydia Sigourney records in her autobiography the same phenomenon about her own wedding in actual life (*Letters* 262). For a striving and achieving woman, marriage, in conventional ideology, spelled what seemed to be the end of conscious endeavor and the beginning of "the swoon / God sends us Women—," as Emily Dickinson so aptly put it (1072). The loss of consciousness may well begin with the swoon of sexual ecstasy authorized to a woman by marriage, but it is also profoundly associated with loss of visibility—or identity—in the larger world. As Edna recovers from her marital "swoon," the first words she hears from her new husband are: "To-day I snap the fetters of your literary bondage. There shall be no more books written: No more study, no more toil, no more anxiety, no more heartache: And that dear public you love so well, must even help itself, and whistle for a new pet. You belong solely to me now" (489).

Elizabeth Oakes Smith's sonnet, "The Wife," highlights the lack of consciousness expected of the conventional wife. Particularly significant because it comes from a writer who later abandoned poetry, suggesting it was an inadequate medium with which "to reveal woman to herself," the poem, while overtly extolling the virtues of this "caged" woman, reveals also a great deal of the ambivalence Cheryl Walker notes as pervasive in women's poems about marriage (50–52).

> All day, like some sweet bird, content to sing
>   In its small cage, she moveth to and fro—
> And ever and anon will upward spring
>   To her sweet lips, fresh from the fount below,
> The murmured melody of pleasant thought,
>   Unconscious uttered, gentle-toned and low.

Light household duties, evermore inwrought
　　With placid fancies of one trusting heart
That lives but in her smile, and turns
　　From life's cold seeming and the busy mart,
With tenderness, that heavenward ever yearns
To be refreshed where one pure altar burns.
　　Shut out from hence, the mockery of life,
　　Thus liveth she content, the meek, fond, trusting wife.

(Griswold 187)

The wife's song is "unconscious." Her fancies are "placid." In her cage she is the singer of the unwritten poetry of household deeds, and will never be the composer of poetry that is written.

Although women writers may have approached the subject of marriage ambivalently, we should not overread this ambivalence. The cultural mythos may have implied that marriage was the end of the story, but it also, and more enticingly, promised power in the form of a mystical transformation—what A.D.T. Whitney calls, so tellingly, "the *unseen* sacredness" (*Hitherto* 164, my emphasis). At the close of *Queechy*, Susan Warner, through Fleda's benumbed newly married consciousness, expresses the common hyperbole. "His wife!" Fleda muses, "had so marvellous a change really been wrought in her?—the little asparagus-picker of Queechy transformed into the mistress of all this domain. . . . And his wife!" (II 389). Dickinson herself displays similar, but even more heightened, rhetoric in a note to her friend Emily Ford after attending her wedding in 1853: "it seemed to me translation, not any earthly thing, and if a little after you'd ridden on the wind, it would not have surprised me" (L 146). In the cultural mythos a new and transcendent identity awaited the married woman—one that was not available to the single woman. It is the seductive lure of this promised mystical transformation co-existing alongside the nagging awareness of identity loss in conventional marriage that informs the complex and self-contradictory figure of the wife/bride in Dickinson's highly charged marriage poems.[11]

I'm "wife"—I've finished that—
That other state—
I'm Czar—I'm "Woman" now—
It's safer so—

How odd the Girl's life looks
Behind this soft Eclipse—
I think that Earth feels so
To folks in Heaven—now—

> This being comfort—then
> That other kind—was pain—
> But why compare?
> I'm "Wife"! Stop there!

(199)

Of the several "wife" poems in Dickinson's canon, this poem pays the most attention to defining the terms. The use of quotation marks around the two key terms, "wife" and "woman," focuses attention squarely upon them. The words do not announce themselves boldly as known entities, but rather float like protean bubbles in a sea of potential meaning. The known experience, on the other hand, "the Girl's life," while introduced hesitantly as "that— / That other state," immediately becomes the base term of reference, compared with Earth in contrast to Heaven, and thus, by analogy, with life in contrast to death.

Marriage, in Dickinson's metaphor, is the "soft Eclipse," which at one and the same time transforms the self *and* makes it invisible. In her investigation of the significance of this word "wife," which beyond all others defined the ideal female self in her era, Dickinson aligns the "safety" and "comfort" of marriage with a state of afterlife. While this afterlife is ostensibly heaven, it is a fairly ambiguous paradise; are safety and comfort worth the "eclipse" of a life? This question is implicit in the equation as Dickinson places marriage in contradistinction to "that— / That other state" for which society seems to offer no identifying term. Certainly "woman" does not seem to be available, having immediately equated itself with "wife."

This speaker, however, although initially stammering for want of a precise term, goes on to identify "That other state" *as* life, "the Girl's life." Further she is reluctant to recognize the "pain" that according to received definitions must have been attached to this solitary state: "This being comfort—then / That other kind—was pain—." The tone is one of hesitant acknowledgment of some "truth" not intuitively recognized as valid; she may well have found "the Girl's life" quite satisfactory. "But why compare?" she continues quickly, "I'm 'Wife'! Stop there!" The persona of "wife,"—or, more precisely, the persona trying on the role of "wife"— will not permit further investigation, suggesting by the abruptness of her termination of the discussion that she is afraid the results will be unfavorable. Having linguistically "tried on" this married identity, the speaker thinks it prudent, like the novels of her era, to "stop there." The poem, begun in a tone of triumph, closes in ambiguity.

In the poem above, the word "marriage" is never mentioned. The operative term is "this soft Eclipse." In other words, marriage as Dickinson

sees it here means not only transformation, but also an obscuration—
whether of life or of the self is not specified. This eclipse may be painless,
even comfortable, perhaps even ecstatic, but it is nonetheless real. One
cannot be seen when one is eclipsed. Other wife poems also contain elements of invisibility. Dickinson's most overt exploration of the effect of
marriage on the individual woman is in poem 732:

> She rose to His Requirement—dropt
> The Playthings of Her Life
> To take the honorable Work
> Of Woman, and of Wife—
>
> If ought She missed in Her new Day,
> Of Amplitude, or Awe—
> Or first Prospective—Or the Gold
> In using, wear away,
>
> It lay unmentioned—as the Sea
> Develope Pearl, and Weed,
> But only to Himself—be known
> The Fathoms they abide—

Here being "Woman" and "Wife" is once again equated, and defined,
sincerely I think, as "honorable Work." In order to attain this identity,
however, the woman described in this poem must sink her own potential;
"Fathoms" deep, in invisibility and silence, her capacity for "Amplitude,
or Awe" lies unrecognized and "unmentioned." And in poem 461, "A
Wife—at Daybreak I shall be—," the consummation of the marriage, the
making of a wife, is implicitly equated with death. "Eternity, I'm coming—
Sir," the bride says to her approaching husband, "Savior—I've seen the
face—before!" Christ, Death, and the husband are indistinguishable one
from the other here, and the marriage experience is thoroughly overlaid
with implications of death—the final invisibility.

Loss of consciousness, invisibility, silence: these are the qualities of
death. They are also qualities that contemporary women's literature attached, if only in a secondary manner, to marriage. For Dickinson, too,
these qualities are inextricably linked to the idea of marriage. *Her* dilemma
in the face of marriage is heightened by her awareness of her own "Amplitude," of just how much it is she has to lose. Marriage or death were
the options offered to protagonists in most of the novels by her American
female contemporaries, and they were often related, especially if the

woman was gifted in any significant way. Eva in *The Sinless Child* explicitly states that she can never marry because she possesses "one unearthly gift . . . the gift of thought, / Whence all will shrink away" (77). Thus when she reaches marriageable age and falls in love, her only recourse is to die. Mara in *The Pearl of Orr's Island* astonishes everyone with her intellectual capacity. On her deathbed she tells her fiancé, Moses, that, in effect, he is better off without her because she is so superior to him: "I have felt that in all that was deepest and dearest to me, I was alone. You did not come near to me, nor touch me where I feel most deeply" (390). The housing of great intellect or spirituality in a female body almost always dooms the unfortunate woman to an early death.

The only other option given is the renunciation of the capacity for greatness. Edna Earl of *St. Elmo* has written two brilliant books while still in her early youth, but renounces her "literary bondage" (489) for what promises to be the even greater bondage of marriage. Avis, the gifted artist of *The Story of Avis* by the younger Elizabeth Stuart Phelps, reluctantly accepts a proposal of marriage. "I love you. . . . " she says, "It is like—death" (105–06). What dies in this novel is the talent with which she has begun to attract the acclaim of the art world. For the brilliant woman, then, marriage promised, either through death or renunciation, the loss of those qualities that most distinguished her.

We have seen that Dickinson equates "woman" and "wife." It is only by becoming "The Wife—without the Sign," that is to say by realizing her capacities as an adult woman without taking on the legal identity of wife, that her persona can avoid "the swoon God sends us women." The loss of consciousness may be initiated by the swoon of sexual passion, but it extends in the ideology to all but domestic achievements. Dickinson sees this loss as being an integral component of marriage that can be evaded by becoming a "woman" through some means other than marriage.

> Title divine—is mine!
> The Wife—without the Sign!
> Acute Degree—conferred on me—
> Empress of Calvary!
> Royal—all but the Crown!
> Bethrothed—without the swoon
> God sends us Women—
> When you—hold—Garnet to Garnet—
> Gold—to Gold—
> Born—Bridalled—Shrouded—
> In a Day—
> "My Husband"—women say—

Stroking the Melody—
Is *this*—the way?

(1072)

This poem appears, at one level at least, to reflect Dickinson's decision to "marry" her art and achieve the divine identity of poet. When we look at it in the context of conventions of marriage that her writing community mandated, the terms of the "marriage" to poetry are clarified. If becoming a wife—allowing oneself the swoon of orgasm—is equated with courting the "swoon" of death or of artistic renunciation, it is incompatible with her decision to be a poet. Yet "wife" is the highest "title" that society offers, and to become a wife *does* promise a mystical transformation, an opportunity to "ride the wind" as she has earlier said. Dickinson co-opts that transformation and at the same time both renounces and avoids the "swoon" by becoming the "Wife—without the Sign." In other words it is as a woman poet, not as a wife-adjunct to a husband, that she is transformed. After all, it is only within a literary work that one can be "Born— Bridalled—Shrouded— / In a Day"; little girl, happy bride, old woman linked with death: she saw it constantly in the literature that surrounded her. On the other hand, she perceives great writers as "Women, now, queens, now!" as she said about her contemporaries Elizabeth Barrett Browning and George Sand (L 234). And, in the poem above she puts herself on a level with these women writers, calling herself an "Empress . . . / Royal—all but the Crown!"

The poem begins with an affirmation and proceeds with a series of triumphant statements, but it ends with a question that stands in contradistinction to all that has gone before. " 'My Husband'—women say—" (and *she* has just said so much more) "Stroking the Melody— / Is *this*—the way?" The poetry of a conventional woman's life is contained in two words, "My Husband." The wife strokes the limited melody of these three syllables as if committing an act of love. She expresses herself through her relationship to her husband; she does not write. Dickinson, on the other hand, questions the expressive scope of this relationship. "Is *this* the way?" she wonders, and leaves the question unanswered.

As a woman steeped in the literary conventions of a community of expression that encouraged women to write while insisting that they remain, in essence, silent, Dickinson was attracted to the stereotypes of the little girl and the wife/bride with which women writers attempted to circumvent the "gospel of silence" and fill the expressive void at the heart of nineteenth-century American women's literature. She was, however, uncertain of the adequacy of these figures to express the complexities of an adult woman's experience. For her poetry she takes what she can from them—pathos from the little girl and mystical transformation from the wife/ bride—and exploits the emotional options offered by these figures. At the same time she presents the images in such a way that it is difficult to miss the deadly contradictions involved. It is life depicted in the acceptable modes that is the true "distorted act," to appropriate the terms of Stephens's disclaimer that Sigourney's life contained "no distorted acts, no wild search." Dickinson's conventional figures *do* conduct a "wild search," and it is precisely those "unattainable sympathies and transcendental delusions" Stephens condemns that her personae are after. Their ultimate fate, however, is to fail in their quests, to be frozen and diminished.

Although those in society who have defined what of her experience a woman may recognize and transcribe may have designated Dickinson's life as "small" ("The Sages—call it small—" she says in poem 271), and Dickinson adopts insignificance as one mode of self-presentation, she also feels her own potential for "Amplitude." "Ceasing to be an Invisible Lady," Higginson concludes in his essay, woman "must become a visible force: there is no middle ground" (69). For Emily Dickinson "becoming visible" posed many problems, as it did for her contemporaries. Her use of the conventions they employed to approximate the reality of their lives constitutes a serious effort to envision herself in available modes of being. The ambivalence and self-contradiction of the conventional figures as she brings them to life on the page, however, show her to have found them as inadequate for self-representation as they indeed were.

IV

"THE GRIEVED—ARE MANY—
I AM TOLD—"

THE WOMAN WRITER
AND PUBLIC DISCOURSE

> "I dont know anything more about affairs
> in the world, than if I was in a trance."
>
> —Emily Dickinson, 1847

The arena of public concerns seems an unlikely one in which to investigate Emily Dickinson's life and work. A discussion of Dickinson and public issues is to some degree a discourse in negative terms, a chronicling of what isn't there. Dickinson is a quintessentially private poet. Although she was living and writing in a time of great social tumult, when major issues of human freedom and responsibility—abolition of slavery, women's rights, urban poverty, exploitation of the working poor—were in frequent contest at the polls, in the press and pulpit, and on the battlefield, her direct commentary on these matters is virtually nonexistent. Only a few remarks can be found in her letters, and the poetry is almost entirely free of public reference. If public affairs affect Dickinson's poetry at all, it is, as Shira Wolosky claims, in the realm of the metaphysical, rather than in the arena of active political engagement or of concern with the larger political, economic, and civil factors that motivated them.[1]

Yet an investigation of Dickinson's relationship—at least in her writing—with social issues will prove rewarding nonetheless, because here we see quite clearly an important line of demarcation between Dickinson's poetics and conventional nineteenth-century literary expectations. In her exploration of conventional images of the feminine, we have seen Dickinson exhibit an attraction toward and a conflicted conformity with cultural norms; in her treatment of social concerns, or rather her avoidance of them, she breaks radically from those norms. Here Dickinson's expression is given impetus by a dynamic of articulation directly in opposition to that of her female contemporaries. The writing of by far the largest group of women writers found motivation, or, at least, rationale, in the desire to be—as Lydia Sigourney in her autobiography states it—"an instrument of good" (*Letters* 324). Interpreted altruistically by writers, their "instrumentality" meant a mandate to speak for moral betterment, either that of the reader or that of the world. In other words, women's writing was to be personally inspirational, to effect conversion in spirit or in behavior, or to alter conditions in the world. In any case, literary endeavor was for the sake of others. Dickinson's articulation, on the other hand, although occasionally didactic, is not altruistic; concerned overwhelmingly with the interests of the self, with the metaphysical implications of the self, and with the process of articulation itself, Dickinson's expression, even in the arena of public issues, cleaves stubbornly to its creator and to the process of its creation. In contrasting her few recorded comments on public matters with the social concerns of her contemporaries, we see that Dickinson was far more interested in the linguistic and poetic possibilities of the *language* of social concern than in the issues to which that language ostensibly referred.

Where her contemporaries used language to refer outward to economic and social reality, Dickinson's sparse language of public issues, both in her letters and her poetry, is either referenced strikingly to the nature and potential of language itself, or it is strongly allusive or metaphoric, referring almost inevitably to personal rather than to public issues. In her letters Dickinson co-opts the images, language, and concerns of public issues to affirm affectional bonds between herself and her correspondents. Often, too, in those letters, she employs images of social concern as linguistic and imagistic counters in an experimental aesthetic of wordplay and wit. In her poetry she uses these elements, when she uses them at all, metaphorically, as referential tools with which to evoke powerful insights and emotions about her own psychological and existential situation.

In Dickinson's era most women writers used language motivationally, "to make people think and act in a particular way," as Jane Tompkins notes (xi). Accordingly the language employed was familiar, communicative, nonobstructive. As Nina Baym says: "nineteenth-century popular American women writers . . . were vitally concerned to gain access to the public sphere in order to transform it by their social and domestic idealism; for this goal, none other than the language in use could possibly serve" ("Madwoman" 51). Whereas many women writers used language in an attempt to reform the world, Dickinson, in her poetry reformed language. As David Porter points out, defects in syntax and grammar, unreasonable transpositions, extreme ellipsis, and lost connectives are among the features that

indicate Dickinson's role as "language founder" (38). These language features unsettle readers in a manner enhancing the unsettling content of
much of Dickinson's discourse; they also create communicative barriers
between the text and the untutored reader and highlight Dickinson's opposition to the communal literary aims of the majority of her female contemporaries. Had she, like them, been primarily concerned with bringing
a message to a large group of readers, her freedom to revolutionize the
language of poetry would have been severely curtailed. But her focus on
self and on a few close friends—who would have grown accustomed to,
and tolerant of, her manner of expression—liberated her from the necessity
of communicating on a large scale, and freed her to violate the conventions
of language. Thus she was enabled to experiment radically with the elements of poetry, ultimately creating a poetics that addressed issues far
from the literary concerns of her female contemporaries.

Although Amherst was a bit of a backwater at mid-century, Dickinson's
lack of social reference was not due to social or geographical isolation. Her
family and friends constitute as politically and publicly active a milieu as
one could have found anywhere in the country. Her father, Edward Dickinson, was a state senator and a U.S. congressman. Samuel Bowles, a
personal and family friend, was editor of the *Springfield Republican* and was
involved in politics at the local, state, and national level. Otis Lord, a
lifelong friend with whom she was in love in her later years, was judge of
the Superior Court of Massachusetts, an associate justice of the Supreme
Judicial Court of Massachusetts, speaker of the state House of Representatives, and a state senator. Helen Hunt Jackson, a friend from childhood,
was a well-known writer; her book *A Century of Dishonor* (1881) traced the
government's mistreatment of Indians and succeeded in winning her a
government commission to review the needs of California's Mission
Indians. Thomas Wentworth Higginson, a long-time Dickinson correspon-
dent, was a reformer involved in many of the liberal causes of mid-
nineteenth-century America.

We have no way of knowing what occupied Dickinson's mind and conversation on a daily basis; records simply don't exist. Because of her social
milieu we can assume an awareness of public issues. We can also posit a
certain amount of social concern because we know that in 1864 she con-
tributed three poems to *The Drum Beat*, a publication in Brooklyn designed
to raise funds for the United States Sanitary Commission, the organization
that supervised military field hospitals during the Civil War. Further, in
1880 she asked Thomas Wentworth Higginson for his advice about poems

she had promised to a charity that would "aid unfortunate Children" (L 676).

Nonetheless, where it concerns us, "on the page," as R. J. Wilson states it, social commentary is noticeably absent. Wilson mentions the lack of "a kind of social middle ground, a realm of institutions, of social groups and classes, of contests for power, of law and custom . . . a middle landscape that we might call simply *society*" (454). What makes Dickinson's lack of public reference so very curious in its cultural context is that Dickinson was writing at a time when the strongest and the freest voices of women writers were heard on issues germane to the structure and needs of society as a whole. In the sometimes sensationalized reform literature of the era, a focus on labor abuses, alcoholism, prostitution, and slavery provided a popular base for the discourse of advocacy, and although certainly not all women writers were writing on public issues, strong moral concern for social betterment was the impetus for a considerable number. In speaking out on major social wrongs women writers could be, and were, more forceful in style and statement and more comprehensive in subject matter than feminine expressive constraints would otherwise have allowed. Harriet Beecher Stowe's exploration of the history of sexual exploitation suffered by Cassy, the black woman who was Simon Legree's mistress, is an excellent example of the way in which women's writing was liberated from taboos—in this case from the proscription against expression of sexual issues—by strong social concern. The literature of social advocacy, less fettered than other genres, had access to otherwise forbidden areas of investigation, and outrage fueled compelling literary voices. From Sedgwick's *Hope Leslie* (1827) through Stowe's *Uncle Tom's Cabin* (1852), Davis's "Life in the Iron Mills" (1861), and Jackson's *Ramona* (1884), there exists in nineteenth-century American women's novels a powerful tradition of social realism and advocacy for Indians, blacks, and the working poor.[2]

Women writers who worked in this vein—Stowe and Rebecca Harding Davis, for instance—tended to be socially liberal in their thinking. For those who were more conservative, the ideology of femininity did sanction a non-involvement in social concerns. As Lydia Maria Child said regarding the majority of her contemporaries, they "have, from long habit, become accustomed to. . . . consider it feminine and pretty to abjure all such use of their faculties, as would make them co-workers with men in the advancement of those great principles, on which the progress of society depends" (Jeffrey 123). And even among those women who *were* seriously concerned about the state of society, women's influence for good was often thought to be best utilized indirectly and in the domestic arena.

There has been a tendency in this century to deride the reform movements of the previous century—particularly those in which women were
predominantly involved—as soft-hearted and soft-headed do-goodism.
The reality is, however, that in a nation beset by serious social problems,
municipal and state institutions for relief were simply inadequate. In the
burgeoning urban areas, for example, desperate poverty, starvation, home-
lessness, prostitution, alcoholism, and labor abuses were rampant. It was
upon the efforts of the churches and of private individuals that much ame-
lioration of distress and initiative for reform depended. Because women
were expected to be more sensitive to moral issues than men, they were
in the forefront of social activism. If we allow ourselves to see past the
bonnets and petticoats of some of the reform rhetoric, we will recognize
the importance and validity of their concerns, many of which continue to
beset us today.

Dickinson, however, not only rejected the public involvement of such
women reformers as Child—who was an ardent abolitionist—and of Elizabeth Stuart Phelps—who was involved in the women's rights, temperance,
and anti-vivisection movements—but she seems to have scorned the private, domestically based charities of the sewing circle as well. Evidence
exists that Phelps may have written to Dickinson in 1872, most likely asking
for a literary contribution. A sardonic account by Dickinson in a letter to
her cousin Louise Norcross refers to a letter of solicitation from a "Miss P
_____" and reveals contempt for her and impatience with her reformist
stance:

> Of Miss P _____ I know but this, dear. She wrote me in October, requesting
> me to aid the world by my chirrup more. Perhaps she stated it as my duty,
> I don't distinctly remember, and always burn such letters, so I cannot obtain
> it now. I replied declining. She did not write to me again—she might have
> been offended, or perhaps is extricating humanity from some hopeless ditch.
> (L 380)

Much earlier, in 1850, Dickinson had used a similar sardonic tone to
describe the charitable work of a local women's group.

> The Sewing Society has commenced again . . . now all the poor will be
> helped—the cold warmed—the warm cooled—the hungry fed—the thirsty
> attended to—the ragged clothed—and this suffering—tumbled down world
> will be helped to it's [sic] feet again—which will be quite pleasant to all. I
> dont attend—notwithstanding my high approbation. . . . (L 30)

Dickinson's attitude toward society at large, in comparison with many
other contemporary women, can hardly be considered progressive. While

women like Abba May Alcott were doing social work in the slums of Boston, the young Dickinson was writing to her brother who was teaching there (and having trouble disciplining his charges): "Vinnie and I say masses for poor Irish boys [sic] souls. So far as *I* am concerned I should like to have you kill some—there are so many now, there is no room for the Americans" (L 43). Karl Keller goes so far as to call her a "cracked conservative" (222), adding that "she tended to be suspicious of the Woman of the Nineteenth Century she might often have felt she was expected to be" (222–23). Although I deplore Keller's diction, I can't help but notice, as he does, certain strongly conservative tendencies in Dickinson's psychological makeup, and this is one of them: the slow but radical changes in the contemporary perception of women's role in the affairs of the world did not engage her at all, and of a rich and tumultuous matrix of socially involved women and publicly aware women writers, Dickinson's writing took no account.

Richard Sewall, Dickinson's biographer, notes the lack of social reference in her many letters to Higginson, the nationally known reformer and writer she had chosen as mentor:

> Save for a few poignant references, it is characteristic that, in her letters to Higginson, she all but ignored the stirring events of the time and said nothing at all about the great national causes with which he had for years been publicly identified—Abolition, women's rights, the plight of the Northern poor. Long before the spring of 1862, his name had appeared frequently in the *Springfield Republican* in connection with such matters; she could hardly have helped reading about him, and them. (*Life* 535)

Of the three major contemporary social concerns that Sewall mentions—abolition, women's rights, and the plight of the northern poor—the last would have been the most visible to Dickinson. The closest she ever came to the South and to slavery was a trip to Washington, D.C., in 1855, and she seems to have had no interest in the women's rights movement. On trips to Springfield and Boston, however, she must have been aware of the presence of dire poverty, and, closer at hand, she could hardly have helped but know of the squalid conditions in the shanties of the Irish laborers in Amherst—the destitution of the Irish was notorious throughout the northeastern states at mid-century. The records, however, show little written reaction. Poverty and the related issues of prison reform, labor abuses, and hunger were not, as we will see, matters that engaged Dickinson's literary imagination other than as opportunities for wordplay or metaphor.

Poverty, however, was an important issue for many other contemporary women writers. Ellen Moers, in a discussion of the English social activist writers, has noted that in the early nineteenth century fiction and poetry were women's only instruments of social action (30). American women too, especially the fiction writers, used their talents as instruments to educate readers into an awareness of the suffering of the socially disadvantaged. As Phelps in *The Story of Avis* has her leading character, an artist, say, these women had "a passion to express the moan of human famine" (292). Often they did their job well and convincingly; Phelps said of the effect of reading "Life in the Iron Mills," "one could never again say that one did not understand" (Olsen 139). Her own "Tenth of January" (1868) and *The Silent Partner* (1871) were directly inspired by Davis's work. As with all polemical writing, this fiction dealing with social oppression was didactic in intent, designed to motivate much-needed social changes.

A didactic element does exist in Dickinson's poetry. However, it is never addressed to the larger social issues that often engaged her contemporaries. "Didactic" is a difficult word to define precisely; all poetry, perhaps, can be said to teach. But the difference lies here: where the writing of Dickinson's contemporaries points outward toward the world of human beings and their institutions, Dickinson's refers largely to the personal. Her "didactic" writing tends to be limited to generalized psychological and philosophical insights into human nature and the living of one's life, as in this 1860 verse:

> It's such a little thing to weep—
> So short a thing to sigh—
> And yet—by Trades—the size of *these*
> We men and women die!
>
> (189)

On those few occasions when Dickinson does mention public issues, the intention is usually not didactic. Two consistent qualities of expression become apparent in these utterances: either the event is co-opted to the personal, as in her letters, becoming an avowal of personal affection or, as in her poetry, a metaphor for personal experience, or the comment becomes an opportunity for linguistic indulgence in wordplay or wit. Both tendencies are strongly consistent in her sparse commentary on public issues, significant elements in her deviation from the discourse of her writing community on the same issues.

In letters throughout the years we can see evidence of Dickinson's almost automatic leap from the public into the private realm. To Susan Gilbert who was teaching school in Baltimore (where the Whig Convention was meeting), June 11, 1852, she writes:

Why cant [sic] *I* be a Delegate to the great Whig Convention?—dont [sic] I know all about Daniel Webster, and the Tariff, and the Law? *Then, Susie I could see you*, during a pause in the session—. (L 94)

To Elizabeth Holland, January 1879:

I am glad you are not hung—like the "Mollie Maguires," tho' doubtless heinous as themselves—in a sweet way—. (L 589)

To Elizabeth Holland, August 1881:

When I look in the Morning Paper to see how the President is, *I know you are looking too*. . . . (L 721)

To Mabel Todd in Europe, Summer 1885:

"Sweet Land of Liberty" is a superfluous Carol *till it concern ourselves*. . . . (L 1004, all italics mine)

In each case what purports to be a comment on, or at least a recognition of, some public event or attitude is revealed to be actually an occasion for an avowal of personal affection. The wide, wide world narrows down to a few cared-for souls; "forgive the Tears that fell for few, but that few too many, for was not each a World?" she says to Elizabeth Holland toward the end of her life (March 1884, L 890).

Writing that is concerned only with the self or with a chosen few readers is bound to manifest qualities different from writing that attempts to reach large audiences with shared concerns. Jane Tompkins calls modernist literature "a form of discourse that has no designs on the world" (125),[3] and this aspect of modernism provides insight into what differentiates Emily Dickinson's poetry from the writing of her contemporaries. As one element in its proto-modernism, Dickinson's work had "no designs on the world." On the other hand, in "Life in the Iron Mills" Rebecca Harding Davis's tendency is to move outward to the world in an attempt to effect change. Her writing makes certain claims upon the reader, claims about which Davis is quite explicit:

Stop a moment. I am going to be honest. This is what I want you to do. I want you to hide your disgust, take no heed to your clean clothes, and come right down with me,—here, into the thickest of the fog and mud and foul effluvia. I want you to hear this story. There is a secret down here, in this nightmare fog, that has lain dumb for centuries: I want to make it a real thing to you. ("Iron Mills" 13–14)

Her intention in involving the reader, in dirtying the "clean clothes" of the reader's perception of reality, is single-minded—to effect social change:[4] "if your eyes are free as mine are to look deeper, no perfume-tinted dawn will be so fair with promise of the day that shall surely come" (14). That "day" will see a realization of social justice in America; Davis's writing is aimed at the transformation of the world. The language is interactional, mediating with society in an attempt to motivate change; "I want you to hear. . . . I want to make it a real thing to you."

Davis hints at social revolution; Harriet Beecher Stowe, too, in *Uncle Tom's Cabin*, speaks of a *"dies irae,"* a day of judgment. She sees "a mustering among the masses, the world over. . . . in Europe, in England, and in this country" (344), that will eventually transform the oppressive social structure. "The slave-owner can whip his refractory slave to death—the capitalist can starve him to death" (340), her ambivalent slave-owner, Augustine St. Clare, says. Stowe's *Uncle Tom's Cabin* is an attempt to rectify one major component of social injustice, but she sees slavery as only a part of a larger evil—a class hierarchy that encourages massive exploitation of the powerless and that will inevitably end in social revolution. Stowe's writing, like Davis's, can be seen as expressive insurgence—its intention, the radical alteration of society.

Dickinson's writing, on the other hand, shows no attempt to transform objective reality. Indeed, we can see that often, in a very curious way, it is a discourse intended not to interact with the social world or even to serve as metaphor, so much as it is intended to interact with itself as language. A review of the random comments on public issues we do find in Dickinson's writing reveals a self-conscious, indeed almost self-referential quality to the language she uses in those cases where one would expect, instead, external reference. In the mainstream discourse on the social evils of poverty, labor abuses, prison conditions, and hunger were pervasive issues, incurring the literary as well as social intervention of many concerned individuals. Dickinson in her letters and poems mentions all three issues, giving us an opportunity for explicit comparisions that highlight the nonconforming nature of her writing.

Ann Stephens's *Fashion and Famine* (1854) focuses on prison conditions. The book provides a valuable description of New York City's "Tombs" in the 1850s, concentrating at length upon the brutalizing conditions of the women's ward. Stephens also includes realistic details of a trial and of preparation for a hanging. With the reform potential of fiction in mind, she openly and passionately condemns the New York City penal code, which imprisoned hapless witnesses to a crime, often children, along with hardened felons.

> This injustice, so glaring that a savage would blush to acknowledge it, exists almost unnoticed in a city overrun with benevolent societies, crowded with churches, and inundated with sympathies for the wronged of every nation or city on earth. If ostentatious charity would for a time, give way to simple justice, New York like all the American cities we know of, would obtain for itself more respect abroad and more real prosperity at home. (282)

In this novel, a curious compound of the excesses of sentimentality and the impact of realism, the writing is concerned with moving readers— moving them to tears and moving them to action. Sentiment and realism are subsumed in a social sermonizing that aims at social change. Through the influence of readers' strong reactions, the author hopes eventually to motivate authorities to action and to "simple justice." As with "Life in the Iron Mills," reference is outward toward the world, and the language makes transformational forays upon society.

Dickinson's recorded commentary on this issue is quite a different matter. In a letter written in 1850, when she was nineteen years old, she briefly mentions prisons:

> But the world is sleeping in ignorance and error, sir, and we must be crowing cocks, and singing larks, and a rising sun to awake her; or else we'll pull society up to the roots, and plant it in a different place. We'll build Alms-houses, and transcendental State prisons, and scaffolds—we will blow out the sun, and the moon, and encourage invention. Alpha shall kiss Omega— we will ride up the hill of glory—Hallelujah, all hail! (L 34)

This hyperbolic *tour de force*, from a Valentine letter to a friend, was published in an Amherst College magazine. Although it takes social reform as its subject, it is an utterance devoid of true social content; "look what I can do with language and with my wit," is the principal message of this passage. Using religious and reformist rhetoric to mock religion and reform, if only ever so lightly, it is a youthful extravaganza and a delightful piece of nonsense. Reformers are roosters and society is a weed, or at best a garden flower. The intangible thus becomes minutely concrete while the paradigmatically tangible—prisons with their iron doors and their scaffolds—becomes mystical, somehow, incredibly, part and parcel of the "transparent eyeball" of Emersonian transcendentalism. Beginnings and ends embrace, nature is extinguished, and roosters and larks will have caused this apocalypse by using their voices to "encourage invention." In itself a comment on the power of language to transform reality on a grand scale, this passage claims great efficacy for poetry, language as "song." But the paragraph restricts itself to the universe of its own potential—of that which it is possible to conceive of in words. It transforms reality into exciting, self-consciously highlighted language; it doesn't do anything for prison reform.[5]

Another contemporary issue about which reformers were beginning to concern themselves was labor abuse. And here again we can see Dickinson's tendency to focus on language rather than on subject. Unsafe conditions were pervasive in the factories of New England. Elizabeth Stuart Phelps earned her first literary recognition with "The Tenth of January," a story which Dickinson most likely read in the *Atlantic Monthly* in 1868; it described the horrific deaths and mutilations of mill workers in Lawrence, Massachusetts, when the Pemberton Mill collapsed and burned.

> A network twenty feet high, of rods and girders, of beams, pillars, stairways, gearing, roofing, ceiling, walling; wrecks of looms, shafts, twisters, pulleys, bobbins, mules, locked and interwoven; wrecks of human creatures wedged in; a face that you know turned up at you from some pit which twenty-four hours' hewing could not open; a voice that you know crying after you from God knows where; a mass of long, fair hair visible here; a foot there; three fingers of a hand over there; the snow bright-red under foot; charred limbs and headless trunks tossed about; strong men carrying covered things by you, at sight of which other strong men have fainted; the little yellow jet that flared up, and died in smoke, and flared again. . . . (360-61)

Seven hundred and fifty millworkers were buried in the ruins; eighty-eight died a "death of exquisite agony" (359). Phelps's concern is with their suffering. With a focus squarely upon her subject, she condemns the short-sighted profiteering that built the mill with faulty materials and forced these young women, whom she has earlier called "prisoners" of the mills, to work under unsafe conditions.

Dickinson's notice of labor abuses is quite different. A letter to the Hollands in 1853 yields a paragraph about newspaper reporting of industrial calamities. Even more than in the rooster/reformer letter she here reveals the self-reflexive impetus of her language:

> Who writes those funny accidents, where railroads meet each other unexpectedly, and gentlemen in factories get their heads cut off quite informally? The author, too, relates them in such a sprightly way, that they are quite attractive. (L 133)

Here the message pulls away from the subject matter; violence and personal calamity in a newly industrialized society are subordinate to matters of literary style, causing a fracture of expectation upon which the success of the passage, as a piece of writing, depends. Through felicitous combinations, words are wrenched away from their meanings: accidents are "funny"; maimings of mill workers (scandalously and tragically common contemporary occurrences) are "informal"; railroad trains do not collide and kill people, they "meet unexpectedly" as if in a casual sidewalk encounter. Social reality is kept at a distance by concentration on the properties of language. Although the subject matter is grisly, the effect is humorous. With its "sprightly" ability to transform the tragic into the "attractive," language triumphs over intractable reality.

In both these passages language is used skillfully and self-consciously, with a focus on itself as true subject, and the imagination reigns supreme. Nowhere, however, is there the slightest suggestion that language might possibly be used in any way to transform an external reality in which such tragic occurrences are possible. Davis attacks just such unconcern in "Life in the Iron Mills," when she reports the incarceration of her protagonist, Hugh Wolfe: "You wish me to make a tragic story out of it?" she says with angry sarcasm, "Why, in the police-reports of the morning paper you can find a dozen such tragedies. . . . Commonplace enough . . . jocose sometimes, done up in rhyme" (50). Although Dickinson and Davis were the same age—born within a year of each other—and came from similar middle-class backgrounds, the thrust of their writing is almost diametrically opposed. For Davis, subject supersedes style and newspaper reports are not "attractive," but truly tragic on a grand scale, indicative of "power . . . lost to heaven" (50).

Hunger was another social issue about which many women were concerned. Phelps's characterization of Avis's artistic motivation as stemming from a desire to "express the moan of human famine" is instructive as we place Emily Dickinson in the context of contemporary women's writing. Here we see not a playful transformation of language on Dickinson's part, but rather a usurpation of the image for the purposes of personal rather than altruistic expression. Literal and metaphoric images of hunger abound in nineteenth-century American women's literature, forming a communal image bank of significant richness. It can be said, and rightly so, that Dickinson herself felt strongly "a passion to express the moan of human famine," and images of starvation abound in her work.[6] But Dickinson's thrust in these instances is almost always metaphoric, pulling away from reference to the social world and evocation of the pangs of actual hunger to locate itself in the individual realm of personal psychology.

In contrast, Ann Stephens in *Fashion and Famine* deals with the actual. With stark realism she contrasts the colorful abundance of the garden markets of lower Manhattan with a minutely detailed account of the starvation of an elderly couple in a squalid basement room nearby. And Davis in "Life in the Iron Mills" has written a furious, dark, and realistic story, the imagery of which is compelled by hunger. Davis combines the literal and the metaphoric to compound her angry message of human exploitation. A giant rough statue of a nude crouching woman, "muscular, grown coarse with labor, the powerful limbs instinct with some one poignant longing" (32), is Davis's metaphor for the instinctive longings of the economically and spiritually oppressed for self-realization. "She be hungry" says Hugh Wolfe, the miner/artist who has sculpted this disconcerting image from iron korl. Her hunger, however, is not for food, he says; she is starving for "summat to make her live" (33). In this she represents her creator, whose instinct for expression is so strong he creates truth and beauty even from the refuse of the process that destroys him. The symbolic hunger of the sculpted figure is central to the story: Davis's characters are suffering from "soul-starvation" (23), and the tale is fueled by this powerful metaphor. But Davis's rendition of the actual physical deprivation of the poverty-stricken is also convincing. She writes of Deborah, a crippled young working-class woman, as at the end of a day in the mill she enters the dank cellar room she shares with several other workers:

> There she found by the half-extinguished fire an iron saucepan filled with cold boiled potatoes, which she put upon a broken chair with a pint-cup of ale. Placing the old candlestick beside this dainty repast, she untied her bonnet, which hung limp and wet over her face, and prepared to eat her supper. It was the first food that had touched her lips since morning. There was enough of it, however: there is not always. (17)

For Davis, the issue of daily physical hunger is as valid a matter for literary attention as the symbolic hunger that represents more abstruse political, sociological, psychological, or philosophical concerns. In "Life in the Iron Mills," issues of bread and roses, sustenance and beauty, the economic and the artistic, are intricately interwoven. Davis's writing is thoroughly grounded in the social world and her aim is to make it clear that the development of the life of the spirit must needs be prefaced by the satisfaction of physical and economic needs.

In Dickinson's writing, on the other hand, famine is solely of the spirit. By explicitly locating it inward, she makes the metaphoric nature of her discourse on hunger clear in a letter to Maria Whitney in 1883: "Is there not a sweet wolf within us that demands its food?" (L 824). In a poem written in 1862, at the height of her creative productivity, she elaborates on the dynamics of emotional or spiritual hunger: "I had been hungry, all the Years— / My Noon had Come—to dine— / I trembling drew the Table near— / And touched the Curious Wine—" (579). This poem instantly announces its subject as a nonliteral, although strongly felt, deprivation; in Dickinson's imagination, table and wine are the furniture of the heart and not of the hovel. "It would have starved a Gnat— / To live so small as I—," she states in poem 612, continuing her investigation of the pain of some unspecified personal deprivation that leaves her constricted, weak, insignificant, virtually non-existent:

> Nor like the Gnat—had I—
> The privilege to fly
> And seek a Dinner for myself—
> How mightier He—than I—

Dickinson, along with other women writers, finds the image of hunger attractive and useful as a vehicle for the expression of deprivation. What is important here, what distinguishes her in this respect from most of the women writers who were her contemporaries, is the leap she makes from the image to the self rather than from the image to the world. Stephens and Davis look outward. For Dickinson the movement to the self is characteristic of her treatment of almost any mention of social issues, in both her poems and letters, and is indicative of the profoundly, almost solipsistically, personal nature of her poetics.

Whatever the origins of Dickinson's consistent attitude of detachment from the suffering of the poor, it was a necessary precondition for her work, part and parcel of the introspective, self-concerned consciousness essential to the development of a modernist poetics. In order to create a literary language capable of communicating the "disabling freedom" (Porter 104) of a mind that to some degree had set itself free not only from nineteenth-century constraints but also from nineteenth-century assurances, Dickinson perforce shifted the locus of literary energy. A comparison of the facetious passages about "transcendental state prisons" and "funny accidents" with those of her writings which do purport to contain a sincere altruistic social content and to address contemporary social concerns reveals a significant phenomenon: in the latter cases the language and the wit have gone flat. In a letter of 1859 she writes to Dr. and Mrs. Holland, "Belong to me! We have no fires yet, and the evenings grow cold. To-morrow, stoves are set. How many barefoot shiver I trust their Father knows who saw not fit to give them shoes" (L 207), and a few poems express concern. A little poem from 1864, for example, expresses altruistic intent:

> If I can stop one Heart from breaking
> I shall not live in vain
> If I can ease one Life the Aching
> Or cool one Pain
>
> Or help one fainting Robin
> Unto his Nest again
> I shall not live in Vain.
>
> (919)

What we have here is a fairly maudlin poem using stock images and flaccid language. Expectably (but not for her), Dickinson rhymes "breaking" and "Aching," "vain" and "Pain." No quick flashes of wit, no taut couplings of words, no breathtaking diction, nothing is striking about this poem except its banality. Although it is one of the very few in all her canon of 1,775 poems that express any overall concern for the needy, it is so non-specific as to be unconvincing.

"The Beggar Lad—dies early" has been cited as a poem that shows "definite sympathy with the poor" (Wells 195), but it too suggests no action and displays no real anger. It simply relates a situation and promises the conventional recompense in heaven.

> The Beggar Lad—dies early—
> It's Somewhat in the Cold—
> And Somewhat in the Trudging feet—
> And haply, in the World—
>
> The Cruel—smiling—bowing World—
> That took it's Cambric Way—
> Nor heard the timid cry for "Bread"—
> "Sweet Lady—Charity"—
> . . . .
>
> (717)

As in the "fainting Robin" poem, the language here lacks excitement and invention, suggesting a wholesale adaptation of the sentimental mode of much women's poetry, and a lack of the personal commitment to the subject that might have engaged Dickinson's powerful linguistic capabilities.[7]

One might argue that Dickinson's lack of public comment is due to her choice of genre; the poetry of American women, in contrast to the fiction, is not much engaged with public issues. Social problem poems, however, are not unknown; as Emily Stipes Watts points out, a peripheral but sincere concern with public inequities does exist. "In fact," says Watts, "the women poets of the early nineteenth century wrote more of this kind of poem than the men did" (67).

The popular and prolific Lydia Sigourney, for instance, devoted a significant portion of her poetry to issues of racial injustice. *Traits of the Aborigines of America* (1822) is a five-canto poem in blank verse with extensive historical notes. Its purpose is to provide a record of the oppression of the Indians, and it offers an impassioned plea for fair treatment. Sigourney was not exploiting public sentiment here; anti-Indian feelings were pervasive in her society. In her autobiography she noted, "the work was singularly unpopular, there existing in the community no reciprocity with the subject" (*Letters* 327). Nonetheless, in spite of the fact that she depended on sales of her poetry for a living, she continued her unpopular defense of the Indians. In her *Poems* (1827) she includes several verses on the exploitation of the Indian. "Pocahontas" (1841), her one attempt at an epic poem, is, as Aaron Kramer puts it, "an apology and a memorial to those 'scorn'd and perish'd people' " (223), and in it, as he has also noted, she decries rampant Anglo-Saxonism. Sigourney did not confine her advocacy to Indians; she took up the cause of black Americans as well. Her poem "To the First Slave Ship" (*Poems* [1827] 176) is a fierce condemnation of slavery. And, though in her later years she was anti-abolitionist, her early works contain many references to slavery, and they are, as Kramer has noted, "not sentimental . . . but outraged and harsh" (104).

Kramer's study of social consciousness in the nineteenth century, *The Prophetic Tradition in American Poetry, 1835–1900*, is the only modern study of that period, other than specifically feminist ones, that takes any of the women poets other than Dickinson seriously. Because Kramer is concerned with social issues rather than with artistic issues, he looks at Sigourney in her proper context, allowing a fair evaluation of her work and influence in terms of her own intentions. Roy Harvey Pearce, on the other hand, reveals a lack of understanding of the cultural context when he says that Sigourney lacked "the intelligence to assume [her] proper responsibilities," that she "catered to and exploited the general . . . reader" (197).[8] It is not necessary to propose Sigourney as a great poet in order to see the short-sightedness of this stance. Just what *are* the "proper responsibilities" of a poet? Sigourney did often "exploit" the reader with sentimentality, but she did so on grounds that were defensible in the tenets of the contemporary writing community, and these grounds underscore the basic preoccupations of that community. They were preoccupations with which Dickinson must have been familiar, but grounded in a differing, no less compelling world view, she chose not to be concerned.

The "proper responsibilities" of a poet are not easily defined and delimited but vary from era to era as poetic emphases shift—now a preoccupation with form, now with the world at large, now with expression of the self, now with the capacities of language. To Sigourney, as we have seen, the proper responsibility of a poet was clear—"to aim at being an instrument of good." In its title her first book, *Moral Pieces, in Prose and Verse*, emphasizes that intent. Other writers, too, found the moral emphasis primary. Augusta Wilson's words about Edna Earl, her writer/protagonist in *St. Elmo* echo Sigourney's: "The fondest hope of Edna's heart was to be useful in 'her day and generation'—to be an instrument of some good to her race" (203). The moral impulse as the primary motivation for expression was, then, pervasive in the writing community. And the discourse of public reform was forceful expression of that moral impulse. It led to some powerful writing and also structured careers in major ways. Helen Hunt Jackson is a good case in point. Although she enjoyed considerable success as a fiction writer and as a poet, she abandoned both light fiction and poetry and turned to advocacy for Indians. At the end of her life she had no regrets about this move, saying that her Indian works were "the only things . . . for which I am glad now. The rest is of no moment. They will live on and they will bear fruit" (Kramer 260).

If Jackson had been born thirty or forty years later, she might have made a fine Imagist poet; her poetic voice is uncluttered and, especially in the poems of nature, her imagery is concrete and evocative. In "October," for instance, the sense of autumnal lushness is realized in an abundance of rich images:

> the waters run
> Too slow, so freighted are the river-ways
> With gold of elms and birches from the maze
> Of forests. Chestnuts, clicking one by one
> Escape from satin burs; her fringes done,
> The gentian spreads them out.

(*Verses* 84)

And "March" evokes an opposing vision, one of natural decomposition:

> Beneath the sheltering walls the thin snow clings,—
> Dead winter's skeleton, left bleaching, white,
> Disjointed, crumbling, on unfriendly fields.

(*Verses* 149)

But Jackson's poetic impulse is thoroughly grounded in contemporary assumptions about the need to present a message; thus, like her fiction, her poetry is characterized by a didacticism uncongenial to the modern reader. In spite of the gloomy picture inspired by the opening lines of "March," the sonnet closes with a conventional affirmation that seems to discount everything that has gone before:

> Ah March! we know thou art
> Kind-hearted, spite of ugly looks and threats,
> And, out of sight, art nursing April's violets!

Jackson's compulsion in her poetry, as here, is usually to make the image secondary to its moral referent, and to state discursively the nature and implications of that referent.

For Dickinson, on the other hand, at least in the poems that have been considered her "greatest" by modern critics, the image rests, unexplicated, on its own merits; certainly lines like "The name—of it—is 'Autumn'— / The hue—of it—is Blood—" (656) would admit of no comforting conventional explication.[9] Furnished already with "the infinite," her images point obliquely to a shifting, insecure, and conflicted moral dimension, seldom given elaboration.

In the writing community of Dickinson's contemporaries expression and its style were bound up closely with a morality that was at once impetus, sanction, and subject matter; that morality often led writers outward to the problems of the world and tied them to an audience. Subordination of the word to the divine Word for the world was what led Jackson to turn from poetry to polemic. Of *Ramona* she said, "I did not write *Ramona*. It was written through me. My life-blood went into it" (Kramer 259). This was the essence of being an "instrument of good."

Dickinson's literary impulse was differently located and differently constituted. She wrote, as Higginson noted, "for the relief of [her] own mind" ("Portfolio" 417), not for the moral betterment of the reader. But in that community of expression, writing was perceived as a hierarchically constituted moral act in which the lines of responsibility ran like a telegraph line directly from heaven through the writer to the world. When Stowe says that God wrote *Uncle Tom's Cabin* (Charles Stowe 156), and Phelps remembers of the creation of *The Gates Ajar* (1868) that "the angel said unto me 'Write!' and I wrote" (*Chapters* 95), neither is displaying empty piety. Each is locating her literary impulse precisely—in a sense of moral obligation that was so strong as to seem divine.

Where Jackson felt morally compelled to abandon poetry for a genre that would allow her a greater opportunity to influence the social attitudes of her readers, Dickinson, in the bulk of her work, seems to have had little or no concern for reader reaction. She uses off-rhymes unusual in contemporary poetry, requiring some adaptation on the part of the reader. Her syntax is sometimes so convoluted that it requires a determined reader to follow it to the point of comprehension. Obscure reference also often complicates the reading of her poems. These features, which put barriers in the way of easy comprehension of her poems, indicate that the enlightenment of the reader is for Dickinson secondary to her obsession with the precise and powerful expression of a complex and often unsettling world view. Further, her persistent refusal to publish—to place her poetry before the reading public—heightens our awareness of her lack of concern with bringing a moral message to readers, with being in this way an "instrument of good."

A study of two poems about suffering, Jackson's "My Legacy" (*Verses* 16–18) and Dickinson's "I measure every Grief I meet,"(561), reveals the profound motivational gap between the two writers. Jackson's poem is long and allegorical. It begins, "They told me I was heir, I turned in haste / And ran to seek my treasure." This unknown "legacy" the poetic speaker imagines initially as material—gold or land—and she journeys to find one who can tell her where to locate it. She is led eventually to Christ, whom she finds to be her brother and "joint heir." Her "share" turns out to be spiritual: "the right like him to know all pain / Which hearts are made for knowing." While the pain here is at first personal, it leads inevitably outward, involving through her connection with Christ an obligation to the suffering of the world, "the right with him to keep / A watch by day and night with all who weep." Further, and more significantly, it involves an expressive mandate, an obligation to spread the message. As the poem moves toward its conclusion, this imperative is stated: "And through my tears I call to each, 'Joint heir / With Christ, make haste to ask him for thy share.' " The purpose of the writing act becomes clear—to influence society, to move individuals to change their lives and thus to change the world. This is indeed a "legacy," the expressive legacy that Jackson as a conforming mid-century woman writer inherited.

In Dickinson's poem the movement is significantly in opposition. "I measure every Grief I meet / With narrow, probing, Eyes—," she says. But what she is searching for is not gold or houses, but from the start an understanding of her own experience. "I wonder if It weighs like *Mine*— / Or has an Easier size" (italics mine). Unlike Jackson, she does not find through her pain a connection with others; her metaphoric movement here is not a journey out into the world, but rather an exercise in conjecture: "I measure," "I wonder," "I note." Her stance is markedly detached from the pain of others, "The Grieved—are many—I am told— / There is the various Cause—." Alien to contact with any but her own grief, this speaker presents herself as knowing only through the report of others ("I am told"), only through the agency of language that somehow fails to allow her to comprehend fully its referred reality, the suffering of others. In no sense does this "telling" unite objective reality with subjective experience. The linguistic distortion of the phrase "the various Cause"—the failure of its adjective to reconcile with its noun—not only draws attention to itself but also suggests reportorial inability to pierce the skin of exclusive self-interest characterizing this speaker. "Grief of Want—and Grief of Cold—" are interesting not as they relate to any needs in society, but only as they serve to define, and thus to "Comfort," her own pain. Language is writer-directed rather than reader-directed. Its purpose is not to motivate action in the world, but rather to provide personal insight and satisfaction and an apt embodiment of alienated anguish. With that intent, language may be private, exaggerated and distorted to serve the needs of the writer rather than of the reader.

Dickinson's own reform movement was to move inward as an advocate for the understanding and precise representation of complex and painful individual human experience. As a poet in *her* sense, she was not heir to the pain of the world but to the pain of being a *self* in the world. Her expressive legacy was herself, "a Fortune— / Exterior—to Time—" as she says in "This was a Poet" (448), and her expressive mandate was to develop a language adequate to communicate the uniqueness of that individual existence. Women's writing, as she would have known it, envisioned the writer as a moral conduit between God and the world. For Dickinson the poet operated in a shifting moral universe in which she was originator of and final field of reference for her own expression. The psychological and metaphysical exploration mandated by that vision demands a new aesthetic to make possible the expression of concerns far outside the literary mandate of Dickinson's contemporaries. Whereas many successful women writers of her generation freed themselves from expressive strictures by engaging in public advocacy, in a dialogue with the world, Dickinson avoided the strictures by other means—her poetic indirection and her non-publication—and poured her energies directly into her exploration of the poetic possibilities of language and of the significance of the *self* in the world:

> The Heart is the Capital of the Mind—
> The Mind is a single State—
> The Heart and the Mind together make
> A single Continent—

One—is the Population—
Numerous enough—
This ecstatic Nation
Seek—it is Yourself.

(1354)

V

"THE RETICENT VOLCANO"
STYLE AND THE PRIVATE WOMAN

This is where Emily Dickinson comes in.
She was the articulate inarticulate. That is
why it so appeals to New England women.

—Sam G. Ward, 1891

In Elizabeth Stuart Phelps's *The Story of Avis*, Susan Jessup, an abused and
abandoned woman, shows up at the protagonist's home to acquaint Avis
with their interlocking histories; it was Avis's husband who had initially
betrayed Susan. Susan leaves Avis with this compelling question: "Why
does a woman trust herself to do any thing [sic], when she's beside herself
with things she can't speak of? That's the worst of being a woman. What
you go through can't be told" (164). As the preceding chapters show, the
awareness of what "can't be told" haunts women's literature in
nineteenth-century America. Indeed it is the primary expressive dilemma:
when they came to consider anything related to personal experience, and
especially to those areas—sexuality, ambition, and anger—that were
specifically proscribed, women writers found themselves to be "beside
[themselves] with things [they couldn't] speak of."

This context of radical reticence, grounded, as we have seen, in cultural
assumptions about the essential morality of feminine nature, reveals a
source for the extreme stylistic indirection that characterizes a significant
portion of Emily Dickinson's poetry; her poetic indirection may well have
roots in her compelling need to express herself on proscribed experiences,
on matters that, because of her acculturation as a woman, couldn't be
spoken of.[1] The "divine reticence" affirmed by Dickinson's friend, the Rev.
John Dudley, reflects conventional thinking, and requires much from the
"exalted" state of femininity, particularly the erasure of self and a radically
reserved demeanor. Dickinson's contemporary, Sam G. Ward, in a letter

to Higginson upon the initial publication of her poems, notes a quality of the "articulate inarticulate" in her poetry and, although this description in some ways applies to all aesthetic creation, Ward specifically indicates a contemporary feminine context, saying "that is why it appeals so to New England women" (Bingham, *Ancestors'* 170).[2] His comment suggests that Dickinson's indirection may well have been attractive to these women because it provided for them a way of alluding to what was in their lives but was, according to the ethos of reticence, not to be spoken of. It would have represented for them a comfortable, even familiar, mode of approaching subjective expression, one that did not threaten to rupture the construct of femininity by which they had achieved cultural identity. Cristanne Miller says that one of the basic effects of the innovations in Dickinson's use of language is "indeterminacy of reference and degree of personal involvement in the poem" (180). Here is a woman who, while manifesting the transcendent ambition of the brilliant creative artist, presents herself, nonetheless, as being, in the Rev. Dudley's terms, "not ambitious of talk, of self-display, of self-manifestation" (Leyda II 171–72). She is there, but at the same time, she is not there; she is somebody, but she is also "Nobody" (288).

The aesthetic sophistication and experimentation of Dickinson's style and her philosophical and psychological complexity take her in many ways beyond the boundaries of the literary expression of her female contemporaries. However, similarities in the use of indirection as an expressive device relate her to them, suggesting a common effort to speak the unspeakable—to evade not only external censors of articulation but also the more troubling internalized inhibitions. Through stylistic means women writers attempted to say or obliquely imply that which had been proscribed. Proscriptions on women's expression thus constitute a common cultural source for Dickinson's indirection and the stylistic tactics of indirection used by other women writers. David Reynolds notes that it is precisely the obliquity and elusiveness of Dickinson's style that make her "representative of American women's culture." Whereas Hawthorne and Whitman, he says, address women's issues, Dickinson "perfects women's *style*" (420). Dickinson brought to full artistic fruition what could be called either a nascent feminine aesthetic or a survival strategy born of conflict and need.

Dickinson's indirection has many aspects—disjunction, compression, radical ellipsis, enigmatic metaphor—but the most characteristic may well be the habitual omission of subject identification. In a poem she included in her third letter to Thomas Wentworth Higginson we find a prime example of omitted subject:

> As if I asked a common Alms,
> And in my wondering hand
> A Stranger pressed a Kingdom,
> And I, bewildered, stand—
> As if I asked the Orient
> Had it for me a Morn—
> And it should lift it's purple Dikes,
> And shatter me with Dawn!

(323)

Aside from its striking omission of reference, this is for Dickinson, a fairly straightforward piece of language. Each of the two sentences of the poem is introduced by an implied main clause—perhaps "it is" or "I feel"—and the dependent clauses that follow are direct in presentation and grammatically correct. The tone, too, is fairly clear—a gratified amazement. But the subject of the poem is replaced by two metaphors, "a Kingdom" and "Dawn," whose reference is not indicated, and out of its immediate context—the letter to Higginson—it is impossible to specify just what this poem means. It could be an expression of religious awe or a response to a declaration of love, as easily as what it seems to be, an expression of profound gratitude for some unstated favor or compliment.

In other Dickinson poems, however, the reader finds, along with omitted reference, tonal devices such as irony and ambivalence and structural devices such as sequential disordering of syntax and narrative. These are stylistic features that can indicate in an oblique manner a meaning that has not been stated, meaning-producing substitutes for the suppressed subject, for that which could not be spoken. To those of us nurtured in the modernist tradition, these stylistic devices are familiar; they constitute an attempt to stretch the limits of language. And, as David Porter suggests, Dickinson's style is often more insistent than her semantics (5). Stylistic devices aimed at expression that goes beyond statement are, of course, not unique in literature to Dickinson or to modernism. In a rudimentary state but with significant frequency and with significant parallels to Dickinson's work, the irony, ambivalence, and sequential disordering that characterize Dickinson's writing are seen in the work of the American women writers who were her contemporaries and who were operating in the same climate of articulation. The work of even the most conforming writers is often characterized by articulate disjunctures between what is being stated and what is—on another level—being communicated, providing a mode of expression predicated on both revelation and concealment. Like Dickinson, these writers punctuate their texts with stylistic scattershot—flashes of

irony, profound ambivalences, unexpected dislocations of sequence—
which provide eloquent unspoken messages. The strategies are either conscious or unintended, depending on the writer in question, but they are
nonetheless expressive. There is at the heart of conventional texts experience that could not be spoken but that could be implied.

In Dickinson's writing and in that of her contemporaries, indirect expressive devices, profound and articulate disjunctures between aspects of
style, tone, and statement, most likely developed as a stylistic adaptation
to social strictures against the intrusion of female subjectivity into the public
arena. Cristanne Miller speaks of the "tension between the poet's partially
articulated desire to speak to an audience, to move her reader, and her
largely unarticulated decision to write the riddling, elliptical poetry she
does" as "the root of the peculiar urgency in Dickinson's poems" (1). Subjectivity presses itself forward in Dickinson's work but is fractured in the
process by psychic resistance to its expression.

In previous chapters I have presented two striking responses on the part
of the majority of women writers to the proscriptions on women's expression: the use of conventional patterns of womanhood—the images of the
little girl and of the wife/bride—to delineate the female self, and the tendency to deal with public rather than with private issues. Both strategies
allowed articulation while avoiding true personal disclosure. To speak honestly and openly in print about oneself or even about a fictional female
character like Ruth Hall or Cassandra Morgeson who might be construed
to contain aspects of one's own experience was another matter. In the
widespread ethos of femininity that characterized middle-class America at
this time, feminine articulation was a venture fraught with obscure dangers.
Mary Kelley quotes Caroline Gilman's account of her reaction at age sixteen
to the publication of her first poem. Gilman's response to seeing herself
in print had been one of "alarm"; she "wept bitterly" and felt "as if I had
been detected in man's apparel" (180).

The desire for self-expression in many of these women was, nonetheless,
strong, as one would expect in intelligent and often quite talented writers.
However, the ethos of divine reticence was also strong. Rufus Griswold
approvingly characterized Elizabeth Oakes Smith in her early work as
"seeking expression, yet shrinking from notoriety" (177), and this is an
apt description of the conflict that faced most women writers. In the quest
for expression and the simultaneous flight from "notoriety," they wrote,
but they omitted whole areas of experience from their texts, indicating
censored emotions and attitudes only through tonal dissonance and articulate ruptures of form. Reynolds speaks, for instance, of "[t]he indirec-
tions and disconnections" of *The Morgesons* as being "typical of the broken

narrative patterns" of women's writing (409). What we are seeing here is most likely not a conscious encoding of forbidden material. Rather, this dynamic of simultaneous revelation and concealment represents, in most cases, a shared unconscious response to a deeply embedded conflict, a common reaction to a common expressive bind. And, like many of her contemporaries, Dickinson may well have internalized social standards of femininity to the point where she was often simply incapable of expressing herself directly on feelings, experiences, and ideas that would have been rife with psychic conflict—sexual passion, for example, or anger at the loss of love.

However, in 1846 poet Frances Locke Osgood—more candid than most women in this era—did openly state the case for feminine literary indirection in her poem "A Reply," subtitled "To One Who Said, 'Write From Your Heart.' " In this poem she indicates clearly the strong social bias that generated women's expressive anxieties—conscious or unconscious:

> Ah! woman still
> Must veil the shrine,
> Where feeling feeds the fire divine,
> Nor sing at will,
> Untaught by art,
> The music prison'd in her heart!
>
> . . . .
>
> The world would say
> 'Twas vain and wild,
> Th' impassion'd lay of Nature's child;
> And Feeling, so,
> Should veil the shrine,
> Where softly glow her fires divine!
>
> (*Poems* 46–47)

Here is an expressive stance predicated overtly upon concealment. "Art" in this case is used in the double sense of conscious craft *and* of deceit. The motivating factor in this strategy is the opinion of the "world," an opinion that would condemn uncensored feminine expression as "vain and wild." The "fires" of a woman's passions must be veiled in her expression. Her articulation must be a screened version of the true music "prison'd" in her being.

Both Cheryl Walker (30) and Emily Stipes Watts (136) have linked this poem with Dickinson's "Tell all the Truth but tell it slant—" (1129), and the resemblance at first seems striking. Certainly Osgood is advising a "slant" mode of articulation. But the Dickinson poem read in its entirety does not carry exactly the same meaning as the Osgood poem:

> Tell all the Truth but tell it slant—
> Success in Circuit lies
> Too bright for our infirm Delight
> The Truth's superb surprise
> As Lightning to the Children eased
> With explanation kind
> The Truth must dazzle gradually
> Or every man be blind—

Rather than an aesthetic of concealment, this poem seems to posit an aesthetic based on gradual revelation of abstract truth; far from being truth fraught with anxiety and danger, as one would expect of utterances that fracture deeply embedded expressive proscriptions, the revelations of this poem are associated with the "Delight" and "superb surprise" of all poetry that deals with great and difficult truths. Other Dickinson "tell it slant" poems, however, *do* exist in a context that suggests a precarious articulative situation—a context of danger, anxiety, and concealment. In the following poem the speaker celebrates what initially seems to be a *game* of articulative concealment:

> Good to hide, and hear 'em hunt!
> Better, to be found,
> If one care to, that is,
> The Fox fits the Hound—
>
> Good to know, and not tell,
> Best, to know and tell,
> Can one find the rare Ear
> Not too dull—
>
> (842)

Tone and imagery, however, are oddly incongruous here, indicating a situation the implications of which are not being fully acknowledged. The first verse presents an image: the speaker as a fox, hiding from hunters. The second verse makes the analogy clear: the situation involves an expressive dilemma. The fox/persona is a speaker, one with knowledge to communicate. While the possession of the knowledge is good in itself, the better situation would be an opportunity for expression of it, if one could find an empathetic or understanding listener.

So far my reading reveals a fairly conventional statement and one that seems straightforward and free of anxiety. But superimposing the imagery of the first verse on the explanatory statement of the second, we perceive a significant disparity. If the speaker is a fox, the persona is not merely playing a reticent game of hide and seek; the penalty for being "found"— for having your meaning understood—in this life-and-death chase is to be torn to shreds by hunting dogs. Virulent censors of articulation, most likely both external and internal, are on the trail here. While she has a strong desire to "tell," as a speaker or a poet, this persona knows the penalties and has adapted her articulation to them: "The Fox fits the Hound." In this puzzling line, the radical ambiguity of the verb forces the reader into extravagant, even irresponsible, interpretations in order to make any sense at all of the statement.[3] These are the ways we can read the line: either the speaker "fits" herself to the situation—adapts, perhaps by hiding; or she, in dialect usage, "fights" the hound; or, in one of Dickinson's appropriations of a noun for the purposes of a verb, she angers the hound, throwing him into "fits"; or, in the only other possible—and horrific— reading of this ambiguous line, she is consumed by the hounds and "fits" into them. "If one care to, that is," is her cool assessment of the option of allowing herself to be "found" by the "Hound."

While the tone of this poem in some ways is light—it seems to trip right along with, for Dickinson, little impediment—the implications of its imagery and of that one recalcitrant verb are mystifying and horrific, creating a stylistic disjuncture not dissimilar to what was happening in other women's texts at the time. In a discussion of major women's novels of the day, historian Mary Kelley points out the disparity between the surface text and the subtextual implications of much of this literature: "the positive, forceful message rode and was partly generated by an undercurrent of dissatisfaction and despair" ("Promise and Betrayal" 437).[4] Conventional literary genres develop, to some degree, as formal vehicles of the ideology they disseminate, and their use constitutes an implicit contract with the reader to fulfill certain ideological expectations manifesting themselves as generic conventions. Violation of these expectations flouts the terms of the contract and thus in itself carries meaning. As I say elsewhere about conventional nineteenth-century women's novels, "[d]isruption of expectations always attracts the attention, and in these novels narrative and characterizational disruptions serve inevitably the purpose of highlighting the problematic nature of the feminine ideal" (Dobson 228). The conventional narrative structure of the sentimental novel, with its recurrent emphasis on the process of training a girl into selflessness, suggests conformity to cultural norms of feminine behavior; the tone and a disrupted narrative realization often indicate dissent.

If disruptions and violations of expectation can in themselves be read as elements of commentary grounded in common cultural experience, then we must, at least to some degree, shift Dickinson's well-known stylistic floutings from the arena of the strictly personal to the terrain of the cultural. Upon the publication of the first edition of the poems, Maurice Thompson, a friend of Higginson's, wrote to him: "Miss Dickinson's verse suggests to me a superb brain that has suffered some obscure lesion which now and again prevents the filling out of a thought" (Bingham, *Ancestors'* 79–80). Yet conflicts and contradictions in a text, as Terry Eagleton tells us, display significance in "the *difference* rather than unity between . . . meanings" (*Marxism and Literary Criticism* 35 [emphasis mine]); gaps and evasions in themselves are carriers of meaning.

In *Ruth Hall* Fanny Fern parodies the retrograde conventional authority that finds itself disturbed by literary "violations." A Professor Stearns (author of "History of the Dark Ages") writes to Ruth, the author-protagonist: "You have written tolerably, all things considered, but you violate all established rules of composition, and are as lawless and erratic as a comet. You may startle and dazzle, but you are fit only to throw people out of their orbits" (166). Raymond Williams tells us that changes and modifications ("lawlessness") in genre conventions are prescient not only of new forms of literary expression but also of new ways of being in the world: "emergent formations (. . . often in the form of modification or disturbance in older forms)" presage new forms of social experience (134). In other words, what is experienced by those deeply embedded in the culture as "erratic and lawless" (or symptomatic of brain damage) may indeed be designed (either consciously or unconsciously) to "throw people out of their orbits."

In the failure of style and substance to cohere or the failure of genre to be consistent with its conventions lay the primary modes of indirect expression characterizing nineteenth-century women writers. This stylistic dislocation stemmed from a clash between the cultural mythos with which women's literature was embued and the cultural reality that affected their lives.[5] Rufus Griswold's description of the "finest" women's poetry as being characterized by "a religious delight in nature, and a contentment with home affections and pleasures" (250) is a prime example of the mythos and an excellent description of the kind of writing many women strove for. But another contemporary observer astutely noted the disparity between this ideal and her observed experience of women's actual lives. "I could wish that women were happier," Gail Hamilton wrote in 1861 in a discussion of marriage and women's stunted development; "this may appear a needless wish to those who look only on the surface; but below the smoothly-flowing surface there is an undercurrent which the world knoweth not of. There is a restlessness, an *unuttered discontent*, a vague longing which frets and wears away the cheerfulness and happiness of life" (138, emphasis mine).

Hamilton was what we might call an expressive deviant. Her lively essays deal in an open and forthright manner with women's problems, and occasionally she attacks the expressive taboos openly: "consume in private your private griefs! No. Take them in a bundle, and bear them to the highest mountain-top; ring the churchbells, hoist the flags, beat the drums, and let the whole world see the bonfire; and if the flame scorches our sensitive friends, let them stand back" (192–93).[6] The energetic vehemence of Hamilton's statement indicates the personal force it takes to break the strictures, and her imagery equates women's speech—the verbal eruption of what she sees as an all too pervasive "unuttered discontent"—with the violent potential of fire. We are familiar with Dickinson's use of explosive and volcanic imagery—her sense of herself as a loaded gun, her often reiterated analogy of the self as a dormant volcano: "Vesuvius dont talk—Etna— dont" she assured her "Master" in an anguished avowal of love. In this image, disclosure is perceived as potentially catastrophic: "One of them— said a syllable—a thousand years ago, and Pompeii heard it, and hid forever" (L 233). The volcanic consequence of just one syllable—the most minute integer of the slightest locution—eradicates an entire society, "forever." For Hamilton and Dickinson the imagery of bonfires, scorching flames, and volcanic eruptions relates to the common belief that women's uncensored expression is potentially incendiary—dangerous, even fatal, to the self and to society.

Images of explosiveness, of the volcano, of catastrophic fire were not uncommon in women's writing at mid-century. We have seen Frances Osgood's admonition that "feeling" "Should veil the shrine, / Where softly glow her fires divine." A well-regulated, confined flicker of feeling, reminiscent of the confined flames of the domestic hearth, warms but does not threaten. On the other hand, many writers had the sense of their duty to restrain what they felt to be the explosive potential of heartfelt speech.

> The Solemn—Torrid—Symbol—
> The lips that never lie—
> Whose hissing Corals part—and shut—
> And Cities—ooze away—
>
> (601)

Dickinson in this poem sees life as being "A still—Volcano—," the eruption of which is specifically compared to speech, more particularly to the expression of a truth, the articulation of which would destroy "Cities," eradicating human community. Her perception is uncannily similar to that of Lydia Maria Child, whose writing often tackled "explosive" issues not only of gender but also of race and class. In a letter to a friend in 1856 on the subject of reforming marriage, Child falls quite naturally into the volcanic idiom:

> I am so well aware that society stands over a heaving volcano, from which it is separated by the thinnest possible crust of appearances, that I am afraid to speak or to think on the subject. (Jeffrey 123)

Note that in both of these images, society is seen as immensely fragile compared to the destructive potential of a woman's truth. Child is referring explicitly to a gender-specific subject, the alteration of gender (and sexual) relations. Dickinson's poem is not manifestly gender-specific; the reference to "Life" is generalized. It would, however, be naive to ignore the elided verbal and genital connotations of the labial imagery: "The lips that never lie— / Whose hissing Corals part—and shut— / And Cities—ooze away—." The destructive power here is as sexual as it is verbal. In a nineteenth-century America still marked by the vestiges of its Puritan origins, the possessor of such power is under divine obligation to Christian civilization to maintain reticence.

> The reticent volcano keeps
> His never slumbering plan;
> Confided are his projects pink
> To no precarious man.
>
> (1748)

David Reynolds has also noticed the frequent use in women's writing of explosive imagery. He quotes Fanny Fern in *Ruth Hall* saying: "[W]henever —you—see—a—blue-eyed—soft-voiced—gentle—woman, —look—out—for a hurricane. I tell you that placid Ruth is a smouldering volcano." And he compares the style of women's writing (at least the kind he calls "the literature of misery") to "a kind of dormant volcano, frequently muted and quietly imagistic but always with explosive implications" (415). These "explosive implications," as we have seen, are both stylistic and imagistic. It wasn't only the more openly dissenting writers like Fanny Fern, however, who made use of the imagery of conflagration. Even the most conforming writers, such as Lydia Sigourney, the beloved "Sweet Singer of Hartford," were attracted to the expressive potential of holocaust. In "The Suttee" (1827) Sigourney creates a complex and, in its own peculiar grotesque manner, fairly brilliant poem. And in a stylistic disjuncture of enormous expressive potential she turns her ostensibly blameless theme, a mother's devotion to her child (a "contentment with home affections") into a scorching indictment of the self-immolation inherent in the conventional definition of marriage.

> The Suttee
>
> She sat upon the pile by her dead lord,
> And in her full, dark eye, and shining hair
> Youth revell'd.—The glad murmur of the crowd
> Applauding her consent to the dread doom,
> And the hoarse chanting of infuriate priests
> She heeded not, for her quick ear had caught
> An infant's wail.—Feeble and low that moan,
> Yet it was answer'd in her heaving heart,
> For the Mimosa in its shrinking fold
> From the rude pressure, is not half so true,
> So tremulous, as is a mother's soul
> Unto her wailing babe.—There was such wo
> In her imploring aspect,—in her tones
> Such thrilling agony, that even the hearts
> Of the flame-kindlers soften'd, and they laid
> The famish'd infant on her yearning breast.
> There with his tear-wet cheek he lay and drew
> Plentiful nourishment from that full fount
> Of infant happiness,—and long he prest
> With eager lip the chalice of his joy.—
> And then his little hands he stretch'd to grasp
> His mother's flower-wove tresses, and with smile
> And gay caress embraced his bloated sire,—
> As if kind Nature taught that innocent one
> With fond delay to cheat the hour which seal'd
> His hopeless orphanage.—But those were near
> Who mock'd such dalliance, as that Spirit malign
> Who twined his serpent length mid Eden's bowers
> Frown'd on our parents' bliss.—The victim mark'd
> Their harsh intent, and clasp'd the unconscious babe
> With such convulsive force, that when they tore
> His writhing form away, the very nerves
> Whose deep-sown fibres rack the inmost soul
> Uprooted seem'd.—
>   With voice of high command
> Tossing her arms, she bade them bring her son,—

And then in maniac rashness sought to leap
Among the astonish'd throng.—But the rough cord
Compress'd her slender limbs, and bound her fast
Down to her loathsome partner.—Quick the fire
In showers was hurl'd upon the reeking pile;—
But yet amid the wild, demoniac shout
Of priest and people, mid the thundering yell
Of the infernal gong,—was heard to rise
Thrice a dire death-shriek.—And the men who stood
Near the red pile and heard that fearful cry,
Call'd on their idol-gods, and stopp'd their ears,
And oft amid their nightly dream would start
As Frighted Fancy echoed in her cell
That burning mother's scream.

What Sigourney gives us here is a poem of seeming cultural consensus. The theme, the devotion of a mother to her child, is pervasive in her poetry and in the writing of her female contemporaries to the point where it becomes a cultural icon. The particular situation, too, is not unusual; impelled by missionaries' accounts of Indian women's immolations on the funeral pyres of their husbands, the image of the suttee was common in women's writing in America. This poem then stands squarely in recognizable Christian and cultural genres; it is a cry of outrage at a barbaric heathen custom and a paean to motherhood. These genres carry with them certain expectations, however, that the poem cleverly manipulates; it focuses on the madonna-like cultural icon of mother suckling child, only to have that child torn from its mother's arms; it begins with a focus on conventional feminine submission, only to end with a scream of rage and despair; and, perhaps most importantly, it portrays a "pagan" custom with—for once—no discursive, culture-specific Christian moralizing.

"The Suttee" is a poem far-distanced culturally, religiously, and geographically from both author and audience. Set in New Delhi, so to speak, and not New England, it presents a situation alien, it would seem, to American women. Yet the most striking characteristic of this poem is the anger that impels it; this is a furious poem. Almost a little too furious, we might think, to be solely an expression of concern about the savage customs of unredeemed "heathen." The poem focuses quite sharply on an image that may well have carried intimate emotional connotations for many readers (as well as for Lydia Sigourney, whose marriage by all accounts seems to have been disastrous): the image of a societally approved feminine self-immolation. At the imagistic heart of the poem is a woman bound to a "loathesome partner." Shackled to this "dead lord," the "bloated sire" of her helpless child, this woman cannot even insure the proper fulfillment of the sacred duty of the mother, the nurturance of her child. As she struggles helplessly against her bonds, the only power left to her is the power of articulation: her "voice of high command," the "thrilling agony" of her tones, her "dire death-shriek."

As well as a poem about suttee, then, this poem can profitably be read as a displaced investigation of the potentially deadly nature of conventional marriage, a young woman's shackling and her futile attempts to free herself. While the poem does not moralize on the superiority of Christianity, neither does it provide a discursive commentary on the nature of American marriage. In an age of discursive, broadly explanatory poetry, these verses offer not one line of commentary; they stand on the power of their own thrillingly resonant images. Thus the poem communicates not through authorial interpretation but through tonal resonance and the flouting of genre expectations. The lack of explication offers a certain indeterminacy to the poetic situation, allowing it to be at once descriptive *and* metaphoric. The disgust and outrage associated with the bonding of this woman and man (the "loathsome partner," the "bloated sire") are in themselves potent communicative elements in either a descriptive or a metaphoric reading. If Sigourney as a poet cannot speak openly about the conditions of her own marriage, she can leave with us the resonant echos of "[t]hat burning mother's scream": the scream that haunts readers as it haunted the by-standers at that Indian immolation. Out of the conflagration that constitutes this marriage comes a wordless, haunting scream.

Tonally indicated contrasts are characteristic of this body of nineteenth-century American women's writing: one meaning conforms to conventional expectation, one flouts it. The Sigourney poem can be read as an outraged Christian condemnation of the horrific practice of suttee or as a conventional woman's oblique investigation of what it feels like to be in a marriage that disgusts her. Tone is of necessity a focal element of a literature of indirection; rather than statement, it involves implication. The author's attitude toward her subject and toward her audience is indicated by a discreet manipulation of content and style that communicates an intangible affective quality. Because of its suggestive rather than definitive nature tonal nuance is largely a matter of reading; what is subtle irony or articulate ambivalence to one reader may well be straightforward assertion to another. Herein lies the author's hedge against condemnation; she can always plead an ingenuous literality.

Fanny Fern is a writer who employs tone consciously and overtly, high-lighting her usage as part of the fun of breaking the rules. She, of course, is a nonconforming writer and can allow herself this openness. In her short sketch "The Tear of a Wife" from *Fern Leaves*, the author raises conventional expectations by presenting a sentimental title and following it with an epigraph quoting conventional wisdom: "The tear of a loving girl is like a dew-drop on a rose; but on the cheek of a wife, is a drop of poison to her husband." The exaggeratedly ironic tone of her parodic sermonizing, however, soon turns her blameless advice into a sarcastic harangue.

> Never mind back-aches, and side-aches, and head-aches, and dropsical complaints, and smoky chimneys, and old coats, and young babies! Smile! It flatters your husband. He wants to be considered the source of your happiness, whether he was baptized Nero or Moses! Your mind never being supposed to be occupied with any other subject than himself, of course a tear is a tacit reproach. Besides, you miserable little whimperer! what have you to cry for? A-i-n-t y-o-u m-a-r-r-i-e-d? Isn't that the *summum bonum,*— the height of feminine ambition? You can't get beyond that! It is the jumping-off place! You've arriv!—got to the end of your journey! Stage puts up there! You have nothing to do but retire on your laurels, and spend the rest of your life endeavoring to be thankful that you are Mrs. John Smith! "Smile!" you simpleton! (324–25)

Although a doggedly literal reading of this text would support the ethos of self-abasement that feminine ideology propounded, the true subject of Fanny Fern's brief sketch is obviously something quite different. Irony of tone indicates conflicts and contradictions embedded within an ostensibly straightforward statement or situation. This sketch in particular reveals the conflict between ideal feminine deportment and the actual conditions of a woman's life. Further, it communicates an obvious anger at the suppression of a woman's personal expression—even tears, her one time-honored medium, are banned. Elsewhere this writer attacks the subject of female self-expression head on: "Write!" she advises her readers in *Folly As It Flies* (1868), "to lift yourselves out of the dead-level of your lives . . . to lessen the number who are yearly added to our lunatic asylums from the ranks of misappreciated, unhappy womanhood, narrowed by lives made up of details. Fight it!" (64). But in this sketch she takes the sting out of her indictment with the humor—albeit caustic—of overt irony.

In more conventional texts the irony is more complex, deeply embedded, and not unmixed with ambivalence; conflicting meanings and values are concurrently present, simultaneously highlighting and negating each other. Frances Osgood's daring address to her estranged husband in "Oh! hasten to my side," depicts a situation fraught with proscribed experience; the poem is generated by anger and takes as its subject illicit sexual attraction—most likely for Edgar Allan Poe, with whom Osgood carried on a passionate correspondence (Walker 31). It is only the stylistic indirection of this poem of passion that permitted its publication. On the surface this is a conventional poem of renunciation, but note that it is full of the explicit and evocative description of just exactly how wonderful this love is that must be renounced, to the point that the attractiveness of the illicit love quite overwhelms the speaker's resolve:

> Oh! hasten to my side, I pray!
>   I dare not be alone!
> The smile that tempts, when thou'rt away,
>   Is fonder than thine own.
>
> The voice that oftenest charms mine ear
>   Hath such beguiling tone,
> 'Twill steal my very *soul*, I fear;
>   Ah! leave me not alone!
>
> It speaks in accents low and deep,
>   It murmurs praise too dear,
> It makes me passionately weep,
>   Then gently soothes my fear;
>
> It calls me sweet, endearing names,
>   With Love's own childlike art:
> My tears, my doubts, it softly blames—
>   'Tis music to my heart!
>
> And dark, deep, eloquent, soul-fill'd eyes
>   Speak tenderly to mine;
> Beneath that gaze what feelings rise!
>   It is more kind than thine!
>
> A hand, even pride can scarce repel,
>   Too fondly seeks mine own;
> It is not safe!—it is not well!
>   Ah! leave me not alone!
>
> I try to calm, in cold repose,
>   Beneath his earnest eye,
> The heart that thrills, the cheek that glows—
>   Alas! in *vain* I try!

A profound personal and cultural irony pervades this poem. The speaker does not call her husband back because she loves him—indeed, he repels her—but because society rigorously requires her compliance to an identity known as "wife" and a code known as "honor":

Oh trust me not—a woman frail—
  To brave the snares of life!
Lest—lonely, sad, unloved—I *fail*
  And shame the name of wife!

Come back! though cold and harsh to me,
  There's *honour* by thy side!
Better unblest, yet safe to be,
  Than lost to truth, to pride.

Subdued anger becomes more apparent here. This speaker feels that affection, as well as sexual passion, must be renounced in order to conform to her perception of society's definition of "truth" and "pride." The poem ends unresolved, but with a final image that chills the reader with the ironic horror of the speaker's choice:

Alas! my peril hourly grows,
  In every thought and dream;
Not—not to *thee* my spirit goes,
  But still—yes! still to *him*!

Return with those cold eyes to me,
  And chill my soul once more
Back to the loveless apathy
  It learn'd so well before!

(Watts 112–13)

Complex in its generation by two proscribed feelings, anger and illicit sexuality, this poem is also complex in its tone: irony *and* ambivalence pervade. The overt statement is morally impeccable in terms of the cultural ideal of the faithful wife who—quite properly—struggles to maintain her "honor" although she is beset on both sides—by a husband who fails to fulfill her emotional needs and by an oh so winsome suitor. The tonal indications of that statement, on the other hand, suggest that her conformity to "honor" would be even more immoral than her seemingly inevitable downfall, condemning this passionate woman, as it would, to a life sentence of "loveless apathy" that sounds rather more like death than life. While the irony of the situation is immediately apparent, the effect of that irony is tempered by an ambivalence carrying its own message—if she "fails" the speaker will "shame the name of wife" and violate a concept that she seems honestly to equate with "truth" and "pride." The speaker reveres the prevailing concept of wifehood—and most likely the poet does as well. But she is caught in a clash between ideals and reality heightened by the poem's unusual—for its time—failure to resolve the situation. The complex irony and ambivalence of this poem carry a message to readers that while a woman's conformity to cultural ideals is right and good, it is often achieved at a cost too terrible to be borne.

A similar message is found in a poem of renunciation written by Emily Dickinson in the early 1860s. In "I should have been too glad, I see," an unresolved clash between ideal reality and actual reality creates a tone of ambivalence and a situation characterized by an irony at least as profound as that in the Osgood poem. How is it possible to be "too glad"? Such a self-contradictory situation could exist only in the language that is used to embody the concept, not in the experience of "gladness" itself—by definition a highly desirable state and by implication a state of which one would want as much as possible.

This poem read in both extant versions indicates that only a hairline difference exists in the language between the expression of passive acceptance and the articulation of explosive fury. Thomas Johnson chose to publish in the *Complete Poems* the version Dickinson sent to her sister-in-law, Susan, but Dickinson herself tied into her fascicle collection of her poetry a version with a slightly different final line. Four minute alterations of punctuation and diction from one version to the other change the tone of the poem from ironic anger to profound ambivalence, and reveal a razor's edge of conflicted passion. Here is the poem as we usually read it:

I should have been too glad, I see—
Too lifted—for the scant degree
Of Life's penurious Round—
My little Circuit would have shamed
This new Circumference—have blamed—
The homelier time behind.

I should have been too saved—I see—
Too rescued—Fear too dim to me
That I could spell the Prayer
I knew so perfect—yesterday—
That Scalding One—Sabachthani—
Recited fluent—here—

Earth would have been too much—I see—
And Heaven—not enough for me—
I should have had the Joy
Without the Fear—to justify—
The Palm—without the Calvary—
So Savior—Crucify—

> Defeat—whets Victory—they say—
> The Reefs—in old Gethsemane—
> Endear the Coast—beyond!
> 'Tis Beggars—Banquets—can define—
> 'Tis Parching—vitalizes Wine—
> "Faith" bleats—to understand!

(*Complete Poems* 313)

One similarity between this poem and Osgood's is that both purport to find renunciation of what is overtly passionate love in the Osgood poem and what *seems* to be passionate love in the Dickinson poem a better fate than fulfillment. In actuality, however, both concentrate on how wonderful fulfillment would be—or would have been. One must, however, with the Dickinson poem, first make an assumption that the poem *is* about love, since the subject has not been specified. The reader, then, has a certain amount of reconstruction to do, but it seems a fairly straightforward task. The language is from a religious context, so it may be a poem about assurance of salvation. As Dickinson, in Amherst, was brought up in a particularly conservatively religious segment of society, we cannot discount this possibility, as alien as it may seem to many twentieth-century readers. However, a wholehearted sense of personal redemption and assurance of heaven's rewards would scarcely have made "Earth . . . too much . . . And Heaven not enough." I think we are justified in reading the religious language and imagery comparatively rather than literally. What in life would have made this speaker "too glad" to appreciate heaven? Well, it might be love or it might, given this author, be a career as a poet. When we see in the third verse, however, that the poem is addressed to an individual—called "Savior"—rather than to a goal, we tend to read it as a love poem. Having so determined, we find that the speaker quite conventionally approves the loss of her love in that its realization would have overshadowed the glories of heaven, causing her to focus too much on earthly satisfactions and not enough on her spiritual life. To many readers— if she'd had readers other than Susan for this version—this would have been an acceptable and pleasing statement.

The final line, however,—" 'Faith' bleats—to understand!"–throws an entirely new light on the poem and suggests that it may well not be a straightforward statement but rather an elaborate and extended piece of irony that not only deplores the speaker's loss but, further, satirizes Christian rationalizations that would attempt to offer compensation. The "faith" is not truly a deeply felt belief but, as the quotation marks suggest, a mere word, an ostensible attitude, something *called* "faith" as opposed to true conviction. This implication is clinched by the following word; "bleats" is in one sense appropriate diction, if the speaker *is* a lamb in the flock of Christ, the Good Shepherd. But since "faith" is suspect here, in another and overriding sense, a bleat is just the meaningless call of a silly sheep. The compensations the speaker offers herself in the poem are revealed to be a scam, the wool, so to speak, pulled over her eyes. The exclamation point at the end of the line almost certainly indicates ironic emphasis.

A far different tone, however, comes through in what we might consider the "official" version of the poem, the one Dickinson herself chose to "publish," tying it into one of her own handbound volumes. Here a deeply embedded ambivalence is apparent. In this version the final line, so vital in the creation of the ironic meaning of the poem as printed above, is significantly different; the quotation marks around "faith" are omitted, "faints" is offered as a variant for "bleats," the dash in the center of the line is moved to the end, and the exclamation point is deleted. The line reads: "Faith bleats to understand—." These changes alter meaning: "faith" may be the real thing here, adjusting or rendering ambiguous the meaning of "bleats," and the substitution of the dash for the exclamation point makes the line less definite, more open-ended. When Dickinson's nineteenth-century editors published the poem in 1891, they minimized the irony and maximized the ambivalence by selecting the variant of "faints" for "bleats." In the first published edition of her poems, then, the line reads: "Faith faints to understand—." That selection significantly alters the meaning of the poem from the "Susan" version. This version allows a reading that suggests a sincere desire to reconcile oneself to a tragic situation, simultaneous with an awareness that reconciliation is simply too difficult a task, consciousness cannot comprehend it. This editorial change is not so much an example of tampering (after all, Higginson and Todd certainly didn't have Susan's version where the irony is marked), as it is a highlighting of authorial ambivalence. Any one of the three possible final lines allows a coherent reading of the poem, one casting ironic aspersions on the attitude expressed, one ambiguous, one stressing the ambivalence the speaker feels about her situation. This latter, more acceptable to many of her contemporaries, allowed her editors to clinch the conventional renunciation motif by adopting for the poem the title "Too Much."

That the subject of the poem seems to be a passionate sexual attraction, as with Osgood's poem, makes the writer's conflict and unwillingness to settle on a definitive version all too easy to understand. An indirection initiated by omission of subject specification is heightened by markedly divergent tones, stressing the irony in the ambivalence and the ambivalence in the irony. The poem, rooted in passional deprivation and concomitant loss of self, deals with an "incendiary" subject—a proscribed personal passion. While ostensibly celebrating renunciation—saying the "proper" thing—it undercuts itself with irresolvable ambiguities, thus making it very much a product of its expressive era.

In addition to tonal dissonance, Dickinson's poetry also reflects a marked tendency to disorder expected sequences. The relation of this tendency to the expressive context provided by the work of her female contemporaries is more problematic than her characteristic use of tonal ambiguities. In Dickinson's work disorder is syntactical as well as narrative, and the conventional women poets and novelists who were Dickinson's American contemporaries did not disorder language at the level of the sentence. However, some novelists did disrupt conventional narrative patterns with significant effect, especially when they were working in codified genres such as the domestic novel. Syntax and narrative (especially conventional narrative) both provide locutionary order, expectable sequences of language and events. Disorder of the conventional plot line in women's novels often serves the purpose of expressive indirection by allowing the telling of an interlocutory tale that controverts the message of the genre in which the story is being told. Usually, then, the intrusive tale is perfunctorily denied through the medium of a conventional ending. A counterideological message has been expressed and then contained.

In Dickinson's work disorder exists—as David Porter has shown in his discussion of Dickinson and modernism—at a level so fundamental that it distorts not only narrative—but language itself (38). In Dickinson's work, bespeaking the concerns of the experimental artist, disorder is realized in a complex linguistic, narrative, and referential manner rather than in the more direct narrative manner of some of her contemporaries. Nonetheless, it serves a similar purpose; it provides an opportunity to tell and yet to obscure the fact of telling. In this Dickinson's linguistic disorder, like her narrative disruption, certainly has roots in the contemporary idiom of conflicted dissent.

Although popular fiction in nineteenth-century America contained an extraordinarily varied range of expression, from the eccentric to the conventional, from the vulgar to the ideal, "woman's fiction," as Nina Baym designates the conventional novels that made up by far the largest portion of mainstream book-length fiction by and about women, was a dominant mode. These novels are characterized by a rigidly codified narrative sequence. As Baym puts it: "the many novels all tell, with variations, a single tale" (11). The novels open with the protagonist in late childhood or in her early teens, follow her through various trials and triumphs, and end with her marriage. As chapter 3 shows, this constantly reiterated sequence implies that a woman's individuality, her *story*, is concluded when she becomes a wife. When women novelists disrupt or alter this sequence, it is with the effect of providing indirect, dissenting commentary upon the feminine "life story" sanctioned by the conventional narrative.

Mary Jane Holmes was the author of over fifty extremely well received novels for women. These were not works to be taken seriously as art but popular genre works, investigating fantasies of feminine selfhood current in a culture highly curious about the nature of gender. Holmes worked almost exclusively in the genre Baym calls "woman's fiction" and was well versed in its conventions. In one of her early novels, *Marion Grey* (1863), Holmes quite consciously ruptures the conventional plot line with the effect of providing a narrative space in which she can depict a woman moving from a position of complete powerlessness in a marriage to a position of total control. Selfhood and power are the themes of this novel. Marion is an orphan of fifteen in Virginia when the story opens. Red-haired, undeveloped, homely, and slightly uncouth, she is tricked at the beginning— at the very beginning—of the novel into a marriage with a young man who is after her fortune. Frederick is not an evil man, however; he is simply cold-hearted and selfish. He reasons that in marrying Marion he is doing no wrong to her (she *does* love him) or to himself—"she was a child yet; he could mold her to his will and make her what he pleased" (20).

Marion, between the wedding and the wedding night, discovers his intention and runs away—her virginity presumably (although this of course is never mentioned) still intact. This makes her technically, though a bride, not a wife. In New York City she is befriended by old acquaintances who care for her, see to it that she is well educated, and from a distance keep track of Frederick for her. Frederick, and this is the point of the novel, in deep remorse for his evil deed, undergoes a complete and impassioned change of heart. Indeed, for years he devotes much of his time and energy to searching New York for his lost bride. She, however, has changed her appearance to the point of unrecognizability; even when Frederick sits next to her on a public omnibus he doesn't know who she is. Uncouth little Marion has been educated at an elite school, has developed into a young woman, and has lost her red hair in a fever, becoming a ravishing auburn-haired beauty.

The game of hide and seek goes on for five or six years, until Marion takes a position as governess to Frederick's ward and he falls madly in love with her all over again. Now she has *double* power—he loves her as his lost young bride and, with great guilt (because, after all, he is still a married man), as the gorgeous new governess. Finally she reveals her identity, insists on a new wedding, and the novel ends. Holmes, in this conventional genre, can only provide a "story" for Marion as a "married" woman by flouting narrative expectations, disrupting the narrative sequence to provide a six-year hiatus between the wedding and its consummation. Frederick does not "mold [Marion] to his will and make her what he please[s]," as he intended to. Instead, because the break in the conventional narrative allows her her own story, *she* creates her own striking new self, and molds him to *her* will in the bargain. A canny manipulation of popular genre conventions, this novel disrupts narrative sequence to allow in an interlocutory space the telling of a proscribed story—one of feminine power and the completely justified revenge of a good woman.

A.D.T. Whitney's *Hitherto: A Story of Yesterdays* (1869), a more realistic, serious, and detailed study of a woman's life than *Marion Grey*, disrupts narrative sequence in a similar manner. By having the marriage occur in the middle of the novel rather than at the beginning, as in the Holmes novel, or at the end, as is usual in the genre, and then continuing the story for seven years *beyond* marriage, Whitney opens up a space to show us just exactly how miserable conventional marriage—even to a good man— makes her protagonist. We first make the acquaintance of Anstiss Dolbeare as a young girl, intelligent, articulate, and sensitive. Although she is fond of the young farmer she marries, Anstiss has a difficult time becoming the "little wifie" Richard so longs for; on her wedding day she is quick to remove the finery in which she had become "Mrs. Hathaway" and put on her old familiar clothes, "and then, in a minute, I was Anstiss Dolbeare again" (352). Seven years of closely detailed restlessness and dissatisfaction follow, including a passionate love for and intense intellectual communion with another man. This disruption in the conventional narrative expectations, this continuation of the story beyond its ending, may not constitute the moral of the story, but it provides its beating heart. We see in detail Anstiss's anger at her husband, her boredom on the farm, her intellectual restlessness, her sexual attraction to another man, and her husband's pained awareness that the life he has to offer her is too limited for her needs and capabilities. It is Whitney's explicit intention to give voice to the unspoken experience at the heart of women's lives:

> I think it would be a good thing if some old woman were to tell a story,— if anybody, that is, young or old, could ever really tell a whole one. . . . Stories in this world tell themselves by halves. There is always a silent side; many silent sides, perhaps. . . . What can a girl of twenty know, that she should try to say what disappointment and endurance are, and what they come to. (3–4)

Whitney is consciously experimental in attempting to express this "silent side" by providing a narrative vehicle for the "articulate inarticulate." As far as I know, *Hitherto* is unique in American literature of the last century in its use of a fragmented narrative voice that switches from chapter to chapter in an irregular manner.[7] And, by having continued her story beyond its genre-defined conclusion and thus subverting the expressive intentions of that genre, Whitney has addressed the "silent side," articulating the "disappointment and endurance" of actual, rather than ideal, experience. Although she contains dissent through the device of the obligatory "happy ending" in which Anstiss experiences a religious conversion and reconciles herself to her lot as the "little wifie," thus controverting and "correcting" her earlier experience, Whitney has nonetheless offered a prolonged and culturally critical exploration of the problematic nature of marriage.

"I cannot dance upon my toes" (326) is a Dickinson poem that works in a manner similar to both *Marion Gray* and *Hitherto* in that the author interjects a tale into her narrative that the narrative itself denies. The syntax of the poem is complex and its convolutedness is so extreme that it disrupts semantic expectations; the long complex series of qualifying clauses and phrases makes inordinate demands upon the reader and comprehension demands close attention.

> I cannot dance upon my Toes—
> No Man instructed me—
> But oftentimes, among my mind,
> A Glee possesseth me,
>
> That had I Ballet knowledge—
> Would put itself abroad
> In Pirouette to blanch a Troupe—
> Or lay a Prima, mad,
>
> And though I had no Gown of Gauze—
> No Ringlet, to my Hair,
> Nor hopped for Audiences—like Birds,
> One Claw upon the Air,
>
> Nor tossed my shape in Eider Balls,
> Nor rolled on wheels of snow
> Till I was out of sight, in sound,
> The House encore me so—
>
> Nor any know I know the Art
> I mention—easy—Here—

Nor any Placard boast me—
It's full as Opera—

The poem, presented largely in the subjunctive mood, is framed in the indicative but contains only two main clauses that are both indicative and positive: "A Glee possesseth me" in the fourth line and "It's full as Opera" in the final line. Although these two statements present a state of almost ecstatic confidence, we must look closely at their embeddedness in a body of language that extensively detaches itself from them. Introduced by a disclaimer, conventional in women's writing, the poem sets itself in the negative before it ventures the first of its two positive statements: "A Glee possesseth me." That statement is separated from its companion assertion by a breathless fifteen lines of subordinate clauses and phrases, all of them conditional and most of them negative, designed to modify the semantically highlighted phrases. The purpose of this interlocution is to tell the story of what might be but is not. This interlocutory story is full of details of exuberant public success as a dancer, but its presentation, both negative and conditional, serves the purpose of denial, relating to the speaker's initial disclaiming statement, "I cannot dance upon my Toes—," and reinforcing our awareness of being told a story that exists not in reality but only within a state of mind.

The poem tells a story that would have been problematic for a nineteenth-century American woman: a story of ambition in a public arena. For Dickinson, the image of the dancer on the stage most likely stands as a metaphor for public acknowlegement of herself as a poet. The image of the public poet whose "Ballet knowledge," or consummate skill in poetics, is both presented publicly and applauded by the public is enticing. However, the story of public self-presentation and enthusiastic reception so intermingle the poet with her audience's response that she suffers a loss of identity: "Till I was out of sight, in sound, / The House encore me so." Although the performance and its reception are thrilling, the thought of such self-display might well have caused anxiety to a woman acculturated to see herself as essentially private. However, through a grammatical manipulation—negation and removal from the indicative mood, a mode of statement that links a declaration firmly to reality—the story can be distanced and thus safely told. It is told "between the lines," so to speak, in a manner that at once states and denies. Nonetheless, as in *Hitherto*, despite the denial, the story *has* been told.

Because of the expressive restrictions under which women wrote in nineteenth-century America, much of the most interesting women's writing from that era, for fullest understanding, must be read, like these poems and novels, as a literature of implication. Tonal and sequential nuances suggest experiences or make statements missing from the text. Unnameable experience requires cautious articulative approach, and it may well be as a reaction to this expressive reality—this fact of utterance that proved debilitating to other writers—that Dickinson developed the most central characteristic of her style: her "omitted center," as Jay Leyda calls it (I: xxi). Dickinson's poetic tendency to use nonspecific reference indicates an overpowering need to speak of something that must be omitted from the text. She took the dominant gender-specific literary-speech quandary of her era and with her great linguistic power, as in a superb poem like "My Life had stood—a Loaded Gun—," redeemed it, transforming into an effective aesthetic what had been for many women writers something in the nature of a cultural aphasia of personal expression.

In Dickinson's adaptation to the strictures, she employed the same expressive strategies as other writers but took devices that had been diffuse, occasional, and variously effective in contemporary women's literature, concentrated or exaggerated them, and often carried them to startling extremes. Literary devices like irony, ambivalence, and sequential disordering take a certain amount of reconstruction on the part of the reader to provide full meaning. Occasionally and intriguingly, Dickinson transformed these devices into a stylistic barrier that effectively works to render reconstruction of specific personal disclosure impossible, at the same time as the poem indicates its presence and hints at its significance.

"My Life had stood—a Loaded Gun—" as well as being a superb work of art is just such an enigmatic utterance. It is a poem that defies understanding, but its singular images and tantalizing obscurity render it irresistible to commentators, as is attested to by the multitude of readings given it since it was first published in 1929. It is my contention, however, that reading this poem to determine its meaning becomes something in the nature of an exercise in futility. Dickinson's expressive anxiety is at its height here, whatever her subject—whether it is anger, as it may well be, or ambition, as it could very well be, or sexuality, as it certainly might be, or some intertwined combination of the three. Vivian Pollak calls this a "touchstone text," and Adrienne Rich says the poem is central to understanding "Dickinson, and ourselves, and the condition of the woman artist, particularly in the nineteenth century" (66). Certainly in the context of the gender-specific, culture-specific dynamic of women's literary articulation in nineteenth-century America, these gnarled, resistant, enticing verses take on new significance. Pressure to speak vies with the need to "veil" the subject to the point of unintelligibility. As the conflicting conclusions of the many fine attempts to reconstruct it attest, the meaning of this poem is irrecoverable. In the context of the feminine expressive community, then, the most helpful way to read the poem is not to try to understand its meaning, but rather to determine the significance of the impediments to comprehension.

My Life had stood—a Loaded Gun—
In Corners—till a Day
The Owner passed—identified—
And carried Me away—

And now We roam in Sovereign Woods—
And now We hunt the Doe—
And every time I speak for Him—
The Mountains straight reply—

And do I smile, such cordial light
Upon the Valley glow—
It is as a Vesuvian face
Had let it's pleasure through—

And when at Night—Our good Day done—
I guard My Master's Head—
'Tis better than the Eider-Duck's
Deep Pillow—to have shared—

To foe of His—I'm deadly foe—
None stir the second time—
On whom I lay a Yellow Eye—
Or an emphatic Thumb—

Though I than He—may longer live
He longer must—than I—
For I have but the power to kill,
Without—the power to die—

(754)

The major problem in interpreting this poem is not syntactical but reflects disorder at a referential level; subject reference is eradicated. Here the vacuum at the center of the text is complete. Unlike "I should have been too glad, I see—", this poem is impossible to reconstruct authoritatively. Even conjecture is problematic. A crucial feature of communication has been flouted; in her use of a powerful metaphor without the provision of markers to indicate the area of reference, Dickinson intrigues but does not enlighten the reader. She creates a radical disjuncture between text and meaning which indicates that an experience of profound significance is being expressed but refuses to name that experience.

Conjectures provided by Dickinson's commentators regarding the nature of this indicated experience are illuminating as we attempt to determine the significance of this poem. Sharon Cameron sees anger as its subject, "a fury grown larger than life . . . [that] fantasizes its own immortality" (427). Adrienne Rich finds ambition central. She sees in the split between the active hunter and the passive gun an "ambivalence toward power which is extreme" (65). John Cody discusses a "fusion of sexuality and destructiveness" (402). Anger . . . ambition . . . sexuality. . . . As we have seen, this potent trio caused debilitating anxieties in the women's writing of Dickinson's era, and "My Life had stood—a Loaded Gun—" is rife with indications of all three—to the point where each of the above readers can state his or her case convincingly and with authority. It is my proposal that the significance of this poem lies precisely here, in its embodiment of the expressive dilemma faced by any woman writer of Dickinson's time and place. The culture taught women that these experiences were unnameable. Porter's statement that "the gun . . . is the emblem of her inordinate power of language" (215) nicely defines the essence of the poem; it embodies a superb ability and a pressing need to speak, filtered through a profound culturally conditioned anxiety about telling personal experience.

Although it is impossible to read this poem in a conventional way, it is indubitably to some degree a poem about utterance, an expression of the explosive or incendiary potential of speech. We are given enough markers to indicate that: the gun that "speaks" as it fires, the "Vesuvian" or volcanic qualities that we know from other poems are often associated with speech. But how is it that this poem, with its lost field of reference, communicates? How does it speak to us? What is important here are the tonal implications of the speaker's dissociated experience as a speech object rather than a speech subject; although she is the medium through which articulation occurs, she is not the instigator of the impulse to articulation. As Rich noted, an extreme ambivalence characterizes the description of the relationship between the active "owner," the one who initiates the speech, and the passive "gun," the one who speaks; a fascinated yet horrific interplay is detailed. Yet, although both fascination and horror are indicated, neither predominates. The tension between them gives tonal articulation to a consciousness in conflict. And the concluding lines, without being specific, are imbued with a deep sense of tragic irony. To "have the power to kill / Without—the power to die," whatever it *means*, communicates to us more through tone—through the sense of irresolvable and disorienting contradictions—than through statement or even through analogy. Ambivalence and irony, as in other women's writing of the era, are the vehicles of expression that carry the communicative weight of this poem.

The disruption of sequence that we have found used by other writers to create space for life stories outside the realm of conventional narrative is carried to extraordinary lengths here. The final verse wrenches life-sequence to the point of utter mystification, standing between the reader and the experience to the point of complete occlusion of meaning, yet implying a life gone horribly awry.

Is "My Life had stood—a Loaded Gun" a successful poem? Or is it a hyberbolic, convoluted, evasive failure? It all depends on how we read it. A reader steeped in a modernist aesthetic recognizes the communicative power of shattered syntax and wrenched expectations combined with potent and enigmatic imagery. A good case for the success of this poem is going to depend heavily on a "modernist" awareness of the significance of indirection, nuance, and disruption. Yet I contend that Dickinson's resort to those modes of expression may well have had more to do with the fact that she was writing as a woman in nineteenth-century America than with any conscious prescience of modernism. Women's writing from that era is often faulted with being a failed literature. But it spoke what it had to say as best it could given the available idiom, and that is a more complex idiom than has previously been suggested.

If we consider literary forms and conventions—the most stringently culturally conforming and the most innovatively aesthetically experimental—not strictly as forms but as reflective of individual experience within a given cultural climate, we must look at this literature as being successful on its own terms and as being transitional. Raymond Williams suggests that we can relate literary conventions to "the articulation . . . of structures of feeling which as living processes are much more widely experienced" (133). In this context we can see new significance in both the conformity of these women writers—the universal need for cultural identity and security—and the disruptions—the inevitable thrust in persons and in cultures toward an ever-altering range of experience; their conflicted, self-contradictory body of expression reflects a society experiencing the initial fermentation of radical change.

The era was characterized, on the one hand, by an "official" body of gender definitions, clearly defined, widely circulated, constantly reinforced, and closely associated with literary conventions and their related expressive strictures. On the other hand, in this period we see an increasingly articulate feminist movement and an obvious fascination, in both mainstream and marginal publications, with what would have been considered "deviant" female experience. This fascination is manifest in more extravagant forms of popular literature by characters such as those Reynolds calls "feminist criminals," "adventure feminists," and "sensual women" (339–40), but more subtly and, for literary change, more significantly by the tonal and structural disruptions in the work of mainstream women writers.[8]

Women writers maneuvered between a rigidly codified set of expressive limitations and a wider range of expressive impulses. Along with the more standard discursive, interpretive mode of expression, they came to rely, for communication of nonconforming experience, on suggestiveness, implication, and evocation, articulative features of indirection that, in the consistency of their use, foreshadowed later, more self-conscious and sophisticated aesthetic strategies.

Williams suggests that often it is in what he calls a "minority generation" of cultural forms that we see modifications connecting that generation to its successors (134). Dickinson's manner of indirection is in its extremity idiosyncratic for her era. Yet her characteristic omission of subject and her use of the devices of tonal dissonance and sequential disordering of syntax and narrative are designed to articulate that which is, and to some degree remains, unarticulated: the "silent side" of individual experience. These strategies suggest the presence of passion and personal significance without specifying the precise nature of the personal experience which has generated such intense feeling. This tendency toward the "articulate inarticulate" locates her poetry firmly in its cultural and literary context—a community of feminine expression where women's articulation was seen as potentially incendiary and women's reticence perceived as a prudent virtue—yet at the same time it foreshadows the precepts of literary modernism.

Given the highly idiosyncratic brilliance of Dickinson's mind and imagination, she transformed the broken articulation offered her by her culture into a transcendently effective aesthetic prism, reflecting a particular time and place, but expressing an intensely human experience made all the more vividly available to us by the aesthetic modes of our own day. Dickinson may well, at times and with a self-contradictory fluctuation characteristic of the interplay of desire and anxiety, have felt that her strong impulse for personal disclosure had "the power to kill." From the vantage point of the twentieth century, however, we see only that the vivid, compelling body of expression she left us is "Without—the power to die—."

APPENDIX I
EMILY DICKINSON AND PUBLICATION

A detailed survey of extant contemporary comments about Dickinson and publication reveals unsuccessful attempts by several people to encourage her to publish her poetry. Dickinson's obituary in the *Springfield Republican* (18 May 1886), written by Susan Dickinson, serves as an introduction to that attempt:

> Her talk and writings were like no one's else, and although she never published a line, now and then some enthusiastic literary friend would turn love to larceny, and cause a few verses surreptitiously obtained to be printed. . . . [F]requently notable persons paid her visits, hoping to overcome the protest of her own nature and gain a promise of occasional contributions, at least, to various magazines. She withstood even the fascinations of Mrs. Helen Jackson, who earnestly sought her co-operation in a novel of the No Name series, although one little poem somehow strayed into the volume of verses which appeared in that series. (Leyda II 473)

Later in 1886, in a letter to *The Century* urging the publication of a Dickinson poem, Susan elaborated on that comment: "Col. Higginson, Dr. Holland, 'H. H.' and many other of her literary friends have long urged her to allow her poems to be printed, but she was never willing to face the world" (Bingham, *Ancestors'* 88). An earlier comment by Mabel Todd indicates that desire on the part of several literary professionals to see Dickinson's work published was public knowledge in Amherst, even before her death. In an 1881 letter to her parents, Todd remarks about Dickinson: "Her poems are perfectly wonderful, and all the literary men are after her to have her writings published" (Leyda II 361).

This solicitation began at least as early in her career as 1852, when the publication of a valentine in the *Springfield Republican* elicited this editorial invitation: "There is certainly no presumption in entertaining a private wish that a correspondence more direct than this may be established between it (the author) and the Republican" (Leyda I 234). We have Dickinsons's own evidence that the editorial requests for her poetry continued. In April 1862 when she initiated her correspondence with Thomas Wentworth Higginson, she told him: "Two Editors of Journals came to my Father's House, this winter—and asked me for my Mind—and when I asked them 'Why,' they said I was penurious—and they, would use it for the World—" (L 261). These editors are widely believed to have been Samuel Bowles and J.G. Holland of the *Springfield Republican*, close friends of the family and frequent visitors to the Dickinson house.

About Bowles's interest in publishing her poetry, we have evidence in his own words. In a letter to Sue in November 1864 he asks: "Speaking of writing, do you & Emily give us some gems for the 'Springfield Market' " (Leyda II 93). Sue's daughter, Martha Bianchi, indicates that Sue responded with at least one poem: "My mother . . . had yielded to Mr. Bowles' repeated requests and let the Republican have her [Emily's] lines about the snake" (Leyda II 110). And Dickinson herself supports the "larceny" theory of publication in a resultant letter to Higginson. "Lest you meet my Snake," she informed him, "and suppose I deceive it was robbed of me—defeated too of the third line by the punctuation. The third and fourth were one—I had told you I did not print—I feared you might think me ostensible" (L 316). Bowles had been interested in Dickinson's poetry from the beginning of his acquaintance with her, as the recently discovered Dickinson poem in the *Republican* of 2 August 1858 indicates. As Karen Dandurand says: "The widely accepted view that Dickinson tried in vain to interest Samuel Bowles . . . in publishing her poems must be rejected in light of new evidence that during the summer when Dickinson began her correspondence with him, Bowles was directly responsible for the publication of her poem" ("Another Dickinson Poem" 434).

With Higginson, Dickinson had been clear about her aversion to publication from the start. Responding, seemingly, to advice that she hone her product before she put it on the market, she says: "I smile when you suggest that I delay 'to publish'— that being foreign to my thought, as Firmament to Fin—If fame belonged to me, I could not escape her—" (L 265). Richard Sewall says: "Emily's disavowal about publishing can hardly be taken literally" (554). However, no evidence exists to indicate that Higginson told her *not* to publish or that she was being coy or defensive with him. There is no reason to think she was lying; in the private manner of a nineteenth-century woman she had chosen him as a literary friend, wishing to share her poetry with a knowledgable and sympathetic reader. It is anachronistic to assume that literary ambition is inevitably public in nature and that Dickinson must have corresponded with Higginson primarily in order to advance a career. Higginson himself clarifies her lack of interest in a career in an article in the *Christian Union* (25 September 1890): "Asked again and again for verses to be published, she scarcely ever yielded, even to a friend so tried and dear as the late Mr. Bowles of the Springfield 'Republican' " ("Open Portfolio" 425).

Another major figure who urged Dickinson to publish was Helen Hunt Jackson. As early as 1876 she was soliciting publications from her reluctant friend, telling her she was "a great poet" (L 444a). Sending Dickinson a circular about a series of anonymous publications by Roberts Bros., she says: "Surely, in the shelter of such *double* anonymousness as that will be, you need not shrink. I want to see some of your verses in print. Unless you forbid me, I will send some that I have. May I?" (L 476a). Dickinson responded with anxiety to this pressure to go public. Writing to Higginson, she sent him the circular, saying: "I said I was incapable and she seemed not to believe me . . . if you would be willing to give me a note saying you disapproved it, and thought me unfit, she would believe you—" (L 476). Higginson sympathized with her anxiety, but did not "disapprove."

Jackson continued her pressure for publication. In 1878 she managed to get a Dickinson poem in the No Name volume of poetry (by well-known but anonymous poets) after urging: "Now—will you send me the poem? No—will you let me send the 'Success'—which I know by heart—to Roberts Bros for the Masque of Poets? If you will, it will give me a great pleasure. I ask it as a personal favor to myself— Can you refuse the only thing I perhaps shall ever ask at your hands?" (L 573b). And she continued her interest for the rest of her life. Shortly before her own death in 1885, Jackson wrote to Dickinson again at length on the subject of publication:

> What portfolios of verses you must have.—
> It is a cruel wrong to your "day & generation" that you will not give them light.—If such a thing should happen as that I should outlive you, I wish you would make me your literary legatee & executor. Surely, after you are what is called "dead," you will be willing that the poor ghosts you have left behind, should be cheered and pleased by your verses, will you not?—You ought to be.—I do not think we have a right to with hold from the world a word or a thought any more than a *deed*, which might help a single soul. (L 937a)

Jackson not only pleaded eloquently with her friend to put her verses before the world, she saw that they were seen by others who were in a position to help. Thomas Niles, editor of Roberts Bros. embarked upon a correspondence with Dickinson after the publication of "Success" in the No Name series. He thanked her for her "valuable contribution which for want of a known sponsor Mr Emerson has generally had to father" (L 573d). And three years later he was writing to her again, saying: " 'H. H.' once told me that she wished you could be induced to publish a volume of poems. I should not want to say how highly she praised them, but to such an extent that I wish also that you could" (L 749b). Dickinson's response was to send him one poem ("How happy is the little Stone"), and a modest disclaimer: "The kind but incredible opinion of 'H. H.' and yourself I would like to deserve—" (L 749). A year later Niles was more explicit in his request for a manuscript. Dickinson had sent him her personal copy of the Brontë sisters' poems which he returned, saying: "I will take instead a M.S. collection of your poems, that is, if you want to give them to the world through the medium of a publisher" (L 813b). She responded by sending one poem, then three more, but said nothing about publication, and the matter was dropped.

Contrary to prevalent opinion that Dickinson was discouraged by her friends from publishing, this continued solicitation by at least three major literary figures reveals that her non-publication was due to her own persistent refusal to publish. Unless we choose to believe that all these contemporary witnesses were deluded or in conspiracy, we can only conclude that Dickinson meant it when she told her cousin Ellen Dickinson: "I would as soon undress in public, as give my poems to the world" (Leyda II 482). Her attitude about publication is consistent with the contemporary cultural ideology of feminine reticence. It suggests that she was influenced in ways that had a profound effect on the decisions she made about expression and its arena of communication by the more conservative ideals of her society. The widespread conservative ideology of femininity that characterized middle-class American culture during the nineteenth century sanctioned women's publication for only two reasons—financial need or moral imperatives. Publication for other reasons—for example, the desire for fame or the impulse to communicate thoughts, feelings, or aesthetic perceptions—was consistently discouraged. Dickinson was in no financial difficulty, nor was her writing characterized by a primary didactic impulse. Therefore, as a woman who conformed in the particulars of her life—if not, by and large, in the subject matter and innovative language of her poetry—she would have felt compelled to keep her writing from the public eye.

APPENDIX II

VERSES BY EMILY DICKINSON (1864)

If Emily Dickinson were to have chosen in 1864, the year we now know saw ten separate Dickinson publications, to have published a small edition of her poems, as her friend Helen Hunt Jackson was to do six years later with *Verses* (1870), she would have had many poems her contemporaries would have enjoyed from which to make her selection. Karen Dandurand's reconstruction of Dickinson's lifetime publication history gives us a new understanding of just how many of her poems would have been acceptable to contemporary editors and readers. We know that Dickinson had at least ten poems published in her lifetime, six of which were reprinted, republished, or quoted in full a total of ten times—amounting to twenty separate publications. Ten of these publications occurred within a two-month period in 1864. The ten published poems are:

(1852) " 'Sic transit gloria mundi' " (3)
(1858) "Nobody knows this little Rose—" (35)
(1861) "I taste a liquor never brewed—" (214)
(1862) "Safe in their Alabaster Chambers—" (216)
(1864) "Success is counted sweetest" (67)
(1864) "These are the days when Birds come back—" (130)
(1864) "Flowers—Well—if anybody" (137)
(1864) "Blazing in Gold and quenching in Purple" (228)
(1864) "Some keep the Sabbath going to Church—" (324)
(1866) "A narrow Fellow in the Grass" (986)

("Publication" *Legacy* 1.1 [Spring 1984]: 7)

The published poems, which include two usually counted among her masterpieces, although often conventional in concept, imagery, and style are not unanimously so. At least two use religious imagery and Christian precepts in unconventional ways to make statements that the most orthodox of her contemporaries might well have found troublesome: "Some keep the Sabbath going to Church—" (324) gently mocks churchgoers and clergy, and "These are the days when Birds come back—" (130) uses imagery of the Christian sacrament of communion to evoke a sense of communion with nature that is close to pagan. Some poems are syntactically or grammatically irregular. Some use slant or off rhymes. Yet the evidence indicates that they were acceptable to editors and to readers as well—one poem was printed four times in three different periodicals within a two-week period and another was printed three times in shortly over a month. If Dickinson had chosen to capitalize on the publishing flurry of 1864 and had submitted a manuscript of verses to one of the many publishers then welcoming women's poetry, she certainly could have included the poems above and found many others that editors would have appreciated.

Below is a hypothetical Table of Contents for a volume of *Verses by Emily Dickinson* that could well have been published in 1864. I have chosen fifty of her verses that would have contained little to offend contemporary readers and much to delight them. Conservative in my choices, I have selected and given titles only to poems that do not violate contemporary strictures on feminine expression and whose style or use of language would not have created a barrier between the poem and the mid-nineteenth-century reader. That such a book or one like it, self-published like Jackson's first book of verses or published perhaps by Roberts Brothers in 1883 when Thomas Niles asked Dickinson for a manuscript collection of her poems (L 813b), does not exist in reality is one more indication that Dickinson did not experience the burning desire for publication postulated by some Dickinson critics.

Verses by Emily Dickinson

A Valentine
   ("Sic transit gloria mundi," 3)

The Loss
   (I had a guinea golden—, 23)

Adrift!
   (Adrift! A little boat adrift!, 30)

The Rose
   (Nobody knows this little Rose—, 35)

The Beggar
   (I never lost as much but twice, 49)

Success
   (Success is counted sweetest, 67)

The Funeral
   (One dignity delays for all—, 98)

The Grave
   (What Inn is this, 115)

The Battle
   (To fight aloud, is very brave—, 126)

October
   (These are the days when Birds come back—, 130)

Flowers
   (Flowers—Well—if anybody, 137)

Miss Brontë
   (All overgrown by cunning moss, 148)

Home in Heaven
   (Except to Heaven, she is nought, 154)

The Little King
   (I met a King this afternoon!, 166)

A Carol
   (To learn the Transport by the Pain—, 167)

The Crumb
   (If I should'nt be alive, 182)

Indolent Housewife
  (How many times these low feet staggered—, 187)

Sorrow
  (I shall know why—when Time is over—, 193)

The Storm
  (An awful Tempest mashed the air—, 198)

The May-Wine
  (I taste a liquor never brewed—, 214)

The Sleeping
  (Safe in their Alabaster Chambers—, 216)

Twilight
  (She sweeps with many-colored Brooms—, 219)

Sunset
  (Blazing in Gold and quenching in Purple, 228)

Anguish
  (I like a look of Agony, 241)

Hope
  ("Hope" is the thing with feathers—, 254)

Winter Afternoons
  (There's a certain Slant of light, 258)

Dedication
  (Tie the Strings to my Life, My Lord, 279)

Little Nobody
  (I'm Nobody! Who are you?, 288)

The Choice
  (The Soul selects her own Society—, 303)

Snow
  (It sifts from Leaden Sieves—, 311)

My Sabbath
  (Some keep the Sabbath going to Church—, 324)

Ecstasy
  (Dare you see a Soul *at the White Heat?*, 365)

Death in the Village
  (There's been a Death, in the Opposite House, 389)

The Dark
  (We grow accustomed to the Dark—, 419)

Madness
  (Much Madness is divinest Sense—, 435)

My Letter
  (This is my letter to the World, 441)

The Fly
  (I heard a Fly buzz—when I died—, 465)

The Cat
  (She sights a Bird—she chuckles—, 507)

Waiting
  (If you were coming in the Fall, 511)

The Sea
  (I started Early—Took my Dog—, 520)

The Chariot
  (Because I could not stop for Death—, 712)

Famine
  (God gave a Loaf to every Bird—, 791)

The Long Sleep
  (Ample make this Bed—, 829)

The Child
  (They wont frown always—some sweet Day, 874)

Experience
  (I stepped from Plank to Plank, 875)

The Coffin
  (A Coffin—is a small Domain, 943)

The Mourner
  (A loss of something ever felt I—, 959)

The Dialogue
  (Death is a Dialogue between, 976)

NOTES

Introduction

1. Traditional studies of Emily Dickinson and women writers have related Dickinson to more familiar British women writers, such as Elizabeth Barrett Browning, Christina Rossetti, Jane Austen, the Brontës, and George Eliot, rather than to the American writers. When American women writers have been mentioned it has been often with a most unproductive dismissive contempt. This attitude has been based on a lack of familiarity with the wide range of contemporary writing, a misunderstanding of its appeal to readers, and a common set of assumptions about greatness: that only greatness is significant in literature, that greatness is always transcendent of its culture, and that great writers should be attracted only to greatness.

Jack Capps, for instance, in his otherwise valuable study of Dickinson's reading, questions, and dismisses, the validity of Dickinson's enjoyment of popular American writers: "Dickinson's apparently omnivorous literary taste and her fallible critical evaluations cast some doubt on her standards of criticism. Her enthusiasm for Ik Marvel's 'reveries,' Helen Hunt's poems, and sentimental newspaper verse are enough to discount her direct appraisals" (23). Not only does this evaluation cast aspersions on Dickinson's competence, it also lumps all popular contemporary writing into one dismissible category. Richard Sewall speaks about Dickinson's enthusiasm for a wide range of contemporary literature as a lifelong "capacity for absorbing what we would consider banalities" (*Life* 671–72). Sewall, like Capps, neglects the opportunity to investigate the significance of Dickinson's enjoyment of a variety of contemporary writing, and thus both critics impoverish their understanding of the ways in which her imagination was nourished by, adapted, and expanded upon certain contemporary literary conventions and strategies.

Even the very sympathetic feminist criticism of the past decade or two, for the most part, has felt compelled to detach Dickinson from her specific milieu and look at her in terms of a community of feminine greatness spanning centuries, continents, and cultures. This era, however, has also seen the beginnings of an effort to evaluate the scope and significance of Dickinson's knowledge of and affinities with contemporary American women writers. Elsa Green in 1972 reminded us that we cannot limit our context for Dickinson to that of her great male contemporaries: "Emily Dickinson *was* a female. She knew it and we know it. She did not, in fact, inhabit the same milieu which influenced Ralph Waldo Emerson and his puritan male forebears; and it is a deadly favor to assume she did. Emerson was not raised to celebrate piety, purity, submissiveness, and domesticity as divinely-commanded attributes of himself. . . . In simply *choosing* the vocation of poetess, Emily Dickinson risked psychic and social penalties unknown to her masculine predecessors" (67). And both Cheryl Walker and Emily Stipes Watts have provided literary histories of American women poets that enable us to place Dickinson more accurately within the developing modes of women's poetry.

Current reconstructive criticism, with its enhanced attention to the interactions of culture and art, creates a climate quite congenial to looking at Dickinson contextually. David Reynolds's recent discussion of the "subversive imagination" of mid-century America has produced the most wide-ranging and enlightening investigation so far of the ways in which cultural phenomena permeated and influenced the imaginations of the classic writers of mid-century. Rather than approaching Dickinson from the perspective of the conventional, as I do, Reynolds emphasizes the subversive imagination represented in newspaper and pamphlet literature and in sensational and reform novels, as well as in a type of women's writing he calls the "literature of misery." In so doing he defines a radical Dickinson. "Dickinson critics," he says, "would do well to turn their attention to the cultural forces that liberated her. By doing this, they will realize that she was not a solitary woman rebel but rather the highest product of a rebellious American sisterhood . . . whose best texts had constituted a literary flowering between 1858 and 1866, the very years that were by far her most productive as a poet" (413). Doubtless Dickinson *was* influenced by the more subversive forms of women's writing, those I characterize in my study as being nonconforming in terms of mainstream gender ideology. But the opportunities and excitements offered by dissenting modes of expression are obviously in conflict with the comforts and reassurances offered by the conventional imagination, by definition the most influential and widespread aspect of the cultural dream life. Dickinson's poetry, in its clashing images and fractured style, shows considerable evidence of trying to have it both ways, of attempting to express dissenting energies without letting go of the solidities and assurances of cultural norms.

2. All quotations from Dickinson's letters are from Thomas Johnson and Theodora Ward's three-volume *The Letters of Emily Dickinson* and are cited by the number these editors assigned to the document. Here "L 268" refers to Letter #268 in the Johnson and Ward edition. Poems are cited according to Johnson's numbering in the three-volume variorum edition, *The Poems of Emily Dickinson*.

3. Jane Tompkins in *Sensational Designs* engages the questions of the critical assumptions underlying much modern discussion of nineteenth-century American literature. She finds chief among these "the notion that literary greatness consists in the power of a work to transcend historical circumstances" (3), and her study reveals the manner in which critical criteria of evaluation are themselves a matter of historical context. Tompkins's work makes clear the necessity of including an investigation of cultural and textual continuities and similarities in any comprehensive evaluation of a writer and his or her work.

1. "A Certain Prejudice": The Community of Expression

1. Reynolds, too, notices ways in which Dickinson adapts the stereotypes and stylistic strategies of her female contemporaries: Chapter 14, "The American Women's Renaissance and Emily Dickinson." He tends to focus, however, on the affinities of Dickinson with the writers he identifies as "Subversives." It is my contention that the conventional was at least as influential an element as the subversive in the creation of her poetic imagination.

2. Polly Longsworth, in her essay " 'Was Mr. Dudley Dear?': Emily Dickinson and John Langdon Dudley" follows a "trail of clues" laid out by Jay Leyda in *The Years and Hours of Emily Dickinson* to suggest that this charismatic clergyman may have been something more to Emily Dickinson than simply a friend.

3. Literary critics Nina Baym, Ann Douglas, Judith Fetterley, David Reynolds, Jane Tompkins, and Sandra Zagarell (see Works Cited) all touch on issues of cultural influence for nineteenth-century American women writers. My discussion owes much also to the work of social and intellectual historians of women's culture, such as Nancy Cott, Mary Kelley, Carroll Smith Rosenberg, and Barbara Welter. Their studies have provided a social history of femininity in nineteenth-century America

and have defined the importance of gender as a primary determinant in the lives of American women.

4. Harriet Beecher Stowe's experience touring Great Britain in 1853 is perhaps the most striking example of the public notoriety of the popular writer. Stowe's train was mobbed at every station as she traveled through Scotland and England, and great throngs of British citizens cheered her wherever she made a public appearance. Forrest Wilson, her biographer, says she experienced "the most astonishing reception ever accorded an American by the British public until Charles Augustus Lindbergh flew across the Atlantic" (349). Of course, there was a strong political component to the fervor of that particular reception. But in its kind, if not in its intensity, the public attention Stowe received was typical of that accorded to the popular writer. Lydia Sigourney speaks wryly of an ongoing harassment by the public that she designates a "persecution" (*Letters of Life* 368). Often she found absolute strangers at her door or wandering through her garden, eager for a glance of this nationally beloved poet and for a few original lines from her pen. Louisa May Alcott, too, found attention from her public burdensome. In 1869, shortly after the publication of *Little Women*, she writes in her journal: "People begin to come and stare at the Alcotts. Reporters haunt the place to look at the authoress, who dodges into the woods *à la* Hawthorne, and won't be even a very small lion" (*Life* 207–8).

5. Throughout this study I refer occasionally to Gail Hamilton's long essay "Men and Women" (1862) as commentary on the contemporary expressive climate for women. Hamilton, herself an intelligent and forceful writer, directly addressed on several fronts the problem for the woman writer. The initial problem was one of identity, she felt, and it operated subtly. For instance, said Hamilton, a male critic will "with a most frank, arch, and engaging smile, inform you that, after all, he would 'rather see a ring on your third finger than an ink-spot on your first.' Stupid!" (*Country Living and Country Thinking* 190–91). She reminds us here that a woman was persistently encouraged on all sides to identify domestically, to see herself as related to a home and husband rather than to a public career. Hamilton also dealt with the prevailing strictures on the strength of women's style: "You do not set half enough value on muscular power. Aesthetic young lady-writers and sentimental penny-a-liners have imbibed and propagated the idea, that feebleness and fragility are womanly and fascinating," she says (120). In a discussion of "tabooed expressions" she writes at length about "drawing-room grammar," specific ways in which women's language is debilitated: "It would be easy to go through a long list of tabooed expressions and show how they are informed and vivified with feminine sweetness, brawny vigor, strength of imagination, the play of fancy, and the flash of wit. Translate them into civilized dialect,—make them presentable at your fireside, and immediately the virtue is gone out of them" (95).

6. I discuss and document this phenomenon in detail in chapter 3.

7. Particularly worth looking at are Fuller's *Woman in the Nineteenth Century* (1845), Gail Hamilton's long essay "Men and Women" in *Country Living and Country Thinking* (1862), selected pieces from Fanny Fern's *Fern Leaves from Fanny's Portfolio* (1853, 1854), Kirkland's *A New Home, Who'll Follow? or Glimpses of Western Life* (1839), and Alice Cary's *Clovernook: or Recollections of our Neighborhood in the West* (1852, 1853). Fuller's famous quote about women, "let them be sea-captains, if you will," (*Woman* 187) is an excellent example of writing that has broken free from constraints—here the proscription against ambition. And Kirkland's veiled presentation of a back-country abortion in her fine description of pioneer living (198–9) is something that her nontraditional genre—what she called "a sort of 'Emigrant's Guide' " (iiv) and what we recognize as early American literary realism—allowed

her. Such an immorality, as it would have been considered, could never have found its way into a novel.

8. Fetterley finds the essayists and regionalists she collects in *Provisions: A Reader from Nineteenth-Century American Women* to "manifest a considerable degree of comfort with the act of writing and with the presentation of themselves as writers" (5), and suggests that by "aiming at less than art and lower than immortality" these women "may have avoided some of the psychic trauma that afflicted those who aimed higher" (6).

9. In her essay defining the largely feminine literary genre she calls "narrative of community," Sandra A. Zagarell stresses a differentiation between this collective vision of the human story and the genre of the novel which has tended to focus individualistically upon one protagonist. The American women regionalists mentioned here did their best work in delineating and particularizing the negotiations and accommodations of human community rather than the passions and strivings of one individual. Understanding the almost oppositional nature of the genres of the regional sketch and the novel and of their connections to ideologies of communalism and individualism helps us understand why women would have felt less inhibited in the former genre.

10. Both Henry David Thoreau in *Walden* (1854) and Walt Whitman in "Song of Myself" (1855) directly address the issue of literary expression, its constraints and its responsibilities. Neither found the act of writing to involve an obligation to be "an influence . . . never exerted but for good," as Griswold said about women in *Female Poets*. Both felt themselves unconstrained by communal morality. "The greater part of what my neighbors call good," says Thoreau, "I believe in my soul to be bad, and if I repent of anything, it is very likely to be my good behavior" (113). And Whitman introduces his great long poem with a declaration that he holds "creeds and schools in abeyance" (25). Renunciation of moral conventions was not, of course, universal for male writers; Josiah Gilbert Holland, Dickinson's friend and a very popular poet and novelist, and T. S. Arthur, author of the best-selling temperance novel, *Ten Nights in a Bar-Room* (1854), were only two of the many male writers who conformed to conventional morality and met expressive expectations. But the climate of expression seems to have been freer for male writers. Both Thoreau and Whitman, although aware of cultural expressive restrictions, scorned them openly and in print, in a way that no American woman of comparable brilliance did. Thoreau advises in *Walden*: "Say what you have to say, not what you ought. Any truth is better than make-believe" (346). And Whitman in "Song of Myself" exults in the taboo-shattering nature of his expression:

> Through me forbidden voices,
> Voices of sexes and lusts, voices veil'd and I remove the veil,
> Voices indecent by me clarified and transfigur'd.

> (42)

It was to their own unique experience rather than to shared assumptions about individual experience that these writers felt an expressive obligation. "I celebrate myself, and sing myself," Whitman says (25), and Thoreau requires "of every writer, first or last, a simple and sincere account of his own life, and not merely what he has heard of other men's lives" (107). Both writers are freed by the mandate of personal expressive honesty to make statements about their lives that the large majority of contemporary readers would have found shocking or even perverse. "Song of Myself" is a paean to the "hankering, gross, mystical, nude" persona in which Whitman delights (38), but it is so outrageous in its flouting of expressive decorum as to be unrepresentative of male writers on the whole. Thoreau, more restrained than Whitman, also explores forbidden but deeply felt instincts, confessing, for instance, to such "a strange thrill of savage delight" at the sight of a woodchuck running across his path that he "was strongly tempted to seize and devour him raw" (260). This incident reveals to Thoreau the animal sensuality that mingles with the spiritual—and culturally acceptable—aspects of human life.

Thoreau and Whitman are not the only male writers who show signs of expressive freedom. By creating protagonists who experience passion in areas largely unaddressed by women writers, other male writers, both the well known and the forgotten, reveal a more comprehensive expressive mandate for men than for women. Ambition and anger, for instance, are central personal motivating forces for Herman Melville's Captain Ahab, whose ambition—whose "one unachieved revengeful desire" (*Moby-Dick* 167)—is to strike at the "inscrutable" divine principle of the universe he feels is represented by the great white whale he pursues. "I'd strike the sun if it insulted me" (139), he says in his overweening and destructive ambition. And his anger is so great that it kills him. "For hate's sake I spit my last breath at thee" (431), he curses in a cosmic rebellion unparalleled in women's writing of the era. Male writers occasionally allowed their female protagonists, too, the characteristics of ambition and fury. Hawthorne's Hester Prynne in *The Scarlet Letter* (1850) has had at one time aspirations to be "the destined prophetess" (261) of woman's freedom, and Hawthorne admires that ambition. He also allows Hester legitimate personal hatred for her detestable husband, Chillingworth.

Sexual passion is the area of most obvious difference between men's writing and women's writing in this era. *Moby-Dick* (1851) is replete with erotic imagery; the symbolic "marriage" of Ishmael and Queequeg and the obviously phallic imagery of the sperm whale breaching, "rising with his utmost velocity from the furthest depths . . . piling up a mountain of dazzling foam" (419) are two of many possible examples. Edgar Allan Poe's short stories "Ligeia" (1838) and "The Fall of the House of Usher" (1839) are suffused with suggestions of perverse and incestuous sexual passion. J. W. De Forest's *Miss Ravenel's Conversion from Secession to Loyalty* (1867) is a minor novel that is unusually frank in its presentation of both male and female sexuality. De Forest describes the sexual attraction between the newly married Lillie Ravenel and her lusty husband, Colonel Carter:

> She frequently blushed at encountering him, as if he were still a lover. If she met the bold gaze of his wide-open brown eyes, she trembled with an inward thrill and wanted to say, "Please don't look at me so!" He could tyrannize over her with his eyes; he could make her come to him and try to hide from them by nestling her head on his shoulder; he used to wonder at his power and gratify his vanity as well as his affection by using it. (327)

Lillie's sexual attraction is so strong that she marries Carter in spite of her father's wise disapproval of the man. And Hawthorne's Hester also violates the dictates of authority in favor of passion, experiencing an adulterous sexual love for Arthur Dimmesdale so great that it transcends religious strictures and has "a consecration of its own" (194). The scene in the forest where, after years of separation, Hester pleads with Dimmesdale to leave Puritan Massachusetts and go with her to Europe, suddenly taking off her cap and letting her hair, "dark and rich" (201), fall down around her shoulders, is one of the most erotic in mid-nineteenth-century American literature.

Men's writing of mid-nineteenth-century America, although not universally free from constraints, is a more passionate, comprehensive, and stylistically self-conscious body of work than women's writing. This is so precisely because the gender identity of men did not oblige them to be "divinely reticent" about their own experience and about human passions at large.

11. But Sedgwick's *Hope Leslie* (1827) indicates that proscriptions may not have been as limiting during the 1820s as they were later, at mid-century. With its lively, decidedly nonsubmissive heroine and its graphic portrayal of violence, *Hope Leslie* exhibits qualities that violate the more stringent ideals of feminine expression. The protagonist, Hope, is so autonomous as to defy the dictates of community leaders on several occasions, leading her more proper friend Esther to chastise her thus: "Hope Leslie, you do allow yourself too much liberty of thought and word" (180). And certainly Sedgwick's portrayal of a massacre in which a baby's head is dashed against a doorstep is a "raw" and "bloody" scene by anyone's definition. That Sedgwick received social approbation for the novel is attested to by its popularity; the novel went into several editions (*Life and Letters* 443). And Sedgwick, a habitually modest woman, said that at the time of its first publication, she heard "from all quarters . . . extravagant praise" (*Life and Letters* 187).

12. Capitola Le Noir, the feisty heroine of E.D.E.N. Southworth's *The Hidden Hand*, is the most striking exception (although there are others) to the typical "chastened" little girl of contemporary women's fiction. *The Hidden Hand* was a newspaper serial, published originally in the New York *Ledger* in 1859; it did not appear in book form until 1888. Southworth's early novels on the whole, however, were characterized by flamboyant females who co-exist nicely with the more conventional women characters. As I suggest in my Introduction to the reprint edition of *The Hidden Hand*, Southworth may well have had Ellen Montgomery in mind in her creation of Capitola (xxviii–xxix).

13. It is also important to note that *Uncle Tom's Cabin* has a male rather than a female protagonist. Cassy, the vital and defiant black woman who comes into the novel toward the end, is a striking candidate for a full-length story of her own. However, Cassy, as Simon Legree's unwilling mistress and as slave-courtesan to several men before him, is characterized by a wide-ranging sexual experience as well as by her strong personal anger at the situation that has enslaved and victimized her. Although her sexual life is not autonomous—she is presented as a victim of the caprice and lust of white males—and she repents her angry defiance of Christian principles and is "redeemed" in the end, she still violates proscriptions to the point of being ineligible by contemporary standards to be a literary protagonist.

14. I must stress here that proscriptions were only *beginning* to break up at this time. More conservative cultural elements continued to proscribe literature. In a study of a literary censorship movement of the late nineteenth century, Dee Garrison tells us that in 1881 the American Library Association made a list of authors "whose works are sometimes excluded from public libraries by reason of sensational or immoral qualities" and circulated it to seventy major public libraries (72). Ironically, in light of what I have shown about the nature of expressive deviance in nineteenth-century America, several of the writers on that list were fairly conservative, conforming women writers. Ann Stephens, E.D.E.N. Southworth, Mary Jane Holmes, Caroline Lee Hentz, and Augusta Jane Evans Wilson offended, Garrison conjectures, by presenting a "much more open discussion of the female's plight" (75) than did other domestic novelists.

15. As a nonconforming writer Elizabeth Stoddard is not bound by the prohibition against profanity. Desmond Somers's "What the hell are you doing here?" in *The Morgesons* (171) is the only oath I've seen in any American woman's text of the period.

16. While Cassandra does fall in love at least once, with Charles Morgeson, the married cousin with whom she makes her home while she attends school, it would be difficult to call this experience a "romance" in the sense that was familiar to

American women readers. Stoddard offers a picture of attempted seduction and resistance characterized by stark realism rather than by the inflated emotionalism of romantic novels like those of the Brontës (which were widely read in America) or by the combination of sensationalism and moral didacticism that characterized Susanna Rowland's *Charlotte Temple*. Cassandra's relationship with Ben Somers is not a romance but rather a wary friendship, and her eventual marriage to his brother, Desmond, is preceded by a "non-relationship" as far as any extended development of character interaction within the narrative.

17. I discuss contemporary attitudes toward women's publication in chapter 2. Mary Kelley's social history, *Private Woman, Public Stage: Literary Domesticity in Nineteenth-Century America*, documents at length the personal conflicts women writers faced in reconciling their roles as writers in the public sphere with their perceptions of themselves as private, domestic individuals.

18. For an in-depth discussion of the dynamic at work in *The Wide, Wide World* and *Hitherto*, see my essay, "The Hidden Hand: Subversion of Cultural Ideology in Three Mid-Nineteenth-Century American Women's Novels," *American Quarterly* 38 (Summer 1986): 225–42.

19. I discuss each of these reactive strategies—the use of the little girl protagonist, the focus on public issues, and the resort to stylistic indirection—at length in later chapters.

20. Jo, the protagonist of *Little Women*, reluctantly rejects her lurid sensation stories and learns the lesson of a woman's "true style." However, Alcott herself published many "lurid" stories anonymously in the pages of newspapers and weekly story papers.

21. The writers I classify as writing to some degree or other in deviance from the community of expression are those writers Reynolds calls "Subversives," creators of a subversive and sensationalized "literature of misery" in whose tradition Dickinson placed herself. Reynolds is correct in defining such a tradition, but he tends to underestimate the ways in which it is connected to conventional expression, the ways in which it is self-contradictory and conflicted, and the ways in which conventional expression itself contained outlets for cultural criticism as well as affirmation.

To say for instance that the conventional female character he calls the "female exemplar" in novels like *The Wide, Wide World* and *The Lamplighter* "resisted all the troublesome paradoxes of Subversive popular culture" in a literary mode that is lacking in "gender-specific elements" (388) is to read without a gender-specific sensitivity to the nuanced manner in which "proper" women expressed their griefs and consolations. Reynolds says that critics have tended to overemphasize the role that "Conventional" literature played in mid-century America, providing a "lopsided view of antebellum culture," and he may well be correct. His point regarding "the immense cultural power of . . . Subversive literature, which was bizarre, nightmarish, and often politically radical" (8) is well taken. Certainly his investigation of the lively and irreverent "Subversive" modes of literary expression provides a bracing and much-needed revisionary reading of antebellum culture. However, conventional women's writing was far more complex and influential than Reynolds, in his desire to resurrect the more culturally hidden literature, suggests. Mainstream literature may have been delimited and restricted, but it was the dominant mode of writing for, by, and about women and it was not without major significance in both cultural and literary terms.

Further, to operate on the assumption that cultural dissent in literature is its primary value is to continue the perpetuation of long-held assumptions about the role of the writer in America—that he, as Melville said of Hawthorne, must say "NO! in thunder." This view has long been held by literary critics and has more recently been adopted by a number of feminist critics. However, for women, there was strength and affirmation in many aspects of women's culture, by which I mean that network of shared values, abilities, affinities, affections, and consolations that sustained women. Dickinson's life and poetry, as I show throughout this study, reveal significant indication of her attraction to domestic identification and accomplishment. It would be a mistake to undervalue the influence of women's culture on her.

22. In much of men's writing, too, personal aspects of *women's* lives were rigidly screened. Cynthia Wolff's essay on stereotypes of women in literature defines the limitations: "She could feel love (especially unrequited or betrayed love) but seldom sexual passion; she could feel sympathy for others . . . but she was . . . incapable of moral outrage. Most strikingly, she was never permitted to feel anger; the absence of rage in these otherwise highly emotional women is truly striking. And of course, she was never moved by public ambitions" (211).

2. "My Author Existence": Lives of Women Writers

1. The recent reprint edition of *Hope Leslie* makes teaching of this novel now a possibility. It works particularly well paired with Cooper's *Last of the Mohicans* or Hawthorne's *Scarlet Letter*, which present far more circumscribed images of both female and Indian characters than does Sedgwick.

2. For an in-depth reading of this poem, see chapter 5.

3. Edgar Allan Poe did not overtly attack Sigourney in his discussion of her in the *Messenger* for January 1836, but he did discuss her at length in the context of certain unscrupulous poets who develop a literary reputation by the "chicanery" of keeping themselves forever in the eye "of that great, overgrown, and majestical gander, the critical and bibliographical rabble" (Haight 80). Among modern critics one might expect the patronizing tone of Gilbert S. Haight's 1930 biography, *Mrs. Sigourney: The Sweet Singer of Hartford*; the title alone is a clue as to what is inside. But Ann Douglas Wood's outright hostility in her 1972 essay, "Mrs. Sigourney and the Sensibility of the Inner Space," is almost incomprehensible. In discussing Sigourney's rise to social prominence and poetic fame she uses the following loaded language: "[Sigourney] was not born to the purple: she struggled hard and *ruthlessly* to wear it. . . . the young Lydia Huntley used her poetry *to get a foot in the door* of Norwich society. . . . she married *well above herself* . . . but this marriage in no way *satiated her ambition.* . . . her success is *a lesson in successful hypocrisy* (164–66, my emphasis).

4. In at least one way Osgood and Dickinson reacted similarly to the awareness of their deviance from expressive codes. Osgood's 1850 edition of poems contains a disclaimer that served a protective purpose. Some poems, she said, "were written to appear in prose sketches and stories, and are expressions of feeling suitable to the persons and incidents with which they were originally involved" (Watts 113). This "supposed person" strategy puts us in mind of Dickinson's comment to Higginson that the emotions expressed in her verse were to be ascribed to a persona, not to the the writer herself (L 268). The climate of expression for women being such that frank utterance of intimate personal truth was prohibited, a public disclaimer (and for Dickinson, Higginson was a "public" of a sort, see note 16 below) of unacceptable emotions was one strategy by which a writer could say all she had to say without facing censure.

5. I discuss this contrast at length in chapter 4.

6. Censure ran from the mild to the severe. Expectably, Stowe was doomed to have her femininity questioned. As Nina Baym tells us, Maria McIntosh in her 1853 novel *The Lofty and the Lowly* took the occasion to contrast "her own womanly writing

behavior with the unnatural militancy of Harriet Beecher Stowe" (98). This verbal censure was easy to take compared with more severe manifestations of hatred. As her biographer, Forrest Wilson, recounts it, the reaction from the South was vicious: "She began to receive anonymous letters from the South, threatening, scurrilous, and obscene, many of them, and once Calvin unwrapped a small parcel out of which fell a black human ear, sliced from the head of some recalcitrant slave and sent to the woman now being widely branded as a fomenter of servile rebellion . . . " (298).

7. Avis, protagonist of the younger Elizabeth Stuart Phelps' *The Story of Avis*, addresses herself, too, to the issue of puddings, but with an emphasis the opposite of Dickinson's: "Very well. Other women might make puddings" (58), but *she* was going to be an artist.

8. Early in her life Dickinson began to feel the burden of housekeeping and to comment on it, albeit in a joking manner, in her letters to her friends. For instance, in a letter to Abiah Root in May 1850 she says: "The circumstances under which I write you this morning are at once glorious, afflicting, and beneficial—glorious in *ends*, afflicting in *means*, and *beneficial* I *trust* in *both*. Twin loaves of bread have just been born into the world under my auspices—fine children—the image of their *mother*—and *here* my dear friend is the *glory*." After apologizing to her old friend in grandiose terms for not having written sooner, she says with whimsy, "besides I have been at work, providing the 'food that perisheth,' scaring the timorous dust, and being obedient, and kind." But she ends her comment on an ominous note: "*I* call it kind obedience in the books the Shadows write in, it may have another name" (L 36). To Jane Humphrey earlier that year she had been more overt in her complaints about domestic responsibilities: "—and really I came to the conclusion that I should be a villain unparralleled [sic] if I took but an inch of time for so unholy a purpose as writing a friendly letter . . . " (L 30). Continuing to grumble, in an unusually overt fashion for her, about the cultural expectation that she, like a good "true woman," should take this opportunity to cultivate "meekness—and patience—and submission—," she concludes, "Somehow or other I incline to other things" (L 30).

9. "When Father lived I remained with him because he would miss me—Now, Mother is helpless—a holier demand—" (L 735).

10. Rufus Griswold, in his introduction of the young Cary sisters to the literary world, stressed the spontaneity of their verse. "Fruits of no literary leisure," he called their poems, "but the mere past times of lives that are spent in prosaic duties" (*Poems* 7). Richard Howard has noted a similar ancillary, or what he calls "sideline" (95), quality in the work of Emily Dickinson. He finds it singular that Dickinson did not make her poetry the central focus of her attention. He refers to the lack of coherence in her body of work—a feature that characterizes every level from the syntactical to the textual. "Dickinson," he says, "produced, day by day, produced and then rid herself of [her poetry]—it was in fact a by-product, a sideline, an obliquity—the most relentless epic of identity in our literature" (95–96). Whether or not this is evidence of the radically existentialist stance that Howard claims for Dickinson is a matter that can only be conjectured. However, in light of the incessant daily domestic obligations of most nineteenth-century women, it is just as likely that the stylistic and textual fragmentation of Dickinson's poetry reflects the conflicting artistic and familial needs that must have divided her loyalties, fragmented her time, and scattered her energies. Her poetry may well have been, to paraphrase Griswold's comment about the Carys, the pastime of a life spent in prosaic duties.

11. R. J. Wilson proposes that Dickinson wrote to Higginson with the idea of enlisting his help to publish her poetry but that she didn't understand the contemporary literary marketplace. He says she approached Higginson with outdated "as-

sumptions that might have gone with the vanished system of clientele and patronage" (459) and that Higginson was not willing to function in that manner. Wilson is wrong on two counts here: he assumes that Dickinson really did want to publish, and he neglects evidence that Higginson did function in a patron-like manner for other women writers—most notably for Helen Hunt Jackson and Harriet Prescott Spofford.

12. This was not merely an American idea. The father of the British writer Charlotte Yonge (1823–1901), told her that "a lady published for three reasons only: love of praise, love of money, or the wish to do good" (Showalter 56).

13. This was written, obviously, before the publication of *Uncle Tom's Cabin* in 1852. After that success, her earnings were considerably higher.

14. A short sampling: Lydia Sigourney turned to writing as a source of income to support her family of five children in the 1820s when her husband's hardware business began to fail. Elizabeth Oakes Smith's husband, the writer Seba Smith, went bankrupt in the 1830s as a result of ill-advised land speculations, and her writing became a major financial support of their family of six. Susan Warner's father lost his considerable fortune in the panic of 1837, and his obsessive lawsuits thereafter drained the income from the Warner sisters' many publications. In 1844 E.D.E.N. Southworth was deserted by her husband on the Wisconsin frontier, and returned home with one small child and another one on the way. She taught school to support them and herself, until her success as a writer freed her from that ill-paid profession. Fanny Fern's unsuccessful attempt to solicit familial aid for her widowed self and two small children became the subject of *Ruth Hall*. Her scandalous *roman à clef* particularly attacked her brother, Nathaniel P. Willis, a successful poet and New York editor who refused to assist her in launching a literary career. The support of her large family fell heavily on Louisa May Alcott, whose brilliant but improvident father, Bronson Alcott, maintained the family in a state of borderline poverty.

15. Jackson even went against the advice of her own publisher, James Fields, in doing this, putting out "520 good hard dollars" of her own money, as Annie Fields wrote in her diary. "We shall see who is right—," Fields wrote, "She or he—The writer or the publisher" (Leyda II 159).

16. Not that she was resolutely against fame, but she seems to have defined it in a unique manner. A comment in a letter to her sister-in-law, Susan, in 1861 indicates that for her, "fame" had very definite connections to her close personal relationships, rather than to a far-flung public: "Could I make you and Austin—proud—sometime—a great way off—'twould give me taller feet—" (L 238), she says. Note, however, that the motivation for accomplishment is not stated as her own; rather her projected achievement would be for the benefit of Susan and Austin. To Higginson she wrote in January 1877, "I thought your approbation Fame—and it's [sic] withdrawal Infamy" (L 486), once again indicating the affectional nature of her definition of fame, which attached itself more to personal relationships than to widespread public awareness of her as an individual or of her work.

3. "Are There Any Lives of Women?":
Conventions of the Female Self in Women's Writing

1. Among the character types David Reynolds defines in his survey of antebellum popular sensation literature are figures he calls the "feminist criminal" and the "sensual woman." "The prominence of these two characters, he says, "in sensational fiction of the 1840s puts the lie to the standard critical view that popular fiction featured only pure, gentle heroines." These figures, he insists, "embodied the boldest, most rebellious fantasies of American women" (363). However, these

character types did not so much embody fantasies *of* American women, as they embodied fantasies *about* American women—fantasies by male writers such as George Lippard, Ned Buntline, and George Thompson. In women's novels from the era, Southworth came closest to presenting the "female rogues" Reynolds describes, with characters like the "damsel errant" Capitola Le Noir and the feminist "man-hater" Britomarte Conyers. Although these characters are social "rogues," defying conventional decorum and constraints, they do not in any way defy conventional morality; at the height of their cultural defiance, they remain chaste, honest, and noble. In some of her minor characters, however, Southworth does portray vicious, scheming, sexually manipulative women such as those Reynolds describes.

2. This is not to say, however, that sexuality is completely eradicated from these texts. That is certainly not the case. In the novels, with or without the use of the little girl protagonist, sexual passion could appear in an oblique, displaced manner. This may well explain the popularity, as Nina Baym reminds me, of such writers as E.D.E.N. Southworth and Mary Jane Holmes. In Susan Warner's phenomenally popular *The Wide, Wide World*, little Ellen is consistently approached by men in intensely threatening ways that to our post-Freudian eyes have distinctly erotic overtones. The amount of kissing that goes on in this novel is also notable. Sexuality was present as well in women's poetry, as Cheryl Walker notes, rarely openly, "but highly charged language sometimes invites one to read certain poems as having a sexual content" (40).

3. Sandra Gilbert and Susan Gubar are explicit about seeing this little girl persona as a factor in Dickinson's life as well as in her writing. "Where Charlotte Brontë projected her anxieties into images of orphan children, Emily Dickinson herself enacted the part of a child" (*Madwoman* 583). Barbara Mossberg also sees the little girl figure as a functional aspect of Dickinson's life. "Saying 'no' to a conventional life as a woman necessarily keeps Dickinson in a kind of childhood; childhood in this sense is not only a metaphor for confinement and repression, but also a place of retreat from the world's limiting expectations for women. . . . Dickinson's child persona is in large measure a crucial aspect of her systematic refusal to become bound in a conventional woman's life" ("Nursery Rhymes" 60). This analysis is most likely correct—at least in Dickinson's case—but it presents as logical and inevitable under the circumstances a behavior that is in fact most deviant. Other women writers may have protected themselves from censure by adopting the rhetoric (as in the Grace Greenwood quote) and narratives of childhood. Most of them, however, in their lives took an adult and professional stance vis-à-vis the world.

4. The poems from which the little girl figure emerges are: " 'Arcturus' is his other name—" 70; "Why—do they shut Me out of Heaven?" 248; "Over the fence—" 251; "Good Morning—Midnight—" 425; "I started Early—Took my Dog—" 520; "I prayed, at first, a little Girl" 576; "I cried at Pity—not at Pain—" 588; "It would have starved a Gnat—"612; "They shut me up in Prose—" 613; "Let Us play Yesterday—" 728; "They wont frown always—some sweet Day" 874; "So I pull my Stockings off" 1201.

5. Nina Baym's *Woman's Fiction* introduces this figure to modern readers. "The many novels all tell, with variations, a single tale. In essence, it is the story of a young girl who is deprived of the supports she had rightly or wrongly depended on to sustain her throughout life and is faced with the necessity of winning her own way in the world" (11). Baym's thesis that these books present models of maturation seems initially to contradict my reading of the little girl figure as evasive of the full consequences of female maturity. Her more recent essay, "Rewriting the Scribbling Women," however, clarifies the precise terms in which that maturation

was perceived. "Rather than seeing these as stories in which 'women' nevertheless succeed in becoming 'individuals,' many reviewers saw them as stories in which 'individuals' nevertheless succeed in remaining 'women' " (8). The cultural definition of womanhood was strictly delimited, and expressions of, for instance, sexual longing, personal anger, or ambition beyond the boundaries of the home were strongly discouraged.

6. Baym also notes this dichotomy in the protagonists. She calls them the "flawed" and the "flawless" heroines.

7. Jane Tompkins gives an extensive analysis of this rationale of compensation as it works in the popular imagination. She shows how "the by-passing of worldly authority ultimately produces a feminist theology in which the god-head is refashioned into an image of maternal authority" (163).

8. Barbara Mossberg also notices the dual aspect of the child figure—or what she calls the daughter persona—in Dickinson's poems. "Both daughters, the dutiful and the rebellious," she says, "are necessary for manufacture of poetry" (*Daughter* 198). The little girl figure as I develop it here is taken from the poems listed in note 4 above.

9. On 1 November 1868 she confided to her journal her resentment of this pressure to "complete" the novel. "Girls write to ask who the little women marry, as if that was the only end and aim of a woman's life. I *won't* marry Jo to Laurie to please anyone" (*Life* 201).

10. Although in reality, of course, many women continued to strive and achieve even after marriage and maturity, these women don't appear in novels or poetry, except as cautionary tales. Their stories were not the stuff of the popular imagination. Prevailing cultural attitudes can be seen in the following quotes: Alexis de Tocqueville noted that "in America, the independence of women is irrevocably lost in the bonds of matrimony" (201). And Dickinson's friend, Samuel Bowles, confirmed this ethos when he wrote to a friend in 1855 regarding the birth of a son: "I am glad it is a boy. Boys are institutions. They have a future, a positive future. Girls are swallowed up" (Merriam I 168). Elizabeth Oakes Smith, in her poignant account of her reluctant marriage at age sixteen to a man much older than herself, notes the sense of identity loss that came with marriage: "I . . . transformed myself to an utterly different creature from what had been native to me. . . . how carefully I folded my wings. . . . I had lost my girlhood, and found nothing better to take its place" (*Autobiography* 45).

11. Poems using the wife/bride figure are: "I'm 'wife'—I've finished that—" 199; "A Wife—at Daybreak I shall be—" 461; "I am ashamed—I hide—" 473; "The World—stands—solemner—to me—" 493; "She rose to His Requirement—dropt" 732; "Given in Marriage unto Thee" 817; "Title divine—is mine!" 1072; "All that I do" 1496; "Rearrange a 'Wife's' affection!" 1737; " 'Twas here my summer paused" 1756; and possibly "I'm ceded—I've stopped being Their's—" 508.

4. "The Grieved—are many—I am told—": The Woman Writer and Public Discourse

1. Some critics, feeling evidently that her lack of public comment somehow reflects negatively on the person Emily Dickinson was, have tried to defend her by attempting to find deep social concern in her poems and letters. This leads not to vindication but merely to strained and tortuous argumentation. Henry Wells, in his 1947 *Introduction to Emily Dickinson*, devotes a chapter to Dickinson and "The Social Scene." He says that her attitude toward society was "on the whole revolutionary" (188), but his attempt to provide a coherent analysis of her social attitudes and a vindication of her as a caring observer of the social scene fails for lack of

evidence. Adrienne Berenson, in a 1952 essay, "Emily Dickinson's Social Attitudes: A Dissenting View," not only misreads Dickinson's poetry but reveals a lack of understanding of the cultural milieu when she says that "in the complacent nineteenth century, social issues were more or less irrelevant to the central religious questions" (351).

Thomas W. Ford in "Emily Dickinson and the Civil War" (1965) proposes only that the war brought her a heightened awareness of death and thus acted to rouse her creative energy. Wisely, he does not attempt to claim for her an active political interest in the issues and causes that impelled the war. Aaron Kramer, in *The Prophetic Tradition in American Poetry* (1968), traces, rather unconvincingly, a strain of social consciousness in her writing. He is more accurate, however, in noting that "if [social] prophecy includes the urge to transmit distressing truths to hostile ears, Emily Dickinson's work . . . cannot be a promising field of exploration" (136). Shira Wolosky in *Emily Dickinson: A Voice of War* (1984) investigates the effect of the Civil War upon Dickinson, noting that "there are in Dickinson's opus many poems that register, directly or indirectly, the civil conflagration raging around her." It is a "metaphysical conflict . . . accompanied by historical trauma" (xviii) that Wolosky finds in Dickinson's work, however, not an open engagement in contemporary affairs.

2. Here I take issue with Ann Douglas who relegates to *male* authors of the period the impulse "to bring their readers into direct confrontation with the more brutal facts of America's explosive development" (*Feminization* 4). Thoreau, Cooper, Melville, and Whitman, she says, "wrote principally about men, not girls and children, and they wrote about men engaged in economically and ecologically significant activities." The biases here are plain, and I will say only that in comparison with the romanticized images in which these writers perceived "America's explosive development," Sedgwick's description of attacks by white settlers on Indian villages, Stowe's rendition of the sexual exploitation of young girls and of the fatal beating of Uncle Tom, and Davis's exploration of conditions in the iron foundries, are far more realistic about the "brutal facts."

3. "In modernist thinking, literature is by definition a form of discourse that has no designs on the world. It does not attempt to change things, but merely to represent them, and it does so in a specifically literary language whose claim to value lies in its uniqueness. Consequently, works whose stated purpose is to influence the course of history, and which therefore employ a language that is not only not unique but common and accessible to everyone, do not qualify as works of art" (Tompkins 125).

4. Aaron Kramer makes a distinction that is useful in defining the reform momentum of this writing: "It is one thing . . . to hear and express the people's grief and yearning, to recognize and condemn . . . evils. . . . It is another matter, however, for the prophet to play a purposely dynamic, shaping role in the events of [her] age by rousing the bemused multitude and goading it into noble action" (31). An exchange between Stowe and her sister-in-law reveals the "purposely dynamic, shaping role" Stowe envisioned for herself. In 1850, her sister-in-law wrote to her, "Hattie, if I could use a pen as you can, I would write something to make this whole nation feel what an accursed thing slavery is!" Stowe responded, "As long as the baby sleeps with me nights I can't do much at anything, but I will do it at last. I will write that thing if I live" (*Life and Letters* 130). "That thing," of course, turned out to be *Uncle Tom's Cabin*.

5. Dickinson's prisons in her poems are metaphoric, built of "Phantasm Steel" (652). See also poems 77, 1166, 1601.

6. See John Cody, *After Great Pain*, Vivian R. Pollak, "Thirst and Starvation in

Emily Dickinson's Poetry," and Barbara Mossberg, "Hunger in the House," chapter 8 in *Emily Dickinson: When a Writer is a Daughter*.

7. The subject of "beggar lads" in women's writing did not automatically necessitate sentimentality. It was possible to write about poverty with realism, with vivacity, and even with wit as shown by E.D.E.N. Southworth in *The Hidden Hand* (1859). Young Cap, an impertinent newsboy and street urchin, turns out not to be a "beggar lad" after all, but a young girl who has been left destitute in the slums, her foster mother dead and her house demolished. Capitola was one "beggar lad" who did not "die early," and Southworth's lively account of Cap's struggle to survive destitution in mid-century New York is a classic statement of non-sentimental self-reliance. Further, as comedy, it completes the range of approaches to social commentary—the sentimental, the realistic, the humorous—that women writers employed in this era.

8. Other critics ignore all women poets but Dickinson or mention them only as occasion for cheap humor. Spiller's *Literary History of America*, for instance, shows typical bias. About Sigourney it says unfairly, "She knew something of the humanitarian movements of the day, but all she did for Negroes, Indians, the poor, and the insane was to embalm them in the amber of her tears" (289). Donald Stauffer in *A Short History of American Poetry* mentions in passing that she was the most well-known poet of the 1820s and then goes on to talk at length about Fitz-Greene Halleck (66). William Charvat in *The Profession of Authorship in America, 1800–1870* doesn't even mention her. Sandra Zagarell in "Imagining 'America' " is, to date, the only modern critic to take Sigourney seriously, investigating at length the ways in which Sigourney's work critiques the racist assumptions upon which this nation was founded and the tragic human consequences of those assumptions.

9. Dickinson herself doesn't quite seem to know what to do with this gruesome imagery, transmuting her arteries, veins, great globules, and basins of blood rather unconvincingly into a rose that eddies away "Upon Vermillion Wheels."

5. "The Reticent Volcano": Style and the Private Woman

1. Cheryl Walker also notes this phenomenon, relating it specifically to the women poets of Dickinson's era: "There is ample evidence that women poets in the nineteenth century felt unable to express their true feelings directly, whether because of internal or external pressures or some combination of both. In Emily Dickinson's words, they 'tell all the truth but tell it slant.' To make this poetry intelligible today we must recover the grounds of its being, which include the historical factors that inhibited free speech to begin with" (32). Walker rightly attributes this indirection of self-expression to the prevalent cultural doctrine of separate spheres for men's and women's action and to the fears women writers felt about loss of femininity in the pursuit of a literary career.

2. Ward writes specifically about the ways in which Dickinson's writing reflects a Puritan ethos that affected all New Englanders, both male and female. However, he does specify the appeal of Dickinson's poetry for women. "If the gift of articulateness was not denied, you had Channing, Emerson, Hawthorne. . . . Mostly it was denied, & became a family fate. This is where Emily Dickinson comes in. She was the articulate inarticulate. That is why it appeals so to New England women."

3. Jack Capps quotes this poem and then, incomprehensibly, goes on to say that Dickinson's "intention was not to be deliberately obscure or abstruse but rather to achieve exactness of expression" (144).

4. Helen Waite Papashvily initiated the discussion of dissatisfaction and dissent in nineteenth-century American women's fiction in her 1956 study, *All the Happy Endings*. Indeed, she finds these texts to be deliberately *subversive*, a veritable

"witches broth, a lethal draught brewed by women and used by women to destroy their common enemy, man" (xvii). Papashvily overreads the novels to support her thesis, but her study is valuable in that it is the first to bring to the attention of modern scholars the disparity between the culturally affirmative surface narratives of these novels and the dissenting messages they sometimes conveyed.

5. Feminist agitation, although a minority movement, was the visible manifestation of the subterranean workings of gender discontent. No ideology is ever completely hegemonic in a culture and eventual shifts in gender definitions were fermenting at various levels of society throughout the century.

6. Hamilton advised women to express themselves freely despite proscriptions: "Girls, do not be deceived. Write. Write poetry, —write in rhyme. . . . Any one of you who refrains from writing for fear of ridicule, is a coward. . . . The more a man tells you not to write, the more do you write" (183–84). Hamilton also unleashes her tart epithets against proscriptions on women's language. Her paragraphs on "tabooed expressions" in "Men and Women" are particularly enlightening: "Men can talk 'slang.' 'Dry up' is nowhere forbidden in the Decalogue. Neither the law nor the prophets frown on 'a thousand of brick.' The Sermon on the Mount does not discountenance 'knuckling to'; but between women and these minor immoralities stands an invisible barrier of propriety,—waves an abstract flaming sword in the hand of Mrs. Grundy,—and we must submit to Mrs. Grundy, though the heavens fall. But who can reckon up the loss which we sustain?" (94).

7. Largely the story is told in Anstiss Dolbeare's direct first-person narration; then the voice of an omniscient author telling the tale of the orphan Hope Devine enters the narration; most intriguing is a voice called "the silent side," which concentrates on the thoughts and feelings of Richard Hathaway, Anstiss's husband-to-be. In a manner presaging stream-of-consciousness narration, this voice adds a pre-modern complexity to the tale. "The silent side is fragmentary," it informs us, "a man doesn't think on in a straight line through a mile-long chapter; neither does he think all on one thread" (51).

8. Myra Jehlen proposes that formal assumptions upon which the structure of the novel depends reflect the assumptions of the culture about sex roles. "It seems reasonable to suppose that the novel, envisioning the encounter of the individual with his world in the modern idiom, posits as one of its structuring assumptions (an assumption that transcends the merely thematic, to function formally) the special form that sexual hierarchy has taken in modern times" (595). For the popular women's novels of mid-nineteenth-century America there is no question but that formal aspects are fundamentally shaped by cultural sex-role assumptions, but the distortions and articulate disorderings of those narratives reflect the nascent uneasiness with those roles that was to eventuate in cultural change.

WORKS CITED

Abbott, Rev. John S. C. *The Mother at Home*. New York: American Tract Society, 1833.

Alcott, Louisa May. *Life, Letters, and Journals*. Ed. Ednah D. Cheney. Boston: Little, Brown, 1889.

Ames, Mary Clemmer. *A Memorial of Alice and Phoebe Cary with Some of Their Later Poems*. New York: Hurd and Houghton, 1873.

Baym, Nina. *Woman's Fiction: A Guide to Novels by and about Women in America: 1820–1870*. Ithaca: Cornell University Press, 1978.

———.*Novels, Readers, and Reviewers: Responses to Fiction in Antebellum America*. Ithaca: Cornell University Press, 1984.

———."Rewriting the Scribbling Women." *Legacy* 2.2 (Fall 1985):3–12.

———."The Madwoman and Her Languages: Why I Don't Do Feminist Literary Theory." *Feminist Issues in Literary Scholarship*. Ed. Shari Benstock. Bloomington: Indiana University Press, 1987.

Beecher, Catharine, and Harriet Beecher Stowe. *The American Woman's Home*. New York: J. B. Ford and Co., 1869.

Berenson, Adrienne. "Emily Dickinson's Social Attitudes: A Dissenting View." *Western Humanities Review* 6.4 (1952):351–62.

Bingham, Millicent Todd. *Ancestors' Brocades: The Literary Discovery of Emily Dickinson: The Editing and Publication of Her Letters and Poems*. 1945. New York: Dover, 1967.

———. *Emily Dickinson's Home: Letters of Edward Dickinson and His Family*. New York: Harper and Brothers, 1955.

Browning, Elizabeth Barrett. *The Letters of Elizabeth Barrett Browning to Mary Russell Mitford, 1836–1854*. 3 vols. Ed. Meredith B. Raymond and Mary Rose Sullivan. Winfield, Kans.: Wedgestone, 1983.

Cameron, Sharon. "A Loaded Gun: Dickinson and the Dialectic of Rage." *PMLA* 93 (1978): 423–37.

Capps, Jack L. *Emily Dickinson's Reading: 1836–1886*. Cambridge: Harvard University Press, 1966.

Cary, Alice. *Clovernook Sketches and Other Stories*. Ed. Judith Fetterley. New Brunswick, N.J.: Rutgers University Press, 1987.

———. *Ballads, Lyrics, and Hymns*. New York: Hurd and Houghton, 1865.

Chapman, Raymond. *Linguistics and Literature: An Introduction to Literary Stylistics*. London: Edward Arnold, 1973.

Cody, John. *After Great Pain: The Inner Life of Emily Dickinson*. Cambridge: Belknap Press of Harvard University Press, 1971.

Cooke, Rose Terry. *"How Celia Changed Her Mind" and Selected Stories*. Ed. Elizabeth Ammons. New Brunswick, N.J.: Rutgers University Press, 1986.

Cott, Nancy F. *The Bonds of Womanhood: "Woman's Sphere" in New England, 1780–1835*. New Haven: Yale University Press, 1977.

Cummins, Maria Susanna. *The Lamplighter*. 1854. Ed. Nina Baym. New Brunswick, N.J.: Rutgers University Press, 1988.

Dandurand, Karen. "Another Dickinson Poem Published in Her Lifetime." *American Literature* 54.3 (October 1982):434–37.

————."New Dickinson Civil War Publications." *American Literature* 56.1 (March 1984):17–27.

————."Publication of Dickinson's Poems in Her Lifetime." *Legacy* 1.1 (Spring 1984):7.

Davis, Rebecca Harding. *Life in the Iron Mills*. 1861. Ed. Tillie Olsen. Old Westbury, N.Y.: Feminist Press, 1972.

————."The Wife's Story." *Atlantic Monthly* 14 (July 1864):1–19.

————."Marcia." *Silhouettes of American Life*. 1892. New York: Garnett Press, 1968.

De Forest, John William. *Miss Ravenel's Conversion from Secession to Loyalty*. 1867. New York: Rinehart, 1955.

Degler, Carl N. *At Odds: Women and the Family in America from the Revolution to the Present*. Oxford: Oxford University Press, 1980.

de Tocqueville, Alexis. *Democracy in America*. 1835. Ed. Phillips Bradley. New York: Alfred A. Knopf, 1945.

Dickinson, Emily. *The Poems of Emily Dickinson*. 3 vols. Ed. Thomas H. Johnson. Cambridge: Harvard University Press, 1955.

————. *The Letters of Emily Dickinson*. 3 vols. Ed. Thomas H. Johnson and Theodora Ward. Cambridge: Harvard University Press, 1958.

Dobson, Joanne. "The Hidden Hand: Subversion of Cultural Ideology in Three Mid-Nineteenth-Century American Women's Novels." *American Quarterly* 38.2 (Summer 1986):223–42.

Douglas, Ann. *The Feminization of American Culture*. New York: Avon, 1977.

Eagleton, Terence. *Marxism and Literary Criticism*. Berkeley: University of California Press, 1976.

Emerson, Ralph Waldo. *Miscellanies*. 1904. New York: AMS, 1968.

————. *Selected Writings of Ralph Waldo Emerson*. Ed. William H. Gilman. New York: New American Library, 1965.

Fern, Fanny (Sara Parton). *Fern Leaves from Fanny's Portfolio*. Auburn, N.Y.: Derby and Miller, 1853.

————. *Ruth Hall: And Other Writings*. Ed. Joyce W. Warren. New Brunswick, N.J.: Rutgers University Press, 1986.

————. *Folly As It Flies*. New York: G. W. Carleton, 1868.

Fetterley, Judith. "*Little Women*: Alcott's Civil War." *Feminist Studies* 5 (1979):369–83.

————. ed. *Provisions: A Reader from 19th-Century American Women*. Bloomington: Indiana University Press, 1985.

Ford, Thomas W. "Emily Dickinson and the Civil War." *University Review* 31.3 (1965):199–203.

Foster, Edward Halsey. *Susan and Anna Warner*. Boston: Twayne, 1978.

Fowler, Roger. *Understanding Language: An Introduction to Linguistics*. London: Routledge and Kegan Paul, 1974.

Fuller (Ossoli), Margaret. *Woman in the Nineteenth Century*. 1845. *Margaret Fuller: American Romantic*. Ed. Perry Miller. Ithaca, N.Y.: Cornell University Press, 1963.

————."American Literature: Its Position in the Present Time, and Prospects for the Future." 1846. *Margaret Fuller: American Romantic*. Ed. Perry Miller. Ithaca, N.Y.: Cornell University Press, 1963.

Garrison, Dee. "Immoral Fiction in the Late Victorian Library." *American Quarterly* 28.1 (Spring 1976):71–89.

Giglioli, Pier Paolo, ed. *Language and Social Context*. Harmondsworth: Penguin, 1972.

Gilbert, Sandra M. and Susan Gubar. *The Madwoman in the Attic: The Woman Writer and the Nineteenth-Century Literary Imagination*. New Haven: Yale University Press, 1979.

Gilman, Caroline. *Recollections of a Southern Matron and a New England Bride.* Philadelphia: G. G. Evans, 1859.

Godey's Lady's Book 14 (January 1837): 1–5.

Green, Elsa. "Emily Dickinson was a Poetess." *College English* 34 (1972):63–70.

Griswold, Rufus, ed. *The Female Poets of America.* 1848. Rev. by R. H. Stoddard. New York: James Miller, 1874.

Haight, Gordon S. *Mrs. Sigourney: The Sweet Singer of Hartford.* New Haven: Yale University Press, 1930.

Hamilton, Gail (Mary Abigail Dodge). *Country Living and Country Thinking.* 4th ed. Boston: Ticknor and Fields, 1862.

Harland, Marion (Mary Virginia Terhune). *The Hidden Path.* New York: Derby and Jackson, 1855.

Hart, James D. *The Popular Book: A History of America's Literary Taste.* New York: Oxford University Press, 1950.

Hart, John Seely. *Female Prose Writers of America.* 1851. Philadelphia: E. H. Butler, 1855.

Hawthorne, Nathaniel. *The Scarlet Letter.* 1850. Boston: Houghton Mifflin, 1960.

———. *Letters of Hawthorne to William D. Ticknor: 1851–1864.* Newark: Carteret Book Club, 1910.

Higginson, Thomas Wentworth. *Women and the Alphabet: A Series of Essays.* 1881. New York: Arno, 1972.

———."An Open Portfolio." 1890. *American Poetry and Poetics: Poems and Critical Documents.* Ed. Daniel G. Hoffman. New York: Anchor Books, 1962.

———."Emily Dickinson's Letters." *Atlantic Monthly* 68 (October 1891):444–56.

Holland, J. G. *Miss Gilbert's Career: An American Story.* New York: Charles Scribner's Sons, 1860.

Holmes, Mary Jane. *Dora Deane, or the East India Uncle.* 1859. New York: F. M. Lupton, n. d.

———. *Marian Grey.* 1863. New York: A. L. Burt, n.d.

Howard, Richard. "A Consideration of the Writings of Emily Dickinson." *Prose* 6 (1973):67–97.

Jackson, Helen Hunt (pseud. H. H.). *Verses.* Boston: Roberts Brothers, 1875.

Jameson, Fredric. *The Political Unconscious: Narrative as a Socially Symbolic Act.* Ithaca, N.Y.: Cornell University Press, 1981.

Jeffrey, Kirk. "Marriage, Career, and Feminine Ideology in Nineteenth-Century America: Reconstructing the Marital Experience of Lydia Maria Child, 1828–1874." *Feminist Studies* 2 (1975):113–30.

Jehlen, Myra. "Archimedes and the Paradox of Feminist Literary Criticism." *Signs* 6.4 (1981):575–601.

Juhasz, Suzanne. *Naked and Fiery Forms: Modern American Poetry by Women, A New Tradition.* New York: Harper and Row, 1976.

Keller, Karl. *The Only Kangaroo Among the Beauty: Emily Dickinson and America.* Baltimore: Johns Hopkins University Press, 1979.

Kelley, Mary. "A Woman Alone: Catharine Maria Sedgwick's Spinsterhood in Nineteenth-Century America." *New England Quarterly* 51.2 (June 1978):209–25.

———."The Sentimentalists: Promise and Betrayal in the Home." *Signs* 4.3 (1979):434–46.

———. *Private Woman, Public Stage: Literary Domesticity in Nineteenth-Century America.* New York: Oxford University Press, 1984.

Kirkland, Caroline (pseud. Mary Clavers). *A New Home—Who'll Follow? or Glimpses of Western Life.* 1839. 2nd ed. New York: C. S. Francis, 1840.

Kramer, Aaron. *The Prophetic Tradition in American Poetry, 1839–1900.* Rutherford, N.J.: Fairleigh Dickinson University Press, 1968.

Larcom, Lucy. *A New England Girlhood.* 1889. Gloucester, Mass.: Peter Smith, 1973.

Leyda, Jay. *The Years and Hours of Emily Dickinson.* 2 vols. New Haven: Yale University Press, 1960.

Longsworth, Polly. " 'Was Mr. Dudley Dear?': Emily Dickinson and John Langdon Dudley." *Massachusetts Review* 26.2 & 3 (Summer/Autumn 1985):360–72.

Martineau, Harriet. *Society in America.* 1837. Gloucester, Mass.: Peter Smith, 1968.

May, Caroline. *American Female Poets.* Philadelphia: Lindsay and Blakiston, 1848.

McNall, Sally Allen. *Who Is in the House?: A Psychological Study of Two Centuries of Women's Fiction in America, 1795 to the Present.* New York: Elsevier, 1981.

Melville, Herman. *Moby-Dick.* 1851. Boston: Houghton Mifflin, 1956.

Menken, Adah Isaacs. *Infelicia.* 1868. Philadelphia: J. B. Lippincott, 1875.

Merriam, George S. *The Life and Times of Samuel Bowles.* 2 vols. New York: Century, 1885.

Miller, Cristanne. *Emily Dickinson: A Poet's Grammar.* New York: Harvard University Press, 1987.

Miller, Ruth. *The Poetry of Emily Dickinson.* Middletown, Conn.: Wesleyan University Press, 1968.

Mossberg, Barbara. *Emily Dickinson: When a Writer Is a Daughter.* Bloomington: Indiana University Press, 1982.

Olsen, Tillie. *Silences.* New York: Dell, 1978.

Osgood, Frances Sargent Locke. *Poems.* New York: Clark, Austin, 1850.

Papashvily, Helen Waite. *All the Happy Endings.* New York: Harper, 1956.

Parker, Gail, ed. *The Oven Birds: American Women on Womanhood, 1820–1920.* Garden City, N.Y.: Doubleday, 1972.

Pearce, Roy Harvey. *The Continuity of American Poetry.* Princeton, N.J.: Princeton University Press, 1961.

Phelps, Elizabeth Stuart. *The Sunnyside; or, The Country Minister's Wife.* Philadelphia: American Sunday School Union, 1851.

———. *The Angel over the Right Shoulder.* 1852. Pp. 203–59 in *Provisions: A Reader from 19th-Century American Women.* Ed. Judith Fetterley. Bloomington: Indiana University Press, 1985

———. *The Last Leaf from Sunnyside.* Boston: Phillips, Sampson, 1853.

Phelps (Ward), Elizabeth Stuart. "The Tenth of January." *Atlantic Monthly* 21 (March 1868):345–62.

———. *The Story of Avis.* 1877. Ed. Carol Farley Kessler. New Brunswick, N.J.: Rutgers University Press, 1985.

———. *Chapters From a Life.* Boston: Houghton, Mifflin, 1896.

Pollak, Vivian. "Thirst and Starvation in Emily Dickinson's Poetry." *American Literature* 51.1 (March 1979):33–49.

———. *Dickinson: The Anxiety of Gender.* Ithaca, N.Y.: Cornell University Press, 1984.

Porter, David T. *Dickinson: The Modern Idiom.* Cambridge: Harvard University Press, 1981.

Pratt, Annis. *Archetypal Patterns in Women's Fiction.* Bloomington: Indiana University Press, 1981.

Reynolds, David. *Beneath the American Renaissance: The Subversive Imagination in the Age of Emerson and Melville.* New York: Alfred A. Knopf, 1988.

Rich, Adrienne. "Vesuvius at Home: The Power of Emily Dickinson." *Parnassus* 5.1 (1976):49–74.

Saxton, Martha. *Louisa May: A Modern Biography of Louisa May Alcott.* Boston: Houghton Mifflin, 1977.

Sedgwick, Catharine Maria. *Hope Leslie*. 1827. Ed. Mary Kelley. New Brunswick, N.J.: Rutgers University Press, 1987.

———. *The Life and Letters of Catharine Maria Sedgwick*. Ed. Mary E. Dewey. New York: Harper and Brothers, 1872.

Sewall, Richard B. *The Life of Emily Dickinson*. 1974. New York: Farrar, Straus and Giroux, 1980.

Showalter, Elaine. *A Literature of Their Own: British Women Novelists from Brontë to Lessing*. Princeton, N.J.: Princeton University Press, 1977.

Sigourney, Lydia Huntley. *Poems*. Boston: S. G. Goodrich, 1827.

———. *Letters of Life*. New York: D. Appleton, 1866.

Smith, Elizabeth Oakes. *The Sinless Child and Other Poems*. Ed. John Keese. New York: Wiley and Putnam, 1843.

———. *Selections from the Autobiography of Elizabeth Oakes Smith*. Ed. Mary Alice Wyman. Lewiston, Maine: Lewiston Journal, 1924.

Southworth, Emma D.E.N. *The Hidden Hand*. 1859. Ed. Joanne Dobson. New Brunswick, N.J.: Rutgers University Press, 1988.

Spiller, Robert E. et al. *Literary History of the United States*. New York: Macmillan, 1949.

St. Armand, Barton Levi. *Emily Dickinson and Her Culture: The Soul's Society*. Cambridge: Cambridge University Press, 1984.

Stauffer, Donald Barlow. *A Short History of American Poetry*. New York: E. P. Dutton, 1974.

Stephens, Ann. *Fashion and Famine*. New York: Bunce and Brother, 1854.

Stern, Madeline. *Books and Book People*. New York: Bowker, 1978.

———. *Publishers for Mass Entertainment in Nineteenth-Century America*. Boston: G. K. Hall, 1980.

Stoddard, Elizabeth. *The Morgesons*. 1862. Ed. Lawrence Buell and Sandra A. Zagarell. Philadelphia: University of Pennsylvania Press, 1984.

Stowe, Charles E. *The Life of Harriet Beecher Stowe*. Boston: Houghton Mifflin, 1891.

Stowe, Harriet Beecher. *Uncle Tom's Cabin: or, Life Among the Lowly*. 1852. Harmondsworth: Penguin, 1981.

———. *The Pearl of Orr's Island*. 1862. Boston: Houghton Mifflin, n.d.

———. *Life and Letters of Harriet Beecher Stowe*. Ed. Annie Fields. Boston: Houghton Mifflin, 1898.

Strasser, Susan. *Never Done: A History of American Housework*. New York: Pantheon, 1982.

Thoreau, Henry David. *Walden*. 1854. *Thoreau: Walden and Other Writings*. Ed. Joseph Wood Krutch. New York: Bantam, 1962

Tompkins, Jane. *Sensational Designs: The Cultural Work of American Fiction, 1790–1860*. New York: Oxford University Press, 1985.

Walker, Cheryl. *The Nightingale's Burden: Women Poets and American Culture before 1900*. Bloomington: Indiana University Press, 1982.

Warner, Anna. *Susan Warner*. New York: G. P. Putnam's Sons, 1909.

Warner, Susan. *The Wide, Wide World*. 1850. Ed. Jane Tompkins. New York: Feminist Press, 1987.

———. *Queechy*. 2 vols. New York: George P. Putnam, 1852.

Watts, Emily Stipes. *The Poetry of American Women from 1632 to 1945*. Austin: University of Texas Press, 1977.

Wells, Henry. *An Introduction to Emily Dickinson*. Chicago: Hendricks House, 1947.

Whicher, George. "Emily Dickinson Among the Victorians." *The Recognition of Emily Dickinson*. Ed. Caesar R. Blake and Carlton F. Wells. 1964. Ann Arbor: Ann Arbor Paperbacks, 1968.

Whitman, Walt. *Complete Poetry and Selected Prose*. Ed. James E. Miller, Jr. Boston: Houghton Mifflin, 1959.

Whitney, A. D. T. *Hitherto; A Story of Yesterdays*. Boston: Loring, 1869.

Williams, Raymond. *Marxism and Literature*. New York: Oxford University Press, 1977.

Wilson, Augusta Jane Evans. *St. Elmo*. 1866. New York: Grosset and Dunlap, 1896.

Wilson, Forrest. *Crusader in Crinoline: The Life of Harriet Beecher Stowe*. Philadelphia: J. B. Lippincott, 1941.

Wilson, R. J. "Emily Dickinson and the Problem of Career." *Massachusetts Review* 20.3 (1979):451–61.

Wolff, Cynthia. "A Mirror for Men: Stereotypes of Women in Literature." In *Woman: An Issue*. Ed. Lee R. Edwards et al. Boston: Little, Brown, 1972.

Wolosky, Shira. *Emily Dickinson: A Voice of War*. New Haven: Yale University Press, 1984.

Wood, Ann D(ouglas). "The 'Scribbling Women' and Fanny Fern: Why Women Wrote." *American Quarterly* 23 (Spring 1971):3–24.

———."Mrs. Sigourney and the Sensibility of the Inner Space." *New England Quarterly* 45 (June 1972):163–81.

Zagarell, Sandra A. "Narrative of Community: The Identification of a Genre." *Signs* 13.31 (1988):498–527.

———."Expanding 'America': Lydia Sigourney's *Sketch of Connecticut*, Catharine Sedgwick's *Hope Leslie*." *Tulsa Studies in Women's Literature* 6 (1987):225–45.

INDEX TO POEMS CITED

GENERAL INDEX